Politics and Administration
at the Top

Published by the University of Pittsburgh Press, Pittsburgh, Pa. 15261
Copyright © 1997, University of Pittsburgh Press
All rights reserved
Manufactured in the United States of America
Printed on acid-free paper
10 9 8 7 6 5 4 3 2 1

Dunn, Delmer D.
    Politics and administration at the top : lessons from down under / Delmer D.
Dunn.
        p.   cm. — (Pitt series in policy and institutional studies)
    Includes bibliographical references (p.) and index.
    ISBN 0-8229-4045-0 (cloth : acid-free paper) . —ISBN 0-8229-5650-0 (pbk. :
acid-free paper)
        1. Australia—Politics and government—1945– 2. Bureaucracy—Australia.
3. Cabinet system—Australia.   4. Democracy—Australia.   5. Political planning—
Australia.   I. Title.   II. Series.
JQ4031.D86   1997
352.3'0994—dc21   97-4770

A CIP catalog record for this book is available from the British Library.

This book is dedicated

to my wife, Ann,

and to our son, John,

and our daughter, Kielly.

Contents

Acknowledgments   ix

1. Responsiveness in Democratic Public Administration   1

2. Issues in Administrative Responsiveness to Elected Officials   18

3. The Department Secretary   43

4. The Ministerial Staff   74

5. The Minister   109

6. Lessons for U.S. Public Administration   144

Bibliiography   175

Index   187

Acknowledgments

The idea for this book began while I was teaching a graduate course, Public Administration and Democracy, in the University of Georgia public administration graduate program. It developed in several conversations with colleagues, both at Georgia and later at the Australian National University (ANU). The relationship between elected and career officials is an important one in democracies, and that relationship comprises the focus of this book. Many of the findings of this research were unanticipated, especially that a major conclusion would be to affirm several of the traditional values of the "old" public administration. But this is where the findings led, as readers will see.

I gratefully acknowledge support from both the University of Georgia and the Australian National University. My research was conducted while I was appointed Visiting Fellow in the Department of Political Science, Faculty of Arts, ANU, in 1992 and while I was working as a visiting faculty member in 1996. John Hart arranged both visits and has been an invaluable and supportive ally throughout the research project. I also acknowledge with much appreciation the assistance of David Adams, Brian Galligan, the late Leonard Hume, Will Sanders, and John Uhr, all of ANU at the time (Brian Galligan has subsequently moved to the University of Melbourne), and of John Halligan at the University of Canberra for their advice and assistance in my learning about Australia and Australian government. I also appreciate helpful comments on the research from several colleagues at the University of Georgia, including Thomas Lauth, Eugene

Miller, Hal Rainey, and Laurence O'Toole, as well as Robert Durant, a former colleague now at the University of Baltimore, and two excellent readers from the University of Pittsburgh Press. I also benefited from discussions with three ANU political science students doing research on Australian government. They were Ian Beckett, now of the University of Tasmania, Maria Maley, and Peter Vickary.

None of these individuals should be accountable either for advice not taken or for advice taken but implemented badly. My appreciation goes also to Yvonne Ramsey for her excellent work in transcribing the audio tapes of the 1992 interviews, to Craig Davis who provided valuable research assistance over a lengthy period of time, and to Serena Wilson who recently succeeded him. The administrative and secretarial staff at both ANU and Georgia have been extremely helpful, including Geneva Bradberry, Clarice Pilcher, Nancy Power, Pam Smith, Jerrie Teet, and Teresa Wood at Georgia, and Polly Ball, Jackie Lipsham, Sharon Merten, and Thelma Williams at ANU. I also acknowledge with appreciation the assistance of Jill Adams of the Australian Public Service Commission, and Gillian Evans of the Research School for Social Sciences at ANU, for assistance in gathering data for the study. I am also grateful for the support and help of the staff of the University of Pittsburgh Press in bringing this book to fruition. These include Cynthia Miller, Jane Flanders, Kathy McLaughlin, Margie Bachman, Lisa Leppo, Pippa Letsky, and Kathy Bennett.

More general debts are owed to many others. Jeffrey Brudney, James Feldt, the late Frank Gibson, Robert Golembiewski, Edward Kellough, Jerome Legge, Felix Nigro, and Joe Whorton, in addition to those named above, have been excellent colleagues at Georgia and have added immensely to my education in public administration, as did my professors at Wisconsin, including James Davis, Gerald Haag, and Clara Penniman. Finally, I am deeply indebted to the Australian public servants who agreed to be interviewed for this study. They gave time that was scarce to them. For that I am deeply grateful.

Politics and Administration
at the Top

theory, which provides no obvious answers when it comes to defining clearly the responsibility of the bureaucracy or the most appropriate ways in which it can be held accountable. Democratic theory also does not define which particular representative institutions are meant to hold the bureaucracy accountable for its responsibilities or how these institutions can best perform this task. Nor is it altogether clear which forms of taking account are most appropriate to which oversight institutions (Bradshaw and Pring 1972, 355–58; Kernaghan and Langford 1990, 157, 162–63; Lijphart 1992, 11–21).

There is agreement that both the politician and the bureaucrat have unique contributions to make to the policy process. But at this time there is no broad agreement in the United States about the appropriate mix between the expertise and experience provided by the bureaucracy and the political direction provided by elected officials to the activities of bureaucracy. The purpose of this book is to attempt to define better what that mix might be. The method for doing this is to look at another country—Australia—and with a comparative and institutional approach to explore the relationship between politics and administration. The goal is to distill as finely as possible the fundamentals of the relationship between elected officials and the public service in one country, to use the findings for understanding that relationship in the United States, and to develop ideas for improvement of the politics-administration connection in the United States. Another goal is to develop greater understanding of the more general concerns of accountability and responsibility of bureaucrats in a democratic system of government. To be sure, there are other channels through which the democratic polity seeks either responsiveness from the bureaucracy or control of it. (The courts most readily come to mind.) But this study will focus upon that direction which comes from the politician or through the staff of the politician.

The Australian Commonwealth Government

The primary data for this study come from two sets of interviews with officials in the Australian national government. One set of interviews was held in October through December 1992, and the other in October 1996. The Australian Commonwealth government represents a hybrid in the family of democratic nations. It derives more directly from the Westminster system, which was developed originally in Great Britain, than does that of the United States. It is a parliamentary system. But its form of government is somewhere between the American and the British, because it does have some features of the U.S. government. Hence, it has been described as "the Washminster system" in reference to its combination of Westminster-derived principles of the British model of responsible parliamentary government and United States–inspired principles of federalism, a written constitution, and a bicameral legislature, with each house having substantial powers (Thompson 1980). In contrast to the American system, however, it does have responsible political parties in that they require members of parliament to vote with their party unless a given vote is not considered a party vote, and it operates as a parliamentary democracy, although not in so pure a Westminster fashion as Great Britain (Emy and Hughes 1991, 343–50).

There are three major political parties in Australian government, the Australian Labor Party, the Liberal Party, and the National Party. The Liberals and Nationals form an ongoing partnership, known as the Coalition, which contests national elections with a common platform. The Coalition parties usually coordinate the electorates in which they contest, although from time to time they have fielded candidates in opposition to each other. When the Coalition attained power in the March 1996 election, the Liberal Party leader became prime minister and the National Party leader became the deputy prime minister.

Power in Australia at the national level thus alternates on a bipartisan basis between the Labor Party and the Coalition. At the time of the first set of interviews in late 1992 the Labor Party had nearly ten years in power, having been first elected in 1983 with Robert Hawke as prime minister. Since the leader of the governing party becomes prime minister in a parliamentary democracy, parliamentary systems permit changing prime minister between elections, and this occurred in Australia in December 1991, less than a year prior to the first set of interviews. Paul Keating, the former treasurer, at that time successfully challenged Prime Minister Hawke for leadership of the Labor Party, and became prime minister (Kelly 1992, 615–59).

During the early period of the 1992 interviews, polling data indicated that the Labor government led by Mr. Keating would probably lose the coming election. But by the time the interviews ended, public support for the Keating government had increased, though the party still trailed the Coalition in public opinion polls. Subsequent to the interviews, Labor strength improved and the party won another term in elections held in March 1993, and it governed until March 1996, when the Liberal-National

Coalition, led by John Howard, won decisively in the House of Representatives.

In Australia control of the House of Representatives determines which party forms the government. The prime minister and other ministers will then come from that party, or in the case of the Coalition, from the two political parties that it contains. Unlike some parliamentary systems, ministers must be members of parliament. Ministers may come from either the House or Senate. The Australian Constitution does not require it, but by practice the prime minister must be a member of the House.

Australian House members are elected from single-member election districts based on population, except that no state can have fewer than five members. The Australian Capital Territory has two representatives and the Northern Territory has one. The Australian Constitution stipulates that the House must be "as nearly as practicable" twice the size of the Senate. In the early 1990s there were 147 members. The Senate is composed of twelve members from each of the six Australian states, plus two each from the Northern Territory and the Australian Capital Territory, for a total of seventy-six (*Parliamentary Handbook* 1991, 13–14). The terms are ordinarily three-year terms for the House, and six-year terms for the Senate, with one-half of each state's or territory's Senate delegation being elected every three years on a territory or statewide basis. As in other Westminster-based systems, elections can be called prior to the end of the term of office. Because House members are elected from single-member districts, Labor and the Coalition usually hold all but a few seats in the House. One or the other forms the government and the government must maintain majority support in the House.

In contrast to the House, Senate members are elected on a proportional representation basis. Because six senators are elected at-large in each election in the states, a party polling about 14.29 percent of the vote gains one seat (Lucy 1993, 91–92). The proportional election rule in the Senate means that minor parties stand a very good chance of being represented in the Senate. The largest bloc of minor parties is usually the Democrats, but the Greens and various independents are also present. Since this election system for the Senate was adopted in 1948, the party forming the government has held a majority of the Senate as well as the House for only fifteen years (Emy and Hughes 1991, 365). This necessitates the governing party forming a coalition with senators from minor parties to achieve a majority to pass the government's program in the Senate.

In the years Labor held power from 1983 to 1993, the Australian

Democrats were often a coalition partner for winning passage of the government program in the Senate. But after the March 1993 election, the combination of Labor and Democrats fell short of a majority, which required more negotiation between government and various independents (as well as Democrats) in the Senate in order to win the majority necessary to pass legislation. The divided party control of the Senate continued after the Liberal-National Coalition parties resumed power after the March 1996 election. But the Coalition needed only two additional votes in the Senate to pass legislation. They could thus develop alliances with the Democrats, or with individual independents. The power of the Senate in Australia is greater than in most Westminster systems. The Senate must approve the budget and is virtually co-equal with the House on legislative matters (Emy and Hughes 1991, 366).

For those unfamiliar with parliamentary systems of government, a few words of explanation regarding ministers, portfolios, and government departments will make this study more accessible. In parliamentary systems, executive and legislative power is not separated. The party or parties that can muster a majority in the legislature form what is called the government. Executive power is held collectively by the prime minister and a set of ministers, who form the cabinet. Often the terms *cabinet* and *government* are used interchangeably, although the latter term connotes the parliamentary majority forming the government as well as the cabinet. In almost all cases of parliamentary democracy, ministers are members of parliament, and thus elected to the legislature by a constituency. Their selection as minister varies by party in Australia. The Labor Party elects ministers by caucus, whereas the Liberal and National parties utilize a more centralized procedure centering on the party leader. A government retains power as long as it maintains a parliamentary majority on major legislation. In Australia, as in other Westminster systems, an election can be called prior to the end of a given term, but it must be called by the end of the term in office.

The responsibilities for governing are parceled out among the ministers by assigning each a portfolio. A portfolio consists of a set of responsibilities, usually a department or in some cases a part of a department, in the executive branch of government. In Australia a given minister can be assigned a responsibility for a general area rather than a department (or in addition to a department), for example, to assist the prime minister with the public service, with women's issues, or with privatization. Further, ministers can be named a member of cabinet but not assigned responsibility for a department or a set of issues. The prime minister and designated ministers make up the cabinet, which, unlike the United States, must collectively approve the budget and new legislative initiatives. In Australia, not all ministers belong to the cabinet, and the government determines the size of cabinet. For example, the Labor government in 1992 utilized a cabinet of sixteen, not including the prime minister, with a total of twenty-nine ministers. When the Labor government left office in 1996, the cabinet numbered sixteen, with a total of thirty ministers. The Coalition government in 1996 had a cabinet of fourteen, with a total of twenty-seven ministers (*Commonwealth Government Directory*, August 1992, 48–49; December 1995–February 1996, 50–51; June 1996, 50–51). In addition to ministers, who may or may not be members of the cabinet, governments also include parliamentary secretaries. These individuals are assigned a more minor role in given departments than are ministers.

Ministers are responsible for a department or other areas that comprise their portfolio, and they oversee the delivery of the government's program in the areas to which they are assigned. They must secure approval for the budget each year, and for changes in the law that require parliamentary approval. In these cases, the minister must secure approval of the cabinet.

Approval by cabinet is not automatic. Debate is often vigorous. The minister who is unprepared or who fails to argue deftly and strongly for his or her position can at this juncture face defeat of a policy or budget proposal. At times, depending on the issue and the relationship of cabinet to the party caucus, the minister might also need approval of the caucus in order to achieve approval of a new program. In fact, at least in the Labor governments of the 1980s and 1990s, debate in caucus was likely to be more decisive than debate in parliament (Emy and Hughes 1991, 347–50). Caucuses include all members of the party in parliament just as in U.S. legislative bodies. Unlike the United States, Australian caucus votes are binding on members of the party when legislation moves to the floor of the House or Senate. In Australia the government controls the House, which assures that cabinet-approved measures receive passage of authorization or appropriation legislation. Since the governing party does not usually control the Senate, the minister responsible for a given initiative must negotiate with a minor party, minor parties, or individual independents in the Senate in order to achieve a majority vote.

The Coalition or the Labor Party form what is called the opposition when they do not form the government. The opposition includes shadow ministers, meaning that they shadow or maintain a vigil over the portfolio of a given government minister. From that vantage point the shadow minister critiques the performance of the minister and department for which he or she is responsible. Much of that responsibility is publicly manifest during question time. This is a period of one hour per day, set aside in the House and Senate when parliament is in session. During this period the prime minister and other ministers must explain and defend their actions. Both the government and opposition attempt to score political points with the public as the media focuses coverage on this event.

Ministers can also be asked questions by members of their own party. These are often arranged to announce a favorable action or to permit a minister to build support for a given action or to announce an action that is designed to build political support for the government. (Such questions are called "Dorothy Dixes" in Australia.) In addition to these responsibilities the shadow ministers form a government-in-waiting by becoming knowledgeable about the issues relevant to the minister and department they cover. This provides training in case the opposition wins the next election and forms the government. There is no guarantee, however, that serving as a shadow minister will lead to a ministerial assignment when power changes hands.

Members of parliament whose party is in power but who are not ministers or parliamentary secretaries are called backbenchers, simply because they do not sit on the front bench when parliament convenes. Members of the opposition who are not part of the shadow ministry are also termed backbenchers, and those who are members of minor parties are backbenchers in Australia because they are not named as ministers or parliamentary secretaries for the government or as shadow ministers for the opposition.

A second key group in the Australian government is formed by the staff members of ministers. Those who have policy-related responsibilities are often called advisers. These staff member posts have grown in both number and responsibility since the early 1970s. Staff members assist ministers as they perform their responsibilities as minister.

Department heads in Australia are responsible for departments. They are not elected but are appointed to their position by the government of the day. They are usually appointed for their professional skills, not for their previous experience in politics. The Westminster system has traditionally emphasized professional competence as the primary basis for serving in a department head position. Most have served many years in the Australian bureaucracy before serving as department head.

The relationship between ministers and department heads is important because it is through that relationship that politics and administration meet in Australia. That meeting is much more focused in Australia than in a separated power system like that of the United States. But the connection between politics and administration occurs in all democracies, which means that what can be learned about that connection in any democracy has relevance for other democracies, including the United States. The advantage of studying how the connection occurs in Australia lies in the more focused way that politics and administration meet or connect there. The stronger focus permits a better unraveling of the fundamentals of this connection than can occur in a system of government where the connection is more diffused.

Reforms in Australian Commonwealth Government

Australia constitutes a good choice for study in many ways. It offers a unique definition of government that lies somewhere between the U.S. government and that of Great Britain. Further, the recent experience in Australia, especially during the period when the Labor Party held power between 1983 and 1996, is especially pertinent to considering reforms designed to provide a better mix between politics and administration because the relationship between elected officials and the Australian public service received substantial attention in those years.

There have been many developments in Australia designed to improve the political responsiveness of the bureaucracy and coordinate policy development by the government, but three developments pertain directly to this study. Two of these focus on reforms that sought increased responsiveness of the bureaucracy to ministers. Campbell and Halligan write that by the 1970s in Australia, "The bureaucracy was seen as too elitist, too independent, too unrepresentative and insufficiently responsive. . . . The reaction was to challenge the public servants' monopoly over advice to ministers and to question their indispensability to the processes of government" (1992, 201–02). The impetus for these reforms did not include "bashing" the bureaucracy, questioning its competence, nor assuming that it could not be responsive. The argument for these reforms thus never achieved what Campbell has called "open warfare against the career civil servant" that has marked some U.S. reforms (1993, 116). But the general concern of recent Australian Labor governments with the responsiveness of the bureaucracy mirrors the concern of many American politicians, career public servants, and scholars.

One of these reforms focused on enhancing the ability of ministers to achieve responsiveness from departments by providing them more staff resources. This began in the early 1970s with the advent of the Gough Whitlam Labor government after the Labor Party had served more than twenty years in opposition. The movement diminished in the first years of the Liberal-National Coalition government led by Malcolm Fraser, which began in the mid-1970s, and was emphasized again when the Labor Party, led by Robert Hawke, resumed power in 1983 (Campbell and Halligan 1992, 202–03; Forward 1977; Halligan and Power 1992, 75, 76, 81–84; Mediansky and Nockles 1975, 1981; Smith 1977; Walter 1986, 51–59; Warhurst 1988, 336–39; Weller 1983; Yeend 1979).

These changes can be noted by the number of ministerial staff during this time, as seen in table 1.1. The increase in the Whitlam years compared to the prior government is not large. But the Whitlam government emphasized for the first time ministerial staff as sources of policy advice to ministers that did not come from the department. Hence staff tended more often than previously to be recruited from outside the bureaucracy, and those who were from the bureaucracy were expected to work for the minister's policy objectives, not the department's. The early deemphasis of ministerial staff by the Fraser Coalition government, which displaced the Whitlam Labor government in 1975, can be seen from the decrease in staff that occurred then. But that was only temporary. By the end of the Fraser years the number of ministerial staff exceeded that of the Whitlam government's. The Labor Party's emphasis on ministerial staff can be noted by the increase in ministerial staff between 1983 and 1996 in the Hawke and Keating Labor governments. Although the new Coalition government elected in March 1996 reduced the size of the ministerial staff, the numerical reduction does not signify a return to the early days of the previous Coalition (Fraser) government.

A second reform in the 1983–1996 Labor government years centered on the non-elected officials who head the departments in the Commonwealth government. At one time the title of these individuals was Permanent Head, and they held office for lengthy periods of time. That has been changed to the title of Department Secretary. Further, the Labor government during this period began appointing department heads to five-year terms, although some were replaced prior to the end of their appoint-

Table 1.1

Ministerial Staff in Australia, 1972–1996

Coalition	Labor	Coalition	Coalition	Labor	Labor	Coalition
McMahon	Whitlam	Fraser	Fraser	Hawke	Keating	Howard
1972	1974	1976	1983	1983	1995	1996
155	207	138	217	224	481	423

Sources: For 1972, 1974, and 1976, see Forward 1977, 160; for 1983, see Walter 1986, 115; for 1995, see Ministerial Directory, October 1995; for 1996, see Ministerial Directory, June 1996.

ments or were shifted to other departments during Labor government rule.

Finally, control over these appointments moved more decisively to the prime minister and the minister. Prior to 1987 when a vacancy in one of these positions occurred, the Public Service Board developed a shortlist of public servants available to fill it, with the minister and prime minister usually choosing from the list. Since 1987 the function of the Public Service Board and its chair has been replaced by the Secretary of the Department of Prime Minister and Cabinet, the department that serves the prime minister. This has had the impact of shifting more control over these appointments to the government of the day (Campbell and Halligan 1992, 50, 206–08; Halligan and Power 1992, 89–91; Hawke 1989; and Hyslop 1993, 73–75).

The initial signals from the Coalition government of John Howard indicate that the new government has accepted these reforms and may add some more. One of the first acts of the new government was replacing six of the twenty department heads in the previous government with new department heads, some of whom came from outside the bureaucracy (although in most cases they had experience in Commonwealth departments in the past). Another department head departed shortly after the new government assumed power, and an eighth left in late 1996. In addition, the new government, as a part of a plan for general public service reform, has proposed to place department heads under performance contracts and to change their title to Chief Executive Officer. The initial discussion paper on these reforms indicated that the process for developing the contracts would lie with the minister of a given portfolio. It did not specify that approval would be required by the cabinet, the prime minister, or the Department of Prime Minister and Cabinet (Reith 1996).

A third development of recent years in Australia, which relates to the study, did not achieve the status of a reform but nevertheless centers on the relationship between politics and administration. In Australia there has been persistent pressure by parliament to broaden reporting and accountability lines by departments from the traditional Westminster model, which emphasizes ministers, to also include committees of the two houses (Uhr 1982; Emy and Hughes 1991, 359–70). Since the cabinet has so much influence in a parliamentary system, those not a part of the majority party (whose members can influence the cabinet through the party caucus) often have few ways to influence policy outcomes. This has led to an increasing tendency of Senate committees to engage in oversight activities. Senate committees review departments' spending requests twice each year. Other committees in both the Australian House and Senate conduct studies that may have policy implications. These activities of legislative committees create the possibility of requiring more accountability of departments to these committees, possibly diluting the lines of accountability to the minister (Campbell and Halligan 1992, 214–17). The case for broad accountability of department to parliament is embodied in a report issued by a committee of the House of Representatives (HRSCFPA 1990).

The tensions resulting from these pressures are most noticeable in a project sponsored by the Management Advisory Board (MAB). This board is chaired by the secretary of the Department of Prime Minister and Cabinet, and most of its members are other department secretaries (Halligan and Power 1992, 99–100). In 1993, MAB published a report on *Accountability in the Commonwealth Public Sector,* strongly supportive of the tradition of ministerial responsibility and protective of the autonomy and political neutrality of the public service (MAB 1993). This report and the sentiment that it sought to address indicates that the issue of bureaucratic responsiveness is very important in Australia as it is in the United States. The report had been published in draft form prior to the first set of interviews and was very salient to the department heads interviewed for the study, thus enhancing their discussion of the relationship of the bureaucracy to elected officials during these interviews (MAB 1991).

The emphasis on responsiveness in the bureaucracy—as noted by the development of greater ministerial staff resources, greater input by elected officials in the selection of department heads, and the pressure by members of parliament for injecting greater influence over department activities by broadening reporting lines for departments to include parliamentary committees—indicate that the question of achieving better responsiveness from the bureaucracy is very much an issue in Australia as it is in the United States. Thus, those interested in this issue in the United States will find the ways that Australia has sought to gain greater responsiveness of the bureaucracy to be pertinent to their interest in this issue.

A Comparative and Institutional Approach

The study utilizes a comparative and institutional approach. Although the United States borrowed heavily from Great Britain's nineteenth-century civil service reforms, the study of public administration in America has tended to neglect developments in other countries. But there is a growing literature that is comparative in focus. The rationale of a comparative approach was put well by Richard Neustadt who wrote, "looking at another system helps illuminate our own" (1980, Foreword). Guy Peters cogently states the case for comparative public bureaucracy studies. These include, among others, the need to develop theory on more than a single national experience, the provision of a better context in which to understand U.S. public administration, and the ease of comparing the common threads in bureaucracies and executive offices in different countries (Peters 1988, 1–25). This study focuses on the connection between politics and administration in Australia, one of the democracies that, like the United States, traces its roots to Great Britain.

The study also focuses on institutions at a time in which there has been more scholarly emphasis on institutions. This emphasis has sometimes been called the New Institutionalism, because its ultimate aim is to facilitate analysis and develop theory rather than to emphasize description in the manner of the "old" institutionalism (Grafstein 1992; March and Olsen 1984; Thelen and Steinmo 1992). This study is both comparative and institutional in its focus. In recent years there have been several such studies, including several that focus on the Anglo-based democracies of the United States, Canada, Great Britain, New Zealand, and Australia (see Campbell 1983, 1993; Campbell and Wyszomirski, 1991; Campbell and Halligan 1992; Mascarenhas 1993; and Rose and Suleiman 1980). The institutional approach guides one toward studies that examine relations among governmental institutions, among other areas of interest (Thelen and Steinmo 1992, 2). Thus, this study centers on two institutions—the bureaucracy and the ministerial office—with the query being how the latter politically directs the former. Those findings will then be compared with those focusing on the politics-administration connection in U.S. institutions.

Over time, scholars using a comparative focus have examined both policy and institutions. The latest phase in comparative public policy studies offers lessons in methods appropriate to comparing institutions. According to Castles, who has focused on comparative policy studies, these studies have at times suffered from a narrow conceptualization that does not ask the right questions because of the methodological constraints imposed by quantitative methodology. In an effort to overcome these deficiencies, comparative analysis has rediscovered the value of critical or anomalous cases and the place of selective examinations of the distinctiveness of related cases, where subtle differences instruct more than do superficial institutional similarities (Castles 1989, 9–10, and 1991, 1–14). This approach suggests that, by focusing on institutions providing for the connection between politics and administration, this study will provide findings that will be pertinent to those interested in that connection in other countries.

The Data for the Study

The data for this study come from two sets of interviews, conducted with those in the Australian Commonwealth government through whom political direction of the public service is exercised. The first set of interviews was conducted between October and December 1992. At the time of these interviews the Australian Commonwealth government had sixteen senior ministers, plus the prime minister, who were members of the cabinet. There were an additional number of "junior" ministers, who each had responsibility for some of a given department's functions.

The 1992 interviews include seven current or former cabinet ministers. Almost all the ministers interviewed in the first set of interviews had served in at least two portfolios since the Labor Party regained power in 1983. A second group of respondents consisted of nine persons who headed departments in the Australian national government. All but one of these had the title of department secretary. All prior to their present appointment had served in the Australian public service and were appointed to their present positions by the Labor Party government. A third group important to the study were staff members to the ministers. Nine staff members to the ministers—six of whom held the designation of Senior Adviser—were interviewed.

The second set of interviews was conducted in October 1996. This set of interviews was designed to follow up on the 1992 interviews, to ascertain any changes in the relationship between ministers and departments and ministers and their staffs since the Labor government, after thirteen years in power, had been defeated by the Coalition in March 1996. Although the Coalition government reduced the number of departments from twenty to eighteen, it basically maintained the department organization of the previous Labor government, with the concomitant continuation of senior and junior ministers. The new government incorporated fourteen ministers, in addition to the prime minister, as cabinet ministers. The 1996 interviews included five cabinet ministers, four senior staff members of the remaining nine cabinet members, four former Labor government cabinet ministers (all of whom had been interviewed in the previous set of interviews), five current department heads (one of whom had been included in the previous set of interviews), and two former department heads (both of whom had been interviewed in the previous round of interviews).

The second set of interviews occurred early in the term of the new government and included interviews with relatively new ministers as well as with ministers who had served many years in the Labor government. The interviews also included department heads, some of whom had served both Labor and Coalition governments and some who had served either the Labor or Coalition government. Finally, all staff members interviewed in the second set of interviews were relatively new, whereas in most cases the staff members previously interviewed had served several years in their positions. The second set of interviews thus added more diversity to the perspectives to the first set of interviews.

The interviews with the ministers averaged about thirty minutes in length, with the staff members about forty-five minutes in the first set of interviews and about thirty-five minutes in the second set, and with the secretaries about one hour in the first set of interviews and about forty-five minutes in the second set. All interviews were recorded and transcribed, with the respondents being promised, in return for their agreeing to the interview, that they would not be identified with any quotations used in the study.

The Study's Focus and Findings

Those who were interviewed hold the levers of power in the Australian Commonwealth government. They are the ones who manage the processes that seek to elicit political responsiveness from the Australian bureaucracy. This study will focus on the key elements of that relationship to determine the fundamental essentials for generating responsiveness from the bureaucracy to elected government leaders. This study also examines their perceptions of how well this relationship works. The reports and perceptions of these individuals about how the politics-administration connection works are especially useful because it is unusual to have information on this topic from such high-level officials. Although the relationships between these individuals and the public service that serves below department heads in Australia are also important, that inquiry is beyond the scope of this study.

The book also explores the lessons from the Australian findings that can be useful in the United States, especially at the national level of government. Parliamentary-based democracies differ from the separation-of-powers system of the United States. But those associated with parliamentary systems have shared with their U.S. counterparts a concern with the appropriate relationship between politics and administration. Observations and practices of Australian politicians and administrators will thus have relevance to the U.S. system and to other democracies as well. Social science seeks generalizations that apply in more than one place or situation. Certainly members of the family of democratic nations have learned from each other in other areas, and they can learn from each other in this area as well. Australia is a remarkable hybrid that features components similar to both parliamentary and presidential democracies, which makes that government a good candidate for studying the mix between elected and non-elected officials in a democracy. Such a government offers a fertile source for insight into the appropriate mix between elected administration and politics.

Finally, the study examines findings in the context of the concepts of accountability and responsibility, concepts that have been examined in the past by scholars of both public administration and democratic theory. These concepts apply universally to democratic governments, making the findings associated with them relevant for other democratic governments. In addition, by using these concepts, the study adds the goal of seeking greater understanding of responsibility and accountability as well.

The examination of the relationship between politics and bureaucracy in another practicing democracy, as it turns out, does provide several insights for defining effective relationships between politics and administration in democracies. The Australian practice is not perfect by any means, but it provides a useful overall definition of accountability and responsibility that is relevant for other democracies. The study's findings center on some of the traditional values of public administration—notably the politics-administration dichotomy and neutral competence—and their meaning for modern democracies. Relationships between politics and bureaucracy in Australia are marked by an appreciation for a version of the politics-administration dichotomy that is modified (as this study will indicate) in important ways from what most scholars define as the traditional version of that value.

The politics-bureaucracy relationship in Australia, as we shall discover, also emphasizes a respect for neutral competence that serves both sides of the relationship well. The combination of these values as defined in contemporary Australian government posits robust participation by career officials in policy formulation, and career officials' deference to the political direction set by elected officials within which the legal and constitutional framework that departments, agencies, and politicians must work. Each side recognizes the important contributions the other can make to policy development. Supporting all this is an emphasis by political leaders on defining goals as clearly as possible, in order to set the boundaries of responsibility for public servants, and on establishing a set of responsibilities against which accountability can occur. As in the United States, elected officials have sought to make the bureaucracy more responsive to democratically defined preferences.

The quest in Australia has been relatively more successful than in the United States, as judged by comparing the perceptions of elected officials in each country. This has occurred with Australian elected officials making more politically based appointments than in the past, but at considerably more restrained levels than prevail in the United States. Australian governments have also been more disciplined in making these appointments by emphasizing prior public service administrative experience for those appointed by elected officials to positions in the bureaucracy. These findings suggest important implications for other members of the family of democratic nations, including the United States, that should be of interest to scholars and public officials alike.

The Plan of the Book

The next chapter examines in detail the literature that focuses on the relationship between administration and politics. Then the next three chapters trace the relationships between ministers, their staff, and the department secretaries in Australian government. Chapter 3 focuses on the department secretary. Chapter 4 examines how ministerial staff assist the minister, both in keeping the bureaucracy responsive to political preferences and in relating to other ministers, cabinet, and caucus. Chapter 5 centers on ministers and examines ministerial direction of the bureaucracy in Australia. Finally, chapter 6 draws lessons from the Australian experience that are applicable to the quest for appropriate political responsiveness from the bureaucracy in the United States. The final chapter also examines the implications of these findings for traditional concerns of the accountability and responsibility of the bureaucracy in democratic governments. With this as background, let us turn to considering how Australian cabinet ministers, department secretaries, and ministerial staff work to produce responsiveness by administration to democratic preferences.

2

Issues in Administrative Responsiveness to Elected Officials

Earlier in this century, Max Weber observed the growth of both professional politicians and bureaucracy (1958a, 77–128, and 1958b, 196–244). Weber noted the increasing importance of these two entities, as both had grown in size, function, and power. This growth gives the state "an awesome power base" (Dwivedi 1985, 61). In the United States, the period following World War II became a time of important expansion of bureaucracy. This included the emergence of a national security system reflecting the development of the Cold War, the recruitment of science into the public sector, incorporating an increasing reliance upon expertise as a bureaucratic basis for political authority, and the creation of new management structures for fiscal policy and the economy (Crenson and Rourke 1987, 137–39). The expansion of government "meant prominence for bureaucracy" (139).

The growing prominence and power of bureaucracy poses important problems in a democracy, because it means that unelected officials have greater opportunities to influence policy, potentially in ways that disregard public preferences. This in turn makes the task of elected officials especially important since they must oversee the bureaucracy, infuse it with democratic preferences, and make it accountable to democratic processes (Etzioni-Halevy 1983, 148–58). Scores of scholars have studied this relationship. Their findings and observations inform this study and will be cited at appropriate points.

Despite this attention, scholars have reached no consensus on what Joel Aberbach and Bert Rockman call the proper "meshing" of elected and non-elected officials in "an optimal mix" (1988a, 606). The mix between the two is important for democratic theory, because it determines the extent to which the policy machinery of government reflects predominantly the preferences and values of elected officials or the preferences and values of public servants, who are not elected. The relationship between elected and appointed officials has thus attracted much scholarly attention. Most often, particularly in the United States, the study of this relationship has emphasized the conflict between the two.

The conflict between politics and administration derives from more than the growth of the administrative state and the increased skills needed to deliver modern government services. The different values, perspectives, and concerns of politicians and public servants fuel the conflict that often arises between them. The values emanating from democratic politics include responsiveness, accountability, energy, short time lines, revitalization, power, conflict, compromise, and change. These contrast with the values of bureaucracy, which include nonpartisanship, professionalism, continuity, expertise, experience, problem-solving, long-term perspectives, and effectiveness (Aberbach and Rockman 1988a, 606; Burke 1986, 2–5; Durant 1992, 4–5; Lauth 1989, 193, 204; Light 1987, 156; Maranto 1993, 140–41; Nalbanian 1994, 531–33; Rainey, 1991, 1–12; Terry 1995, 171–72). Further, politicians are likely to think in distributive and redistributive terms and emphasize the specific interests in an issue, whereas bureaucrats advocate more collective solutions (Aberbach, Putnam, and Rockman 1981, 109–14). In addition, bureaucrats may amass sufficient power to thwart the direction provided by elected officials. They can do this by obstructing what elected officials want, by manipulating the timing of meetings (so that elected officials favoring an action contrary to the bureaucrats' preferences are absent), and by withholding or providing information, as appropriate, to advance the bureaucrats' position (Etzioni-Halevy 1983, 148–58; Lynn and Jay 1987).

The differences in the values represented by politics and bureaucracy are not abstract. Those who have studied or participated in policy making with either of these power centers provide ample observations of the difficulty of mixing the two. Those most concerned about the values of responsiveness and revitalization, for example, often take a view of the bureaucracy that Robert Durant calls "bureauphobic." This perspective views the bureaucracy as "an independent political actor sapping constitutional powers that belong to the elected officials" (Durant 1992, 307–08).

Perhaps the most extreme version of this attitude is best illustrated by the comments of two appointees of President Ronald Reagan. One stated: "What is actually in place here is a permanent, self-enclosed system that operates on its own terms, toward its own ends, according to its own laws. This system of permanent government defers only reluctantly to manifestations of public sentiment in elections" (Evans 1987, 2). And this was far from an isolated opinion among Reagan appointees. Another observed: "After an election is won, a whole new battle must be waged to actually control the 'permanent government' in Washington—a government which has become, in many cases, not only contemptuous of electoral processes, but of the law itself" (Bernstein 1987, 217).

Several phenomena are at work in the contrasting perspectives between career public servants on the one hand and elected officials or those appointed for political reasons on the other. First, the two groups hold different time perspectives. Politics requires quick results before the next election whereas bureaucracy is cautious about change (Light 1987, 162–63). A second is that careerists often view their politically appointed superiors as not particularly well qualified (Huddleston 1987, 61). They seek to preserve continuity and do this often by seeking autonomy and resisting interference (Caiden 1988, 31–32; Peters 1988, 156–57; Stein 1991, 7). Further, when party control shifts, the newly elected political leadership views careerists as associated with problems that need correcting and with the failed programs of their defeated political adversaries (Peters 1988, 157). The newly elected political leadership emphasizes the intransigence of the bureaucracy rather than its compliance because "they necessarily spend more time pursuing failures in direction and control than savoring successes" (Randall 1979, 795).

Further, there may be differences within a given administration in the degree of antagonism between political appointees and career officials. Robert Maranto, for example, found that Department of Defense career officials in the Reagan administration "trust appointees, see career-noncareer agreement on the organization mission, can express themselves freely, and consider the Reaganites competent. None of this is true outside Defense" (1993, 99).

Robert Durant emphasizes the relationship between cooperation and goal agreement among careerists and political appointees, with greater cooperation occurring when goal agreement is higher. Durant indicates that the extent of resistance depends on several factors, including "(1) the extent to which careerists positively identify with existing agency or program missions, (2) the political clout of their allies, (3) their possession of expertise valued by appointees, and (4) the political prowess they attribute to those appointees" (1992, 293–94). In Durant's view, levels of resistance and cooperation between elected and appointed officials vary as these factors vary.

Cooperation between politicians and bureaucrats is needed for government to work at its best, but the differences and sometimes animosity between them produce difficulties in defining how best to achieve the optimum relationship of one to the other. The Progressive reforms—which offered the rubric that defined the relationship between politicians and bureaucrats for many years—have gradually fallen into decline. In fact, one leading scholar of American public administration believes that reformers rewrote the "living constitution" of the U.S. government during the 1970s, which redefined the relationship between public servants and elected officials by elevating the bureaucracy to the fourth branch of government. Utilizing the Madisonian plan of "checks and balances" that was incorporated into the Constitution and that uses ambition to check ambition, this reformulation of the place of the bureaucracy works as follows:

> Ambitious legislators and chief executives and judges and interest groups would counteract ambitious bureaucrats. New auxiliary precautions would be adopted. The Progressive faith in bureaucratic experts and ordinary citizens would be renounced. Instead of direct democracy and expert management, we would have representative democracy and the management of experts. (Gormley 1989, 59)

Francis E. Rourke laments the diminishing respect that politicians pay to neutral competence, the centerpiece of the Progressive reforms, but notes that political leaders' obsession with bureaucratic responsiveness stems from the increasing power of civil servants (1992, 544). As the Progressive reform vision of the relationship between politicians and bureaucrats has declined in the United States, politicians have adopted several practices in recent years to curb the power of bureaucrats. These practices have been somewhat different in the executive and legislative branches. Let us look separately at ways that the U.S. executive and legislative branches seek to elicit responsiveness from the bureaucracy.

Achieving Responsiveness from the Bureaucracy

A major tactic used by presidents to achieve greater responsiveness from the bureaucracy is to swamp or layer it with political appointees (Rose 1987a, 423–24). For some time now, scholars of American government have chronicled the increasing number of political appointees and their deepening penetration into lower levels of the bureaucratic hierarchy (Heclo 1977, 55–83; Light 1995). The rationale for this strategy is that persons appointed directly by the president are more likely to work to further the goals of the White House, thus achieving a greater degree of responsiveness from the bureaucracy. As noted in one study: "More and more . . . what the White House wants of civil servants . . . is the following: 'When we say jump, the answer should be "how high" ' " (Aberbach and Rockman 1988a, 608). The result is that the U.S. government makes more political appointments than most other democracies. James Fesler, for example, notes:

> New administrations in Britain and France make 100 top political appointments; a new group in power in Germany makes about 80; a change in the White House, however, can result in about 1,400 new political appointments. Since the United States has about 7,500 top career posts, the ratio of high-political to high-career officials is 1:5. The British and French ratios, in contrast, are 1:40, and the German ratio is 1:80. (1984, 88)

Increasing the number of political appointees does not seem to have had the impact that U.S. elected officials had hoped for, however, and may indeed have led to less effective rather than more effective results. Scholars have traced this paradoxical result to (1) ineffective supervision by political appointees, arising from their lack of ability or preparation and their brief tenure in office; (2) communication difficulties, deriving from the larger number of political appointees producing a longer chain of communication; (3) cutting career officials out of policy discussion, which leads to a diminished ability of the government to make effective policy; (4) the lessening attractiveness of a career in the public service; and (5) the reduced capacity of elected officials to exercise accountability in the executive branch of government. Let us examine these explanations for the ineffectiveness of executive branch efforts to achieve greater responsiveness from the bureaucracy in U.S. national government.

Ineffective Supervision by Political Appointees

A growing concern of those studying political direction of the bureau-cracy is the lack of preparation of those who are responsible for providing the direction. Patricia Ingraham, James Pfiffner, and James Sundquist have concluded that high-level political appointees are not well prepared for the job they are given in Washington. Though they may be well educated, they have little suitable experience to run the agencies and departments they are recruited to manage. They are also provided with little help to bridge this gap (Ingraham 1991, 182; Pfiffner 1987, 63; Sundquist 1995, 398).

The reaction of successive administrations has led to a "thickening" of political appointees, which includes added layers of political appoin-tees in the administrative hierarchy, as well as more appointees at each layer (Light 1995). This has increased rather than diminished the prob-lem. Having more appointees increases the likelihood that a greater num-ber will be inadequately prepared for the task of political management (Light 1987, 172; Rose 1987a, 424) and makes it more difficult for the appointment process to take the necessary care to assure that high-quality persons are appointed (Ingraham 1995, 104–05; Lauth 1989, 203; Pfiffner 1987, 63). Increasing the number of appointees also makes it more difficult to place the right person in the right position, and White House staff sometimes make errors in their assessment of potential appointees (West 1995, 90).

Hugh Heclo has stated that "political appointees are unfit managers of our career personnel systems" (1984, 107). Heclo is blunt in his assess-ment of the reasons why political appointees generally fail: they are too distracted by current business, they are uninterested, they do little to build career institutions, and they are too ignorant to manage career personnel systems (107–08). James Sundquist puts the problem of political appoint-ments in an interesting context:

> It has been a century since we stopped putting uniforms on politi-cians and giving them command of army and navy units. Today, no-body would even think of making anyone other than a career mili-tary officer the chief of staff of the army or the air force or the chief of naval operations. A career officer is the manager—or commander, in service terminology. Yet we rarely look inside the career service to find leadership for civilian departments and major agencies. (1995, 399)

Another reason for ineffective supervision is that political appointees, who enter office ill prepared, do not remain in office long enough to acquire the experience they need. Hugh Heclo captured this phenomenon in the title of his book *A Government of Strangers* (1977; see also Rose 1980, 338). Heclo found that "The single most obvious characteristic of Washington's political appointees is their transience. . . . about half of the top political executives can expect to stay in their jobs less than two years" (1977, 103). Later studies indicate that short-term appointments remain the norm (Brauer 1987, 175). Moreover, over 90 percent of these appointments typically hold office only once, so they do not acquire the experience that could be gained in a succession of short-term appointments (Brauer 1987, 182). Short tenures, with some exceptions, are also the rule in cabinet-level appointments as well (Jones 1994, 63–65). Maranto, however, found that Reagan appointees served a mean time longer than has been found in other studies, perhaps because of the two terms that this administration was in office, with no clear policy changes between the terms. The typical political appointee in 1987 had served 4.39 years in the administration, 3.11 years in the current organization, and 2.06 years in the current position (Maranto 1993, 76–77). Significantly, only eight of the 118 appointees that Maranto studied came from positions in the civil service (ibid.).

The election of President Reagan's vice president, George Bush, to succeed him as president also affected the experience of political appointees in the Bush administration. From half to two-thirds of these appointees had served in the Reagan administration (Michaels 1995, 276). But even with this experience, one-third had no previous direct budget experience, and 70 percent had not held responsibility for budgets of more than $10 million. In addition, few had substantial personnel experience (ibid.). The findings of Maranto and Judith Michaels indicate that policy consistency and continuing rule by the same party can impact political appointee tenures. But the Reagan and Bush era was longer than any other in the postwar period, and the relative consistency of policy from one term to the other is not typical of other late twentieth-century presidential administrations in the United States. For these reasons it is likely that short-term tenures for executive branch political appointees will remain the norm.

Political appointees who lack the experience to manage the bureaucracy effectively when they are appointed often do not stay long enough in the position to acquire it. The fallout includes discontinuities in priorities, short-term perspectives, greater emphasis on personal careers than policy development, a reduction in the collective memory, and diminished ability to work effectively in group processes because appointees do not know each other. (See Brauer 1987, 178–79; Heclo 1987, 207–12; Huddleston 1987, 63; Rose 1980, 338–39.)

Communication Problems

Communication difficulties inhibit the effective supervision of bureaucrats by political appointees. Charles Jones wrote, "Adding staff to solve the president's traditional problem of managing and directing the bureaucracy to his own ends can, itself, become a management problem" (1994, 57). The greater the number of appointees, the more difficult for them to agree upon and communicate with a coherent voice on policy development and implementation (Light 1995, 167; Rose 1987a, 424). Francis Rourke, the distinguished student of the politics-bureaucracy interface, has observed that presidential appointees "have minds of their own, and they cannot always be relied upon to remain mere envoys of the White House once they have tasted the pleasures of power themselves in positions of executive authority" (1992, 544).

Paul Light observes that the increasing number of appointees makes it difficult to forge relationships that would enhance cooperation (1987, 156–57). Herbert Kaufman's extensive study of bureau chiefs finds little political direction from above. He suggests that the increased number of persons between the department secretary and the bureau chief was one reason for this. This development "has increased the distance between the department heads and their agency executives, reducing the unity and sense of common purpose in the departments" (Kaufman 1981, 185).

Ingraham has found that the unclear and tenuous linkages between the White House and political appointees in the executive departments permit those appointees great latitude in determining priorities (1991, 191), suggesting that large numbers of these appointees do not enhance a president's ability to establish political direction of the bureaucray. Thomas Weko, after studying the White House personnel office in the post–World War II period, concluded that increasing the size and power of that office has led to conflicts within the White House, and between the White House staff responsible for appointments and the departments where the appointments are made (1995, 149–52). The state of White House–Executive Department linkage led Aaron Wildavsky, after reading the Reagan appointees' chronicles of their battles with bureaucrats, to conclude that the appointees "had more difficulty in persuading the Republican administration to steer in the direction they thought had been agreed upon than in getting the bureaucracy to follow a clear command" (1987, xiii). Maranto also found that disunity within the Reagan administration worked to impede its ability to provide political direction of agencies (1993, 141). Such conflict is not limited to any one president's staff but seems to be typical for the White House.

Effective communication between political appointees and careerists is thwarted by other factors as well. The number of appointees has grown so great that the White House has difficulty filling all the positions. Staff time devoted to selecting appointees might be better allocated to programmatic concerns (Lauth 1989, 203). Further, the growth of the White House personnel office has led to greater conflict between departments and the office, which can lead to deadlock or drift, leaving large numbers of department personnel slots unfilled (Weko 1995, 151). Paul Light notes that vacancies leave careerists without direction, severing the connection between administration and political direction (1987, 163). Furthermore, the proliferation of appointments has left a kind of loss of value in political influence, a kind of "a dime a dozen" impression about these appointments. "Put simply: a call from an assistant secretary does not mean what it once did" (Stillman 1987, 122). Light observes: "Presidents may be deluding themselves that the tonnage of appointments is more important than the clarity of their leadership" (1995, 93).

In sum, the "solution" of adding more political appointees in order to achieve greater responsiveness from the bureaucracy has not worked, although elected executives are likely to continue to promote it as a solution. That they continue to think they need more political appointees despite the fact that the number of these appointees has been growing for many years suggests that this "solution" is an ineffective tool for increasing political responsiveness. The problem of political responsiveness from the bureaucracy is thus not attributable completely to the intransigence of careerists. Heclo observed in his classic study: "Often it seems that political executives are not so much drowned out by forceful bureaucrats as that they themselves fail to perform" (1977, 239).

Cutting Career Public Servants Out of Policy Formation

The growing number of political appointments in the U.S. executive branch has also worked to produce ineffective policy making at the national level of government in another way as well. Making good policy on complex issues requires policy advice from careerists in the bureaucracy, whose experience and expertise is greater than those of the political appointees. In both Great Britain and the United States, the policy advice of public servants has been supplanted in part by policy advice coming from think tanks, consultants, and university-based scholars (Garvey 1993, 37–45; Campbell and Wilson 1995, 67–69). In the United States the number and diversity of think tanks has grown.

At the same time, many think tanks have become more ideologically driven than was the case in the past. Although information from experts outside the bureaucracy may be useful to elected officials, is the information of the same quality as that potentially available from the public service? Can these alternative sources match either the public service's repository of expertise or experience from administering programs that might better inform policy deliberations? At a minimum, policy advice from departments should be a part of the information routinely available in these deliberations. If this policy advice from public servants is excluded deliberately, or the channels of communication made so tenuous that their advice cannot make it to the top levels of the department, the resultant policy is of lower quality than would otherwise be the case.

Many scholars have noted this phenomenon in U.S. policy making. Aberbach and Rockman as well as Laurence Lynn indicate that presidents and their chief advisers have cut operating agencies and careerists out of the action (Aberbach and Rockman 1988a, 608; 1988b, 82; Lynn 1981, 61). Irene Rubin found that the Reagan administration reduced the contact between career officials and those responsible for making policy in several of the agencies and departments she studied (1985, 194–95). Colin Campbell and John Halligan noted that the Reagan administration closed the bureaucracy out of the policy process (1992, 198–99). Richard Rose indicates that additional appointees make it less likely the politician will receive informed advice about the programs for which he is responsible (1987a, 424). We noted earlier Rourke's distress over the diminished respect for neutral competence. He has found a direct relationship between the increase in presidential appointees and the diminished role of careerists in policy development (Rourke 1991, 115). This reduces the impact of professional knowledge and diminishes the deliberative process through which policy is developed (Rourke 1992, 544–45). Aberbach and Rockman argue that it is precisely because presidents do not believe it possible for bureaucrats to be neutral that they must make political appointments in order to assure that their goals and needs are pursued (1988a, 608). Rose notes the reduction in the collective memory of public officials influential in policy making and a growing "amateurization" of the central direction of government (1980, 338). Heclo has indicated the long-term impact of walling off careerists as a source of policy advice:

> When senior political appointees fail to include higher civil servants in substantive policy discussions, there is little reason for permanent career staff to acquire more than a narrowly technical, routine perspective. When careerists are denied access to an understanding of the political rationales for top-level decision making, they inevitably become divorced from the "big picture" and incapable of communicating it to subordinates. When they are denied the sense of having a fair hearing for their views among the top political decision makers, permanent officialdom retreats into disgruntlement, backbiting, and, in extreme cases, sabotage. And so it is that by not being consulted, senior careerists over time become less worth consulting and less worth appointing to the more responsible departmental positions. (1987, 202)

One irony of the impact of increasing numbers of political appointments is noted by Light. The penetration of these appointments into more layers of the bureaucracy makes it more difficult to develop positive relationships: "Appointees eventually come to see their civil servants as competent and responsive, but the realization may come too late to be of much value in promoting cooperation" (Light 1987, 157).

Attracting the Best and the Brightest

The practice of multiplying political appointments not only has an impact on the quality of policy making but also reduces the attractiveness of a career in the public service. Paul Volcker has expressed his concern that government "is increasingly unable to attract, retain, and motivate the kinds of people it will need to do the essential work of the republic in the years and decades ahead" (1988, 2). He finds that the greater number of political appointees truncates the career paths of public servants at lower levels of responsibility (12). Increasing the numbers of political appointees deprives most careerists of hope for appointment to the most challenging and responsible positions in government (Huddleston 1987, 63). This will reduce the attractiveness of the public service to talented young persons who gravitate to meaningful and challenging positions (Rourke 1991, 115). Over time, increasing the number of political appointees will work to bring about a less competent public service.

Finally, the increasing number of political appointees in the executive branch, meant to increase the ability of at least the president to control the bureaucracy or make it more responsive, actually reduces accountability within the executive branch. The increased number of appointments has been accompanied, as noted, by an increasing number of levels in the administrative hierarchy, as well as by an increasing number of appointments at each level. In each case the number of decision points within the bureaucracy has increased. This not only diffuses the ability of the president to achieve responsiveness, but also diffuses decision making in such a way that it is more difficult to pinpoint failure or determine who is responsible for lack of action (Light 1995, 64). Concomitant to this difficulty, it also becomes more difficult to assign credit for superior performance.

Bureaucratic Responsiveness and the Legislative Branch

Much of the analysis, especially by public administration scholars, of achieving political responsiveness from the bureaucracy has centered around presidential activities. Charles Jones recently criticized this approach as not offering a sufficiently broad context in which to evaluate the president's role alongside that of other political actors. Jones observes, "Much of this presidency-centered analysis concludes that the system is not working well, when in fact only a part of the system has been studied—and the most temporary part, at that" (1994, 284). Although his point is well taken, some attention has been devoted to congressional attempts at eliciting responsiveness from the bureaucracy and to the impact of these attempts.

Congressionally imposed reforms have developed in reaction to legislators' perception that presidents were controlling the bureaucracy unilaterally through the administrative presidency, cutting out congressional influence as much as possible (Rourke 1991, 116; 1993). These congressional-based reforms included expanding the interests represented in administrative proceedings, extending procedural due process, increasing legislative oversight, increasing staff to assist legislators in exerting control over the bureaucracy, and developing sunset legislation, among others (Aberbach 1990; Gilmour and Halley 1994; Gormley 1989, 191–93; Khademian 1995; Rourke 1991, 116; Wilson 1989, 241–44). The way in which this works is indicated in a pithy example provided by James Wilson:

Where Congress once unabashedly directed the War Department to give a weapons contract to the Jedidiah Jones Cannon Foundry, it now directs the Defense Department to insure that the contract is awarded to an American firm that tenders the lowest bid, employs the correct mix of women and minorities, makes provisions to aid the handicapped, gives subcontracts to a suitable number of small businesses, is in compliance with the regulations of the Environmental Protection Agency and Occupational Safety and Health Administration, and is not currently under indictment for contract fraud. To insure that these and other constraints are observed, Congress further directs the Pentagon to employ an army of contract officers and contract auditors and to publish its procurement policies in a book of immense length, excruciating detail, and soporific prose. (1989, 240–41)

Have these reforms worked to enhance legislative influence on the bureaucracy in order to achieve greater responsiveness? Although their reasons differ, most scholars tend to agree that recent reforms have not been successful in achieving a more nearly optimal mix of political direction and bureaucratic action. Two criticisms of congressional reform deserve our attention: (1) the continuing complaint by legislators that bureaucrats are not responsive to them; and (2) the tendency of some congressionally imposed reforms to impede effective bureaucratic action.

Bureaucrats' Responsiveness to the Legislature

Despite reforms to bring the public service more in line with congressional direction, the perception persists among members of Congress that civil servants still labor outside the orbit of congressional influence. There are reasons for this perception. Both James Q. Wilson and Herbert Kaufman argue that responsiveness is a matter of perception and that departments and agencies are responsive in some senses, though not perhaps in others. One reason legislators perceive that bureaucrats are not responsive stems from some key characteristics of Congress. It does not speak with one voice. Moreover, it has organized itself so that committees have considerable power, and to the degree that public servants are responsive it is to the powerful committees that determine their authority and budgetary support—and continuously monitor them—rather than to the Congress as a whole. Kaufman, whose detailed study of bureau chiefs provides insight into the agency-congressional relationship, found that

"Congress is, for a bureau chief, the committees with jurisdiction over his agency" (1981, 166). Kaufman found that bureau chiefs visited at least each year all members of committees with jurisdiction over their agencies (53). Indeed these contacts extended to committee staff as well (54–55).

Aberbach, Putnam, and Rockman found that American bureaucrats were more political in their role focus than were their counterparts in other Western democracies (1981, 98). Further, Robert Gilmour and Alexis Halley's findings, based on their analysis of congressional involvement in ten case studies, show that Congress impacted policy implementation and program execution in these cases in such a way that its involvement was more as a co-manager with the White House. In these case studies Congress, relying on its staff resources, became a co-manager as well as an overseer in policy implementation and program execution (Gilmour and Halley 1994, 335). They further found that "particular [Congress] members and staffs were well-known players in the implementation process reviewed in these cases" (368). Aberbach found that congressional oversight had gradually increased since the early 1970s, although the oversight conducted is rarely comprehensive or systematic (1990, 33, 36–38). Thus, it does appear that members of Congress do impact policy implementation and program direction more than they perceive they do. But Congress elicits responsive action from public servants in a fragmentary and decentralized framework.

A second reason legislators charge that bureaucrats are not responsive is because, in our system of government, Congress is not the only politically based entity to which bureaucrats must be responsive. In the U.S. separation-of-powers government system, bureaucrats must be responsive to multiple authorities. James Q. Wilson, in fact, accuses members of Congress of being "disingenuous" when they complain about the lack of responsiveness of agencies or departments. U.S. bureaucrats know full well that they cannot ignore the wishes of Congress. Wilson also notes the potentially competing demands of other legitimate purveyors of democratic direction: the president or White House (Wilson 1989, 237). The perceived lack of responsiveness to Congress by career public servants derives in part from the structure of government.

Thus, most scholars assert that U.S. bureaucrats are indeed more responsive to Congress than members of Congress generally believe, and that elaborate reforms designed to assure responsiveness are not necessary. Yet members of Congress continue to perceive that bureaucrats are not responsive to them, and as long as this perception persists, Congress will continue to take steps to ensure greater influence over the bureaucracy.

Impeding Bureaucratic Effectiveness

A second critique of congressional reforms designed to strengthen democratic responsiveness from administration is that they have actually made it more difficult for public servants to act effectively or for Congress to exercise effective oversight. Rourke, for example, argues that Congress's reforms of the bureaucracy have generated unintended consequences: "Ironically for career officials, this congressional backlash has reinforced the effect of the administrative presidency on the bureaucracy by placing new curbs on the ability of administrators to use their own judgment in exercising their discretionary authority" (1991, 116). One of the effects of these constraints on discretion is that it reduces the ability of bureaucrats to act in a way that would make their actions more responsive to political direction rather than to the multiple rule constraints placed upon them. It also makes bureaucrats more risk adverse (Kettl 1992, 102–04; Khademian 1995, 41). William Gormley concludes that the reforms have failed in their goals of reducing incrementalism, clientelism, and parochialism in the bureaucracy. But the reforms have achieved something else: they have propagated a climate of fear. Gormley writes:

> Bureaucrats fear legislators and for good reasons. Legislators have been impatient, abusive, insistent, and vindictive. As a result legislative pressure makes bureaucrats uncommonly cautious. Although legislative pressure encourages a certain kind of responsibleness (to legislative freelancers in particular), it seldom encourages innovation. . . . The deeper tragedy is that legislative pressure serves often to narrow rather than to broaden the bureaucracy's perspective. (1989, 221)

Although Gilmour and Halley find that Congress can co-manage executive agencies, they do note that this comes with some cost. The cost includes the added workload of new requirements and the erosion of long-term capacity to manage, which in turn leads to morale problems, diminished analytic capacities and leadership on policy initiatives, and greater difficulty in designing complex policy implementation (1994, 358, 366–67). Samuel Krislov and David Rosenbloom conclude that the proliferation of committees and staff in Congress has reduced congressional impact on agency action by reducing the capacity of Congress to act with "dispatch or decisiveness" and, they assert, "the imperial presidency is giving way to an imprecise Congress" (1981, 198).

Are Bureaucrats Responsive to Elected Officials?

These accounts of (mostly) difficulties associated with elected officials eliciting responsiveness from the bureaucracy must also be informed by a number of recent studies, which attempt to examine the impact of elected officials on program direction and policy implementation more specifically than some of the studies examined above. Some of these studies have been based on surveys that ask public servants about the relative influence of several external actors on the bureaucracy. The usual conclusion is that the legislative body exercises the most influence, with the elected executive somewhat behind, at least at the state level (Brudney and Hebert 1987; Abney and Lauth 1986). Another study examined the impact of party strength and preferences in the U.S. Congress from 1947 to 1984 and found that, despite the delegation of major policy tasks to the executive branch, "congressional parties exert a strong and systematic influence upon national policy making!" (Kiewiet and McCubbins 1991, 231–32).

Several studies have utilized case studies to examine the relationship between elected and appointed officials. Ronald Randall examined the Nixon administration's efforts to change direction on aspects of welfare policy in the Department of Health, Education, and Welfare. He found that in the latter half of Nixon's tenure, the White House, by using a series of successful tactics, managed to elicit the policy response it wanted (Randall 1979). John DiIulio's study of the federal Bureau of Prisons (1994) revealed that public servants worked hard and sacrificed much to pursue public and organizational goals above their own. Gilmour and Halley (1994), summarizing the results of ten case studies in a variety of policy areas, concluded that Congress was an effective co-manager of policy with the president, exercising substantial influence on policy implementation and program choices.

Several scholars have examined U.S. federal regulatory agencies. A recent study of policy implementation in eight regulatory agencies concluded that bureaucracy is more responsive to political direction, from both the president and Congress, than is usually posited by politicians, the public, or scholars (Wood and Waterman 1994). In the eight cases examined, the authors found responsiveness in each case, suggesting that bureaucratic intransigence is exaggerated. The authors concluded, "If bureaucracies are not adapting, then the reason is not because bureaucracies are nonadaptive entities. It is because there is nothing to adapt to" (Wood and Waterman 1994, 154). Studies of other regulatory agencies also showed a policy responsiveness to elected officials, including studies of the Occupational Safety and Health Administration (OSHA), the Office of Surface Mining, the Securities and Exchange Commission, and the National Labor Relations Board (Hedge, Menzel, and Krause, 1989; Hedge, Sccichitano, and Metz 1991; Moe 1982, 1985; Scholz, Twombly, and Headrick 1991; Scholz and Wei 1986).

Not all studies confirm an impact of elected officials upon the actions of public servants, however. One study, for example, found that the Reagan administration exerted little impact on antitrust policy (Eisner and Meier 1990). A study of the Interstate Commerce Commission revealed that appointees of one president are no more likely to vote with each other than with appointees of another president (Cohen 1985). Finally, Ingraham found in three case studies that the link between the White House and political appointees in executive departments was "frequently unclear and tenuous" (1991, 191).

So what are we to make of these findings? Certainly one implication is that the image of the recalcitrant or shirking bureaucrats may be overblown. Dan Wood and Richard Waterman observe, for example, that by finding responsiveness in all eight of the agencies they examined, it "is not all that uncommon" (1994, 141). Still, this does not mean that we can disregard concerns about it. First, the findings are not unanimous and it may very well be that responsiveness varies in accordance with a number of factors. Lana Stein, for example, found in her study of policy in St. Louis that some policy areas, such as health, were responsive to elected officials whereas others, such as police, were not (1991, 83, 96).

Second, considerations of elected public officials' concerns about the responsiveness of the public service must be taken into account. How satisfied they are indicates at least one measure of how well they believe they are fulfilling their responsibilities in governing, even if that satisfaction is not based on accurate perceptions. For another, their ability to focus attention on their concerns in this area means that citizens' perceptions of the responsiveness of the bureaucracy may be dependent upon how elected officials depict that responsiveness. Finally, the concern about bureaucratic responsiveness in democracies is a continuing one in democratic theory and is likely to remain so, especially when either scholars or public officials focus on the requirements and robustness of democracies.

Accountability and Responsibility of Public Administrators

The quest for the fundamentals that define the mix between elected officials and the public service in a democracy must be anchored in a consideration of the concepts of accountability and responsibility. This mix defines the relationship between unelected and elected officials that translates public preferences into policy. The ultimate purpose of mechanisms that impose accountability and provide definition of responsibility is to achieve responsiveness. This means acting in accordance with the preferences and expectations of the person or entity to whom one is accountable or responsible. How do accountability and responsibility help achieve this goal?

Accountability at its most basic means answerability for one's actions or behavior (Dwivedi 1985; Dwivedi and Jabbra 1988, 5; Kernaghan and Langford 1990, 157; Pennock 1979, 267; Uhr 1993b, 2). Accountability is the obligation owed by all public officials to the public, the ultimate sovereign in a democracy, for explanation and justification of their use of public office and the delegated powers conferred on the government through constitutional processes. Accountability in general is something demanded of an agent by a principal. It is thus imposed from the outside upon government officials. For example, accountability is the price the people (acting as the principal) extract for conferring substantial administrative discretion and policy responsibility on the agent (collectively summarized as the government), which in this study we will consider the bureaucracy, or the department secretary in particular (Uhr 1992, 1993a; Banfield 1975, 587–88). An accountability plan refers to an arrangement of obligations owed by one set of officials to another and ultimately to the public (Uhr 1992 and 1993a). The scope of accountability may include hierarchical, legal, political, professional, and moral accountability (Dwivedi and Jabbra 1988, 5–8; Romzek and Dubnick 1987). The accountability plan should define to whom one is answerable (Caiden 1988, 34–35). Such arrangements vary widely across modern democracies, but the common feature is that the representatives of the public owe the public an explanation of their tenure in office.

Because unelected officials exercise much influence in democratic governments, effective accountability involves two accountability transactions. An unelected set of officials, such as the bureaucracy, give an account of their activity to an elected set of officials, such as legislators. The elected officials take due account of unelected officials' activities and feed their own considered account back into the political system and, through that mechanism, to the people.

For accountability to sustain responsiveness, it must ultimately be buttressed by sanctions and awards. When examining the relationship between the electorate and elected officials, the sanctioning mechanism is the power of the electorate to defeat the elected officials at the next election. Removal from office constitutes the obvious ultimate sanction. This power may also exist in the relationship between elected and unelected officials, although it does not always exist for public servants who may be protected from dismissal except for criminal conduct. In the principal-agent relationship between elected and unelected officials, however, there are sanctions available other than, or in addition to, removal from office. These might include demotions, embarrassment in the media, investigations, and budgetary penalties, among others (Peters 1978, 207–29). There are also positive rewards for those who account well for their work (Friedrich 1950, 398).

"Responsibility" is another concept that is useful in examining the appropriate mix between appointed and elected officials in democratic government. Responsibility refers to the charter of delegated powers entrusted to the government, to the grants of power conditionally made available by principals to public official agents to do the things that they have the capacity to take charge of as their area of initiative and responsibility. The definition of responsibility often emphasizes empowerment and discretion (Burke 1986, 11–15; Freund 1960, 37; Pennock 1960, 4, 27). Responsibly placed officials are thus expected to show policy and administrative initiative and leadership, but also to accept accountability when initiatives do not work well or become publicly suspect (Friedrich 1960; Pennock 1979, 267; Uhr 1993b).

In this sense, responsibility takes on a second meaning that is important for our consideration. Agents are responsible if they have a sound concept of their duties and act in a way that is based on due deliberation, sound reasoning, and consideration of relevant facts and circumstances (Pennock 1979, 267). A responsible agent is one who can be relied on, who can be left in charge (Lucas 1993, 11). Responsibility may be based on "a course of action derived from some set of ideals" (Burke 1986, 9). Frederick Mosher called this second meaning subjective or psychological responsibility because it is anchored in "to whom or for what one *feels* responsible and *behaves* responsibly" (1968, 8; see also Burke 1986, 8–15; Kernaghan and Langford 1990, 158; Marx 1957, 44–45). The two meanings of responsibility are related because in this second sense agents, to be responsible, must consider the consequences of their actions, for which they are accountable (Freund 1960, 29–30). Implicit but *very* important in this definition is the requirement that principals provide sufficient definition of agents' duties, so that the definition may guide agents' actions as well as provide a basis for principals to appraise agents' actions through accountability mechanisms. Overall, the two senses of responsibility suggest an empowerment of agents by principals through the assignment of authority, an acceptance of the responsibility of that authority by agents, discretion to act on that authority, and the requirement that agents be accountable for the way they exercise that authority and carry out their duties (Caiden 1988, 25; Uhr 1993b, 4).

Although there are differences between accountability and responsibility, they are interrelated in several ways. One interrelationship is noted by John Uhr who writes that accountability "defines the boundaries within which official responsibilities are acted out" (1993b, 4). Another connection is the relationship between accountability mechanisms and the requirement that agents consider the consequences of their actions as they exercise discretion. Without accountability their discretion would be unfettered and might lead to irresponsible actions. A final relationship focuses on responsibilities. If they are not well defined, then agents may not have sufficient guidance to inform discretion and principals may not have a sufficient basis on which to judge agents' actions.

These definitions provide a starting point for considering the appropriate mix between elected officials and the public service in democratic governments. But they are just a starting point, because there is as yet no agreement among scholars of democratic governments just what that mix should be. Different definitions of the appropriate mix of bureaucracy and politics was at the core of the well-known Friedrich-Finer debate of the early 1940s.

Herman Finer presented a very expansive view of accountability, which had the effect of severely limiting the discretion of bureaucrats: "that the servants of the public are not to decide their own course; they are to be responsible to the elected representatives of the public, and these are to determine the course of action of the public servants to the most minute degree that is technically feasible" (1978, 411–12). Finer based his position on his belief on what democratic government required. For a government to be democratic, the wants of the people must be expressed through an elected institution, which had the power to compel officials to "exact obedience to orders" (413). Finer warned against public administrators acting "for the good of the public outside the declared or clearly deducible intention of the representative assembly" (419). Finer clearly feared undemocratic government if administrators acted on their own discretion.

Carl Friedrich, on the other hand, argued for a broader notion of administrative discretion. He espoused a dual standard of administrative responsibility, one in which the public administrator was responsive to technical knowledge and popular sentiment (1978, 403). Friedrich believed that the increasing complexity of public sector problems required technical competence, and that only one's fellow professionals would be able to judge the activities and policies of the public administrator. In this position, Friedrich echoed the earlier position taken by John Gaus, who asserted that an emerging consideration that individual public servants would incorporate in their definition of responsibility derived from the standards and ideals of the public servant's profession, which would provide an "inner check" (Gaus 1936, 39–40).

Most scholars view Friedrich today primarily as one who espoused professional knowledge and norms as a viable basis for guiding a public administrator's actions. He believed that the actions of a public administrator are irresponsible if they have been "adopted without proper regard to the existing sum of human knowledge concerning the technical issues involved" (1978, 403). But he also argued strongly that the public administrator should be guided by popular sentiment, although this part of his argument is sometimes neglected by modern commentators. Friedrich, however, is clear on this point: "We also have a right to call [a policy or action] irresponsible if it can be shown that it was adopted without proper regard for existing preferences in the community, and more particularly its prevailing majority" (ibid.).

These contrasting views set the stage even today for a consideration of accountability and responsibility, which will of necessity be explored in any consideration of the interaction between politicians and bureaucrats in a democratic government. These views suggest that there may be disagreements among both scholars and public officials as to the appropriate mechanisms of accountability and the relationships between accountability and responsibility. That is indeed the case. Both accountability and responsibility still pose important problems that need resolution in democratic theory.

The Problem of Accountability

One problem in establishing the mechanisms of accountability is that they may not be defined clearly. Kenneth Kernaghan and John Langford, who focused on the Canadian parliamentary system, noted, "Public servants are often accountable in several directions at once and can, therefore, receive conflicting signals as to what is expected of them" (1990, 163). One reflection of this manifests itself in the various definitions of account-ability, including hierarchical, legal, professional, and political (Dwivedi and Jabbra 1988, 5–8; Romzek and Dubnick 1987). In this classification, Finer would place more emphasis on hierarchical and legal definitions of accountability and Friedrich would emphasize professional and political definitions. Michael Barzelay has fashioned one of the strongest critiques of the Friedrich position with respect to accountability to profession. He indicates that, at the time when professional knowledge was just becom-ing essential in government, it was reasonable to equate professional stan-dards with citizens' collective needs and requirements. But the problem now is that "Government often fails to produce desired results . . . when each professional community within government is certain that its stan-dards define the public interest" (Barzelay 1992, 119).

The issues outlined in the classic debate also manifest themselves in modern government practices. Although parliamentary systems usually define to whom the public servant is accountable more clearly than do systems that utilize separation of powers in the structure of government, the accountability regimes vary among parliamentary democracies, with varying emphasis upon the power of parliament, of cabinet, of ministers, and of the bureaucracy (Laver and Shepsle 1994, 5–8). In the United States, the ambiguous definition of to whom public servants are accountable is marked by the almost incessant tug of war on this matter between the president and Congress. In Australia, the attempt to strengthen the over-sight function of parliamentary committees constitutes another manifes-tation of this conflict. Were this effort to be successful, the accountability regime in Australia would emphasize parliament more and ministers less as the principal to which the bureaucracy must account.

Another issue that continues from the classic debate centers on lines of accountability outside government. In considering accountability mecha-nisms in democratic governments it is a given that elected officials are answerable directly to the people and that non-elected officials are an-swerable directly to elected officials. What is less clear is the extent to which non-elected officials are also directly answerable to the people. Friedrich's position that bureaucrats are subject to a dual accountability that includes public sentiment strongly implies a direct accountability by bureaucrats to the people, whereas the Finer position would restrict the task of mediating public sentiment only to elected officials.

Present-day public administration scholars continue to reflect this disagreement. Some posit a direct link of answerability between bureaucrats and the public. Campbell and Halligan, for example, indicate that accountability should extend directly to the public at large (1992, 194). And in his study of American, Canadian, and British bureaucrats Campbell found that they indeed did consider accountability to the public as a factor in their decisions, although there were differences between officials in the three countries (1983, 303–05). Perhaps Gary Wamsley states the case for bureaucrats' accountability to the general public most strongly in his plea for an agential perspective for bureaucrats that increases their concern for a broad conception of the public interest and the common good (1990, 128).

But there are scholars who are troubled by public servants accounting directly to the people. Finer believes that the relationship of citizens to the government falls within the exclusive purview of elected officials. Perhaps the nearest modern soul mate to Finer is Theodore Lowi. Lowi emphatically indicates his preference for constrained discretion of public servants. He writes, *"public administration will always be undermined and corrupted by politicization, and it is politicized to the extent that the authority delegated to it is open-ended"* (1995, 491, emphasis in original). Elsewhere, Lowi (1993) states his case that constitutional power in the U.S. system rests with Congress, and all power in the executive is delegated. It is clear that Lowi would prefer strict lines of accountability between public servants and elected, especially congressional, officials.

Other scholars do not go quite so far as Lowi but are, nevertheless, troubled by an accountability mechanism that runs directly from citizens to public servants, or they prefer a mechanism that relies on elected officials. Kernaghan and Langford, for example, believe it is more practical to hold public servants directly accountable to elected officials. They also believe it to be more legitimate (1990, 167). Rose believes that "civil servants are particularly ill-suited to identify and interpret signals from the electorate" (1987b, 215). Rather, the experience of elected officials provides the basis for choosing among signals from the public and interpreting what is appropriate to guide public action (215–29). Charles Hyneman believes that "elective officials must be our primary reliance for directing and controlling the bureaucracy" (1950, 6). One of the factors in these concerns is the strength or focus of the accountability ties between public servants and the public. This is illustrated by a former Australian department head, Arthur Tange: "Ministers coping with question time and urgency and censure motions make more tangible demands on the accountability of public servants at the top of the hierarchy than do vaporous abstractions about accountability to the community at large" (1982, 4).

The discussion of direct accountability of public servants to the public takes place in the U.S. context against the backdrop of almost one hundred years of reforms, which initially sought to insulate and neutralize the public service and has diminished the strength of political parties. At a time in the nineteenth century when political parties were more robust, they had not only more control over nominations of party candidates for political office but also more control over appointments to executive departments and agencies. Although this led to concern about "spoils," it also provided a more powerful context in which public servants might be more accountable to the public at large through the mechanism of the political party than can be the case now. Certainly those who posit direct accountability of unelected public officials to the public at large do not provide details of how the public can sanction or reward performance. Neither do they indicate how public servants can communicate with the public in such a way as to provide the public with the necessary knowledge to evaluate public servants' work.

The Problem of Responsibility

An important problem of responsibility in democratic governments centers on the difficulty of defining the responsibility of public servants clearly enough to furnish them guidance and provide a basis for taking their actions into account. Elected officials do not always establish clear goals, and even if they do they may distance themselves from previously set objectives if it becomes politically expedient for them to do so. Further, political processes are complex enough that almost any given legislation may embody a variety of goals, not all of which can be simultaneously pursued. Also, as with accountability, there may be multiple elected officials, speaking with many different views, attempting to define these responsibilities.

A second problem of responsibility centers on striking a balance between the initiative and discretion of public servants in a democracy and the necessity that they remain responsive to democratic preferences. The tendency of elected officials to control bureaucrats may lead to their acting to avoid risk rather than to energetically carry out their responsibilities.

This discussion of accountability and responsibility makes it clear that these concepts are important in democratic governments, and that it is necessary to pay attention to the way they work in the many relationships in democratic government. As this study unfolds, the concerns of accountability and responsibility will be limited to exploring how they relate to eliciting responsiveness from non-elected officials in a democracy. We shall also be interested in the specific ways that politicians and administrators interact to provide political direction for the bureaucracy. In the Australian setting of this study, the locus of political direction of the bureaucracy centers on the minister, the staff of the minister, and the department secretary. Let us now examine these three groups of officials to discover the mix between politics and administration in that governmental setting, with the goal of seeking the fundamentals of accountability and responsibility in the relationship between elected and appointed officials in a democracy.

3

The Department
Secretary

The department secretary in Australian Commonwealth government is important to this study because he or she constitutes an important conduit through which political direction is funneled to the department from the minister and the minister's office. Ministers and their staffs also contact and interact with others in the department, including the deputy secretaries and first assistant secretaries, the two positions in the hierarchy immediately below the secretary. But the department secretary is in a unique position to describe and oversee the range of relationships between the department and the minister and ministerial staff.

The position of department secretary in Australian Commonwealth government has undergone considerable change in the last several years. Appointment to the position is now less permanent than it once was. The government of the day, especially the prime minister and the minister of a given department, has more impact on selecting the secretary now than it did at one time (Hyslop 1993, 73–75; Halligan and Power 1992, 89–91). Although current rules permit persons from outside the bureaucracy to assume the position of department secretary, persons holding this position during the Hawke and Keating years generally did so after serving in the Australian Commonwealth bureaucracy. Most regard themselves as professional public servants.

Many of the secretaries interviewed previously held positions in one of the three central departments of Australian Commonwealth government, Treasury, Finance, or Prime Minister and Cabinet, prior to first holding a position as a department secretary. This is true for other secretaries as well and has also been the practice in the past (Hyslop 1993, 81–82). Many secretaries have significant foreign experience, either through their education or through service in international bodies of which Australia is a member. At the time of the first set of interviews, all but one of the secretaries had served in their present position longer than the minister of the department had served in his or her present position. In addition, some of the secretaries had served as secretary of more than one department. After the 1993 election, more than half the department secretaries in the Australian Commonwealth government were transferred, all to the same position in another department.

During the Hawke and Keating governments, sixty-eight individuals served as department head, and their total service as department heads ranged from five months to over fourteen years (172 months). The latter time was served by a department head who had begun his tenure in the previous government. Despite the five-year terms of appointment, the average total service as a department secretary was just over four and a half years, which included in some instances service as head of more than one

Table 3.1

Department Heads in Hawke and Keating Governments, 1983–1996

	Length of Service (months)		
Number of Department Heads	Total[a]	Average	Shortest and Longest[b]
68	3,769	55.4	5–172

Sources: From material compiled by Laurie A. Waldron of the Australian Public Service Commission, from *Commonwealth Government Directory* dated 1984, 1986, 1986–1987, 1988, 1988–1989, June and December 1989, June and December 1990, June and December 1991, August and December 1992, February, June–August, September–November 1993, March–May, June–August, September–November 1994, December 1994–February 1995, March–May, and June–August 1995.

a. The data derive from the *Commonwealth Government Directory,* which is published periodically. The appointments for each department head are listed as beginning and ending with the date of the publication. Service may possibly have begun or finished between the publication dates, but the data provide as good an approximation as is available.

b. Includes total service as a department head, which in some cases started prior to the first Hawke government. The total period of the Hawke and Keating governments was 156 months.

Table 3.2

Average Length of Service in Each Department by Department Head,
Hawke and Keating Governments, 1983–1996

| | Length of Service (months) | | |
Number of Tenures Department Heads[a]	Total	Average	Shortest and Longest[b]
97	3,769	38.9	3–94

Sources: Same as sources for table 3.1.

    a. Since department reorganization occurred several times, if a department head remained in what was the major part of the previous department the time count was not interrupted.

    b. The person serving ninety-four months had served part of the tenure in the previous Coalition government. The longest continuous service that began in a given department during the Hawke and Keating governments was ninety months.

Table 3.3

Mobility of Department Heads
in Hawke and Keating Governments, 1983–1996

| | Number of Posts Held | | | |
	One	Two	Three or More	Total
Number of Department Heads	45	18	5	68
(Percent)	(66.1)	(26.4)	(7.3)	(99.8)[a]

Sources: Same as sources for table 3.1.

    a. Error due to rounding.

department (see table 3.1). In fact, the average length of time department secretaries served as head of a given department was about thirty-nine months, just over three years (see table 3.2). Some secretaries did rotate through several posts, but about two-thirds of them served in only one post in the Hawke and Keating years (as noted in table 3.3). Very few served in more than two posts. This tenure of service does not represent total service in the public service, as almost all department secretaries had served many years in the public service before becoming department head. In almost all instances, this service included time in the positions just below department secretary in the Australian bureaucracy.

Table 3.4 provides another view of department head tenure. Almost 30 percent serve less than two years. But fully 20 percent serve five years

Table 3.4

Months Served as Head of a Particular Department,
Hawke and Keating Governments, 1983–1996

	≤12	13–24	25–36	37–48	49–60	>60	Total
Number of							
Department Heads	11	18	26	11	10	21	97
(Percent)	(11.3)	(18.5)	(26.8)	(11.3)	(10.3)	(21.6)	(99.8)[a]

Sources: Same as sources for table 3.1.
   a. Error due to rounding.

or more in the same position. The average time that a department head serves is lengthy by some standards. And even though many of the department heads interviewed in 1992 had served longer than their minister by the end of the Hawke and Keating years, cabinet ministers had usually served longer in cabinet (over five years) than department heads had served in a department head position. But the department head on average served about five months longer as a department secretary than a cabinet minister served in a given portfolio (see chapter 5).

The Howard government, which assumed power in March 1996, removed six department heads and in some cases replaced them with persons who were not currently serving in the Australian Public Service. In some ways this was a logical extension of the changes in department head selection made in the Hawke and Keating years. Those who were brought in from the outside tended to have previous service in the public service, far more so than is typically the case with political appointments in the United States. Further, the Hawke and Keating governments did make occasional appointments from outside the public service, although, like their successors, their appointees usually had prior Commonwealth public service experience. The primary differences were the suddenness of the action by the Howard government and the number of department secretaries affected, about one-third of the total. Many department secretaries who were retained were shifted to other departments.

In this study of the political-administrative interface, we are particularly interested in what role department secretaries play in this interface, and how they view the role of the minister and their relationship to him or her. The key components of this role include administering the department, providing policy advice to the minister, coordinating the portfolio, and keeping the minister informed.

Administering the Department

Previous studies of ministers have noted that ministers have different styles and interests (Heclo and Wildavsky 1981, 130). Australian department secretaries noted this but still voice preferences about the nature of the relationship between minister and secretary, as well as awareness of how the relationship differs from what they would like. Generally, they described ministers as being heavily involved in setting policy direction but leaving department operations to the secretary to manage. As one secretary put it:

> Our current minister . . . doesn't get involved in the day-to-day administration of the organization at all. He . . . believes that he sets the strategic direction, he does the political angle of government. But as far as the day-to-day operations of the department, he says, "That's your business." That's, I think, a very healthy division of labor. (Interview, October 1992)

Another stated: "I would expect him to have a very clear idea of what he wanted from the department, how he wanted the department to relate to his office [and to] other players. But that the *how* that was achieved was left to me" (interview, October 1992). The secretary elaborated: "It doesn't mean he can't express views on the *how* but that he would respect the fact that, in the end, it's something that he would hold me accountable for, rather than . . . [telling me] how to do it" (interview, October 1992).

This view of the minister–department secretary relationship reflects closely the tradition of Westminster-based systems (see Hyslop 1993, 15–18). And they probably track closely what U.S. bureaucrats would like to see in their relationships with elected officials. Nevertheless, secretaries report that ministers vary in the extent to which they involve themselves in details of department administration. Most secretaries who have worked with more than one minister report that their experience includes those who do get involved in the detail. One, for example, stated:

> But, he's a person who is very heavily into detail. He is not a good delegator, and he likes to do just about everything himself. . . . I mean, the principal things he takes an interest in so as not to be viewed with a distorted impression, they're obviously policy issues. But he's a person who is interested in the detail of policy, not just in the big picture and leaving it to other people to fill out. He really does go right to the detail. (Interview, October 1992)

From the perspective of the department secretary, the minister who gets too involved in the details of administering the department risks losing sight of overall policy direction. One secretary put the matter like this:

> Well, at times, there will be some who will nickel and dime you. And that's not terribly helpful from their viewpoint because instead of getting the big picture they're fiddling around on details. It's also not terribly helpful to the department because it distracts you because they're constantly wanting to interfere in detail, which really shouldn't be their business. (Interview, October 1992)

In this respect, the secretaries would agree with Woodrow Wilson, who wrote, "the administrator should have and does have a will of his own in the choice of means for accomplishing his work. He is not and ought not to be a mere passive instrument" (1992, 19). Ministers of the Labor government in the ten years prior to this study became more involved in the administration of departments than ministers in previous governments (Halligan and Power 1992, 84). Although secretaries prefer that ministers emphasize overall policy direction and refrain from meddling in details, in fact the practice of ministers varies. Department secretaries reported that managing the department comprised a major part of their task. But their work also involves other important services for their ministers, in policy development, in portfolio coordination, and in provision of information that ministers need in order to accomplish their responsibilities.

Developing Policy

Secretaries believe that their departments must play a strong role in policy development, and this belief is shared by both ministers and their staffs. With respect to the integral way that ministers, their staffs, and department personnel can interact in this dimension of the department's role, one secretary reported:

> We've had very close relationships with the . . . ministers and their offices. The process of deciding on what issues will be brought to the cabinet in the budget is one which goes through a budget policy committee, and that consists of the minister, some of the members of the minister's staff, and the senior people in the department; . . . it is a genuine attempt to identify what the priorities are, to set down very

clearly what the facts are and what the issues are, and to come up with the right sort of proposals, solutions which can be turned into proposals. (Interview, October 1992)

Not all ministers create such a formal meeting to plan policy initiatives for a given year. But secretaries believe that they and the department should provide policy advice to the minister. Another secretary stated:

> But broadly speaking, . . . I believe the portfolio secretary ought to be responsible for running the department and . . . ought to be listened to in terms of advice, accepting that ministers will have alternative sources of advice. But I don't think there ought to be a major issue that proceeds without the portfolio secretary being involved in the advice that goes forward [to the minister]. Now whether the minister accepts that advice is a totally different issue. (Interview, October 1992)

Most department secretaries, however, would count it a cause for worry if the minister regularly disregarded their advice or modified it substantially. One stated: "I always took the view that the departments weren't the only source of advice, but if you weren't the major source of advice on a continuing basis, then there was something wrong with the department" (interview, October 1996). Most departments play an active role in policy development. A part of this responsibility is to provide recommendations, as noted by one secretary: "But my general view is that the department ought to put forward proposals or recommendations in all cases. And you shouldn't just give options. You can give options but then say, 'Well, I think you ought to go for this one'" (interview, October 1992).

The desire of secretaries to participate in policy advice is reciprocated by ministers who clearly believe that departments play a critical role in policy development. One minister stated: "The adviser [on the minister's personal staff] may have the idea or the minister may have given the adviser the idea or talked about the ideas—but the development of that would be very much dependent on the policy resources of the department" (interview, November 1992).

Most department secretaries believe that providing advice during the development of policy makes the department influential in government. One secretary commented:

> Now we're first amongst equals I guess in terms of a source of advice, although his personal staff are the last advice. But we get an

opportunity that's second to none to present our views to him about
what should be happening, about what we think are the major issues, and about what should be done about them. And I guess that
gives us some power. But it's power to bring things out rather than to
determine them. (Interview, October 1992)

The input into policy development also includes evaluating the positions
of various players in the process. A department head commented: "But
the influence I think that I have, indeed that the department has, is to
bring a balance to the various interest groups to ensure that parliamentar-
ians and indeed the minister, particularly the minister, is made aware of
the likely impacts on the broader economy of any particular . . . interest
group's [position]" (interview, October 1992).

The statements of secretaries are interesting in light of other studies
that examine the relationships between ministers and the Australian Commonwealth bureaucracy. For example, Campbell and Halligan, who write
from a historical perspective, found that the Hawke government "had
established strong political control over the bureaucracy" (1992, 204).
The increasing use of staff and advisers from outside the departments,
including the augmenting of ministerial staffs, means that the advising
and policy development function that departments once exclusively held,
is now shared with others on whom the minister depends (204–08). But
the department secretaries, ministerial staff, and ministers interviewed for
this study indicate that there remains substantial department involvement
in policy advice and development, even if that involvement might be less
than it was at an earlier time.

Coordinating the Portfolio

The Hawke government's reorganization of departments in 1987 consolidated a number of smaller departments into larger ones, creating what
some call mega-departments. The names of some of these departments
suggest the kind of combining that occurred: Department of Foreign
Affairs and Trade; Department of Employment, Education, and Training;
Department of Transport and Communications. The particular programs
combined within one department in some cases changed after the initial
reorganization. But the emphasis on consolidated departments continued
to the end of the Keating government in 1996. There was ample justification
for the reorganization, as indicated by one department secretary:

The small departments which just [included] one policy area were too much prone to be captured by interest groups; . . . they were too focused on one issue of policy rather than the broad scheme of things in government. I think the broader perspectives that the bigger departments are able to take, I mean DEET [Department of Employment, Education, and Training] is no better example, I think, where the linking of education, training, and employment policy . . . is far better for what's needed in the country and still is. . . . Foreign Affairs and Trade, I think, continues to make sense. Our foreign interests are pretty largely being driven by our trade interests. . . . If there are management problems they have to be coped with; . . . it wasn't justified as essentially a management thing. It was only justifiable ever as a policy-related initiative. (Interview, October 1996)

The viability of the reorganization was perhaps best confirmed by the new Howard government's continuing the basic organization in place when it assumed power in 1996.

This reorganization is pertinent for this study, because it affected the relationships between departments and ministers. After the reorganization many of the departments included a minister, who was also a member of the cabinet, and usually at least one and sometimes more than one additional minister who had responsibilities for a part of the portfolio, but who did not sit in cabinet. Added to this mix were assorted parliamentary secretaries, who were considered members of the ministry. Like the junior ministers, they were not members of the cabinet. But they too might have a portion of the portfolio to oversee or regular tasks to perform that affected the department. This assignment of ministers and parliamentary secretaries set up the possibility that the department might be subject to different signals from the different members of the ministry. The characteristics of political parties in Australia enhances the possibility that different signals might be provided to departments by the members of government responsible for the department. The government elected in 1996, for example, is composed of a coalition of the Liberal and National parties, making it not only possible but very likely that several departments will have ministers from different parties. The Labor Party, which governed from 1983 to 1996, is organized into factions (some of which are quite distinct), which again makes it likely that when Labor is in power many departments will have ministers from different factions of the party (Lucy 1993, 121–22).

The use of multiple ministers for a given department will probably continue. There are always pressures in any government to increase the number of ministers. Ministers have more influence than backbenchers. It is a mark of prestige to be a minister. So the number of ministers in any one portfolio is not likely to decrease in Australian government.

How does this impact the relationship between the department and the political leaders? Most department secretaries support the reorganization. Only one voiced concern about the arrangement:

> I always have basked in the belief that one of the principles of good management was [to keep] clear lines of command and accountability. And so I've always been a skeptic about this model of having multiple ministers . . . in the portfolio. I guess I have to confess that I remain a skeptic. It seems to violate a lot of pretty important principles. But nevertheless, one has to make it work. . . . I'm happy to say that that works well, but it is something that could easily run off the rails. (Interview, October 1996)

One impact of multiple ministers in a portfolio is that it places great demands on the time of department officials. One department secretary reported: "I have to deal with the issue just of conflicting demands on my time. I've never had yet a conflicting demand on my policy advice, if you like, in that the ministers are all going in the same direction" (interview, October 1996). Another department head observed:

> There is a difficulty for the department in adequately servicing the junior minister and providing the minister with the sort of status that the minister wants in a situation where time is very short, where the main issues have to be handled with the senior ministers, where there are just so many demands on time that sometimes you don't give as much attention to junior ministers and parliamentary secretaries as you ought to. (Interview, October 1996)

A second impact concerns the almost inevitable struggles for power and influence in the department among those in the ministry. Those with leadership aspirations in politics are not always able to work together as well as would be desirable. One department secretary observed:

> You do have a senior minister. But . . . if the senior minister dominates things, the junior minister tends to get his or her nose out of joint because they are not being taken as a serious ministerial player.

> You've usually also got in those large portfolios a parliamentary sec-
> retary. They're anxious to [become ministers] so they're sort of ac-
> tive doers around the place wanting to get more and more responsi-
> bility. (Interview, October 1996)

The way in which the activist nature of many ministers in a department
works was noted by one department secretary:

> You could never say it's a one-on-one thing where you know this is
> the thing we're doing and this is the person we're doing it for. There
> was also complexity of who does what? What was the relationship
> between the two ministers? How much do we let the senior minister
> know what the junior minister is doing? How much is it in the end
> the [responsibility of the] senior minister to call the shots and ride
> over the junior minister? (Interview, October 1996)

In parsing the relationship between multiple ministers and departments,
most department secretaries believe that they must ultimately observe the
superior position of the senior minister. As one secretary put it:

> At the end of the day the senior minister, the cabinet minister, calls
> the shots. At the end of the day he or she is the one who makes the
> decisions and decides how much rein to give the junior minister. So
> as secretary of the department I always in the end knew that . . . I and
> the senior minister was the relationship that mattered. And if . . . I
> had to keep a little bit in reserve for the junior, so be it. You have to
> take your cares about that because you don't want to be seen to be
> playing games against the junior [minister]. (Interview, October 1996)

There are several ways that the portfolio might be coordinated. One
of the best is to divide responsibilities and then have that division enforced
(and reinforced if necessary) by the senior minister. The way this works
was described colorfully by one department secretary: "Where you have a
strong minister, then in fact the junior minister and the parliamentary
secretary have specific responsibilities. But they know at the end of the day
they're not going to go outside the boundary because they're going to get
their heads kicked in. And that's a reality of life" (interview, October 1996).

A second way that portfolios are coordinated is through formal meetings that include senior department officials, the ministers and any parliamentary secretary in the portfolio, and sometimes senior staff members of
the ministers and secretary. One secretary observed:

> [It] was very sensible also . . . to have things like budget policy com-
> mittees where the minister, the secretary, the senior officials [in the
> department], the senior people from the minister's office, the junior
> minister, the parliamentary secretary would all be involved. And whilst
> some people might argue that this somehow involves some
> politicization of the public service, it was not really the way it oper-
> ated at all. Because you weren't concerned about the party political
> aspects of particular decisions. That is something that the ministers
> had to work out. You were concerned about the issues, what were
> the best options? what were the financial implications? the technical
> feasibilities in terms of IT [information technology] systems? and so
> forth, whether there are industrial relations implications so there won't
> be problems. . . . It is a very sensible way for getting cooperation
> between the minister, the minister's office, and the public service.
> (Interview, October 1996)

Another secretary indicated that such meetings occurred frequently with
the ministers responsible for the department:

> We have a portfolio business meeting whenever parliament is sitting.
> We start at eight o'clock on Monday morning with the [top depart-
> ment officers] and the ministers in the one room. We mostly talk
> about what the parliamentary week's . . . likely to throw up. But we
> also talk about other major issues that are on their deck for the week.
> (Interview, October 1996)

A third device for coordination centers on the ministerial staff. The
department can facilitate this kind of interaction, as noted by one secretary: "You've got to make sure the ministers' offices talk, because if the
staffers aren't communicating with each other, that could create problems
born of suspicion. And a lot of people in the political process are inherently pretty suspicious people. And often with good reason" (interview,
October 1996). In these kinds of cases the ministerial staff might disen-
tangle differences between ministers and facilitate more unity in the signals that are being sent to the department.

Department secretaries themselves may engage in brokering differences between ministers. One secretary noted:

> But you know if you ascertain the senior wanted thus and thus and
> the junior of the partnership wasn't delivering, you had to help the
> senior minister bring him into line. And I had to do that on not many

occasions. Even if the relationship was good they often used me as the go-between because they didn't want to have a direct tussle, because it didn't suit their political relationship to have a direct fight on something. (Interview, October 1996)

Finally, some ministers (but apparently very few) manage to develop a team approach to providing political direction to a department. One secretary explained:

I've had some ministers, but only a few, who have wanted to run their ministerial team very much as I would run a departmental team— in other words, as a team with an idea that the senior minister will be engaged in any issue that's . . . of importance, and that they will work collaboratively together and then the junior minister will have the areas where he or she has a greater degree of flexibility and latitude. . . . But most ministers tend to, senior ministers they tend to actually go towards a demarcation so that they don't cover each other's turf very often. And by and large, politicians don't work like bureaucrats. They don't in fact have anything approaching a management team on the political side of the system. That's my experience over several years working with senior and junior ministers. I'm not suggesting that ministers don't get on well. It's just that they behave rather different, a different way. They tend to be facing outward towards the community, they tend to be engaging with their own electorate, they tend to be engaging with interest groups, and they really come together perhaps more in a party context than they do in a machinery-of-government context. And they come together in cabinet. (Interview, October 1996)

Despite these attempts at coordination, they do not always work because relationships between colleagues are not always optimal and because the stakes with which they are working are often high. One department secretary stated:

I think that illustrates a general point, which is that these relationships at the end of the day are relationships. You can try and inject some clarity into them in terms of who's handling what. But if the two ministers don't have clear understandings, or they don't work together, then they become difficult. I think that's the story. In other portfolios in other administrations there have been times when even though the responsibilities were technically clear in fact the relation-

ships were difficult and therefore it was difficult for the department
to forge a commonality of view amongst them. (Interview, October
1996)

The same secretary also indicated that the "commonality of view" was
not necessarily a problem in another example provided: "So the issues are
not always about policy. The issues can be about who is doing what"
(interview, October 1996). In such situations, it may be difficult for the
department to know who is at the helm on given matters within the
department's sphere of responsibilities.

A second problem of having multiple ministers in large departments
centers on keeping the components of the department working together.
The impetus for the reorganization of 1987 was to provide some synergy
in related areas. But the components of the department often remain organized as recognizable entities within the larger department. When responsibility for these entities are then distributed to different ministers,
the following dynamic can occur, as explained by one department head:

> But in practice the way the portfolio responsibilities are divided it
> tends to mean that [those in various groups report to one minister or
> the other]. . . . Keeping a sense of collegiality in which the sun and
> the sky for some people is the [junior minister] and the sun and the
> sky for other people is the [cabinet minister] is something that needs
> careful thought and attention. It's not so far a problem, but you can
> always see how you could just let the department spin into two groups
> of people who don't have a collegiate view. (Interview, October 1996)

Keeping the Minister Informed

Another task of the department secretary is to keep the minister informed
of developments in the department (see also Hyslop 1993, 17). Secretaries
paint a picture of great diversity among ministers in their interest in and
attention to departmental business. Some are clearly more interested in
party matters than in department affairs, and all must devote considerable
attention to their parliamentary duties. Ministers who are members of the
House must also devote considerable attention to their constituencies,
more so than those in the Senate whose election is determined in large
part by their position on the party ticket. One secretary agreed that ministers may pick issues in which they are interested but that "they have to be

confronted with [some issues] even when they're not interested." The responsibility of the department is to "make sure that they are across [abreast of or informed on] the significant issues. I mean, at the end of the day they're answerable to parliament" (interview, October 1992). No secretary wants the minister to whom he or she is accountable to be uninformed if queried during question time, for example, as explained by one secretary:

> Well, during parliamentary sittings we see him every day. I mean, we have a meeting with him, which is basically to make sure that he's across whatever we think are the most important things to be across. Partly for the benefit of handling question time. But it also provides an opportunity for us to raise with him anything that we want to. (Interview, October 1992)

Departments also prepare what Australians call submissions to cabinet. These submissions offer the information and argument for a given position that the minister will then take to cabinet (usually without ministerial or department staff being present) and that introduce the case for the minister's position. One department head, in discussing a major policy change by the Labor government that involved several ministerial portfolios, explained:

> So our approach was constantly to [a related department] at a bureaucratic level. . . . But similarly, our minister was moving in that direction with his parliamentary politics, and it of course was a decision that was taken by cabinet. And in that process we, of course, provided the normal sort of briefing to our minister. We provided the normal sort of input to the submission that was prepared by the department. (Interview, October 1992)

Developing the budget is an important process in any government, and in the Australian Commonwealth government a committee of the cabinet known as the Expenditure Review Committee carries the responsibility for developing the budget that is presented to cabinet. The membership of this committee varies over time, but at a minimum includes the minister for finance, the treasurer, and the prime minister. Total membership during the Hawke administration varied from five to seven (Walsh 1995, 101–23). Here, ministers must make their case for expenditures. As with submissions to cabinet, they rely heavily on their departments for preparing for this critical meeting. One minister stated: "Anything that we were going to propose in the [budget] process, I had to get on top of all the details so I could go in and argue for or against anything in the cabinet committee" (interview, October 1996).

Since the ministerial office is inherently political and information is an important part of presenting one's viewpoint, whether winning adherents to it or defending it against critics, the relationships between departments and ministerial offices can at times be sensitive. The persons interviewed, though, seemed to agree that there was a line that separated what was proper action or behavior for the minister or ministerial office and what was proper for a department. One department head explained how differences of opinion about exactly where the line was drawn might be discussed:

> There's a good understanding between this department and the minister's office as to what is political and what isn't. And when one or the other oversteps that line, because of the honesty in the relationship that's been developed, we're able to say we don't think we should be providing that particular type of comment on this particular matter. . . . What we would—and this is the sort of line we'd go through: We would suggest that we provide you with the facts of the matter. "Do you want to color it up? That's your prerogative." . . . It doesn't always follow that the factual position is the position that they would follow most usefully. Now, in the case of [a particular issue raised by the opposition], we are very careful not to be seen to be making value statements, value judgments, about opposition policies. At the end of the day we may well . . . indeed be the organization that's required to implement those policies [of the opposition]. And under those circumstances it would be somewhat foolish for a professional public service, or servant, to come out and declare a particular color on issues. I think we have been fairly successful to date in holding that line. But that's a two-way street. I mean, ministers' offices can be difficult things. But it is important to get in early and establish a good working relationship of honesty and openness in that relationship so that they understand why you're not being able to [meet a request]. (Interview, October 1992)

Fortunately, this view is widely shared by ministers, who recognize this norm, regardless of their political party. One minister, describing expectations of the department, said:

> Well, I think it's as simple as [this,] the department is there to serve

the government of the day in a professional way, exercising at all times loyalty, not entering at any time into politics. It's irrelevant to me what the politics—or whether they have individual politics, that is—[for] the individuals in the department, it's just irrelevant. (Interview, October 1996)

Politicizing Department Secretaries?

An interesting controversy in Australia is whether the Australian public service has become too politicized as a result of the new appointing arrangements of the department secretary. In addition, the 1987 reorganization of Australian government permitted the government to appoint new department heads and to exert influence on the appointment of other senior-level positions in each department. These changes were designed to make the bureaucracy more responsive to political direction (Campbell and Halligan 1992, 203). This criticism argues that because secretaries are no longer permanent they are less likely to give independent advice to ministers. Some former department heads, who in their day held the title of permanent heads, hold this position (Hyslop 1993, 74). Campbell and Halligan quote a line officer as indicating that the changes make it less likely that secretaries will provide advice their ministers would not want to hear (1992, 208). One secretary, responding to this general criticism, stated:

> Well, I really think that's nonsense. I think that the quality, the frank and fearless advice that someone gives to a minister, is in my experience much more a function of (a) the personality of the minister, and (b) the personality of the person giving the advice. Some ministers encourage that sort of advice; other ministers discourage it by their attitude. Some people are willing to give it; some are not willing to give it. I don't think that the security of tenure is a major issue in that; . . . while I can see the theory that people might be afraid to give that advice because they might get moved . . . the sort of person who's worried about being moved would find five other things to worry about as well. But secondly, I find that where a person is either personally or politically compatible with the minister, then within that shared framework it's much easier for him or her to say, "Look, I think this is a dopey idea and won't achieve your purposes at all," or whatever it may be. . . . So I wouldn't go so far as to say that

you're more likely to get frank and fearless advice by this system, but I would really say that nobody could possibly empirically show that [with] one system, you know, you've got more frank and fearless advice than [with] the other system. (Interview, October 1992)

The way disagreement between a secretary and minister might be handled was noted by the report of one secretary. He found that a new minister with experience from a previous portfolio wanted to adopt an organization structure similar to that in the former portfolio, which the secretary thought did not apply to the new department because it was more complex. As the secretary tells the story:

> My minister came into this portfolio from [another department], saw our model [of organization], and wanted to apply [the model from the previous department]. We had some fairly interesting debates at the time where I tried to take him through how it [the current department] is different. He tried to push the department into having a stronger central policy role. Stronger than I was totally comfortable with, because my own view (leaving aside the diversity of this department) is I don't like models of administration that separate policy from administration. I believe the two should interact much more closely. We've ended up with a model in this department, which is, as you'd expect, the usual compromise. (Interview, October 1992)

The matter was resolved when the secretary "put a model to him that I thought captured what he wanted but not in a way that was foreign to the essential nature of what this agency is about, and he accepted it in the end" (interview, October 1992).

Another secretary indicated that most ministers want someone who will offer strong policy advice and who will disagree as needed with the minister:

> They're looking for somebody who can tell them when they're wrong. And most ministers, I think, welcome—it's got to be done with a degree of sympathy, not, "Ah, There! You . . . mucked it up again, Minister XXXX!" But most ministers welcome it. So it's not as difficult as is sometimes portrayed. That's one side, whereas on the other hand the government is certainly looking to people who are responsive in the sense of telling them how they can achieve their objectives—not telling why they shouldn't want to achieve their objectives. (Interview, November 1992)

This secretary added:

> You're looking for a balance between being responsive in the sense
> of taking the government's objectives as a starting point, and saying,
> how's the best way of achieving them? That still leaves you plenty of
> scope for quite interesting policy tensions because it's the nature of
> governments that they've got more objectives than they've got in-
> struments, and so there's a trade-off between them. Pointing up the
> nature of those trade-offs . . . is pretty interesting public policy, and
> . . . it's in that context of pointing up the nature of the trade-offs that
> you may tell some of the things that aren't totally palatable or what-
> ever; . . . it's better that they're told by us than by the opposition, if
> there's something wrong. (Interview, November 1992)

In this sense, the department has the responsibility to provide advice based
on their understanding of the government's objectives while at the same
time drawing on its professional knowledge and experience to provide a
good view of the consequences of proposals, including those that might
be negative (Keating 1995, 22–23). In fact, a former British prime minister wrote, the minister "will discover . . . that the civil servant is prepared
to put up every possible objection to his policy, not from a desire to thwart
him, but because it is his duty to see that the Minister understands all the
difficulties and dangers of the course which he wishes to adopt" (Attlee
1954, 308).

As might be expected, ministers interviewed in 1992 did not agree
with the critique that the new method of selecting department heads had
diminished the independence of the department in providing policy advice. One stated, for example: "Only the ignorant have done that [that is,
charged that the current system has politicized the bureaucracy]" (interview, November 1992). Another stated that the new system helps ministers establish the political influence that is needed:

> The minister ultimately controls the fate of the head of the depart-
> ment, and it is clear that the head of the department recognizes that.
> So (a) if you have a good relationship with the top bureaucrat and he
> is sensitive to the concerns that we are talking about, then (b) I think
> that the minister can rely on the chief departmental executive to be
> sure that the minister's views tend to prevail and his concerns are
> met. (Interview, November 1992)

In this respect the minister agreed with the view expressed by one of

Campbell and Halligan's respondents, who indicated that he fearlessly gave advice but was aware of the government's position so that he knew when to "back off" (1992, 208). Other scholars are also skeptical of this claim that the new method of appointment has led to excessive politicization (Weller 1989, 377). This general position is supported by the former prime minister Robert Hawke, who wrote:

> Some critics of the changes made to appointment and tenure provisions for departmental secretaries argued they would lead to politicisation. Four years later, no one could reasonably claim that the portfolio secretaries serving my government are other than highly professional career public servants who have also served previous governments in senior positions. (Hawke 1989, 13)

The action of the new Howard government in replacing six department heads at the beginning of its term raises this question anew. Clearly the action unsettled department heads, in part because of the number involved (about one-third of all department heads) and in part because all were terminated at one time. The reaction was also intensified because similar developments have occurred in some Australian state governments, with the change of the party controlling governments at times producing wholesale turnover of department heads. One department head noted the difference in the way the new government had handled appointing new department heads: "Typically after a change of government, people will go, but over a period of time. And it's usually managed, more, in the past has been managed, with a little more finesse in terms of being able to ease these people out as opposed to how what happened this time" (interview, October 1996).

The potential impact of this move by the Howard government is that it will chill the propensity of the bureaucracy to give advice "without fear or favor." One former department secretary stated: "On the whole I think the government has been very silly about this because they absolutely caused uncertainty in the public service, and in the longer run that is not good in political terms to have the public service uncertain. The public service won't give informed, objective, fearless advice in those sorts of circumstances" (interview, October 1996). Another department head stated the worry in another way:

> I think my fear is that a Labor government at some future stage of

the game . . . will do it again. Maybe you'll sort of have people appointed who are sympathetic to the government of the day regardless of whether they are going to give them the advice that they ought to hear. They'll tend to give them the advice they want to hear; . . . the caravan that goes out and the new caravan that comes in might suit the United States. But I happen to prefer what was the Westminster System where the public service stayed behind. They told the emperor he didn't have any clothes on. (Interview, October 1996)

A former minister considered public servants more likely to perceive that, when "lack of cooperation is going to be punished, then people aren't going to behave as bureaucrats should" (interview, October 1996).

A department head also indicated another concern about the meaning of the large number of department head terminations: "The reality of life is that they'll put their own people in to department heads and the next step from there is they'll put their clones into senior executive jobs. So we will go down the U.S. path—I just think it's inevitable, quite frankly. I don't like it, but I'm saying we'll have it" (interview, October 1996).

Clearly the expectation of the ministers of the Howard government interviewed for this study is that public servants continue to put advice to them that the public service believes ought to be placed. One minister said that, "they should always feel free to put a point of view to [me], politely but firmly put if necessary a counterargument" (interview, October 1996).

Another minister stated, "If they can give me a logical reason why it won't work, then that's terrific. I appreciate that. Sometimes its result is that you get another idea and you can refine the original idea into a practical idea outcome that everybody agrees upon. But . . . I'm not interested in them just providing something they think . . . might make me feel good" (interview, October 1996).

It is too early in the new government to conclude whether the termination of so many department heads will have an impact on the quality of policy advice that departments provide to ministers. The expectation of ministers is for the relationship between them and department secretaries to remain robust. With time it will be possible to ascertain whether this expectation has been adversely affected by changing so many department secretaries so quickly in the early days of the new Coalition government in 1996.

Accountability of Department Secretaries

At about the time of the first set of interviews, the Management Advisory Board (MAB) in Australia had issued a draft study dealing with the issue of accountability of the public service. Thus, it is no surprise that the issue of department accountability to elected officials came up several times in the interviews with department secretaries. Several secretaries expressed concern about the Senate estimates committees. These committees meet twice each year with authority to conduct hearings on department spending requests. In practice the hearings often range widely, with senators questioning departments on a wide variety of matters (Lucy 1993, 201–04). In one secretary's evaluation of these committees: "Parliamentary accountability is actually fairly devalued, because I think that the things that parliament focuses on so often are trivial, . . . it's tabloid accountability, I think. They address their own important issues much more than they address the broader issues" (interview, October 1992). Another stated:

> The most difficult ongoing committee from a bureaucrat's point of view is the Senate Estimates Committee, which is a very unsatisfactory process perhaps to everybody, but certainly from the department's point of view. On almost every occasion, either a whole sort of series of things, nothing to do with the financial affairs of the department are raised, or it becomes a sort of tedious, dull, inconsequential proceeding where half the people in the room are asleep. I think the concern that we have had is the sort of thing that you are seeing . . . at the moment [where an opposition senator was being very critical of a department head for following the policy of the government]. It does seem to me that the committee arrangements in the parliament are open to that kind of behavior. (Interview, October 1992)

One secretary, when asked to whom he was accountable, stated his position very emphatically:

> Very, very simple. The theory and the practice is that I'm accountable to my minister. Now, the minister is then accountable to the parliament. Now, occasionally, I'll have senators say, "But you're accountable to parliament." I'm not! I'm accountable to the minister. The minister is accountable to parliament. But that's not a pedantic difference. That's a very major, very major difference. (Interview, October 1992)

Although most of the secretaries interviewed agreed with this position, most were not quite so emphatic. Several secretaries recognized that the system of government required the primacy of the minister in the line of accountability, but there were also additional considerations affecting departmental decisions and activities. Departments could not be oblivious to the Senate, for example. Still, the potential for a division of responsibilities that could require departments to respond to conflicting direction from ministers and other parliamentary-based institutions was a concern of many of the department secretaries interviewed (see also Hyslop 1993, 55–60).

In addition, some secretaries referenced broader government policy as a guide: "I would be conscious of the broad outlines of government policy; . . . are there benchmarks in the government's philosophical attitudes or stated public attitudes to issues that will help inform my decision?" (interview, October 1996). Another secretary voiced the view that limiting most secretaries to one five-year term in a department also had the tendency to develop in secretaries a governmentwide rather than a more parochial departmental perspective. In discussing the shift of secretaries during the Labor government, this secretary remarked:

> I have no doubt that . . . [secretary of the Department of Prime Minister and Cabinet] Mike Keating's justification for a reason for doing it was that he felt that secretaries being in place for too long got captured [by the department] and a secretary needed to recognize that his or her loyalty in the end was to government as a whole. (Interview, October 1996)

Some secretaries also listed another factor that guided their discretion, and this was information. Harkening to Friedrich's internal guides based on professional training and judgment, these secretaries believe that any decision for which they are responsible must be based upon good information. One commented that one question to be asked in making a decision was "What are the options? Do I understand the options and the facts?" (interview, October 1996). Another stated: "I want to feel that I have the best available information. And that can range from good to sketchy. . . . So I guess that due diligence is the start. Do I have the data that are available?" (interview, October 1996). In both these instances, the secretary indicated a number of other factors that would guide their decisions but included adequate information among them. Closely akin to the internal guidance systems advanced by Friedrich are notions of ethics, which may be derived from a number of sources including professional values. One secretary, for example, commented: "And very important is my own view of ethics and what is an honest and proper decision to make. And that goes whether it's relating to public policy I'm dealing with or personnel type issues, across the whole spectrum" (interview, October 1996).

What about accountability beyond parliament and the minister? Department secretaries also discussed broader lines of accountability that went beyond accountability to ministers. One interpretation of accountability included the department's responsibility to administer the law:

> In what respect is the secretary accountable to the minister? Well, obviously, for the operations of the department. And, I think, generally for the administration of the act as well. But not in respect of each individual decision, although if, for example, there was a pack of individual decisions which seemed to indicate that we weren't applying the law, then I think there is accountability to the minister. . . . Now, in our constitutional situation it's pretty clear that we are in fact responsible to ministers under the constitution, to the executive. . . . But in some way maybe we're accountable to the legislation itself, which is, I suppose, in a sense, it's an aspect of the rule of law that you have to ensure that the legislation is properly applied, and then of course a whole lot of things flow from that that you've got to have—training of your staff, and you've got to have systems in place to ensure that everything operates in accordance with the law, and the crucial thing is to get consistency of decisions in accordance with the law all around the countryside so that you don't have different interpretations of the law or different decisions being taken depending on which office you go to. (Interview, October 1992)

The accountability of department secretaries to law has also been noted by others (Hyslop 1993, 56).

The next step of accountability is accountability to the public, built upon the position of Friedrich and others previously discussed. Michael Keating, who served as secretary of the Department of Prime Minister and Cabinet when Paul Keating was prime minister, has written that "one of the strengths of a democracy is that unelected officials do not have the power to define what is in the best interests of the public. What exactly would legitimise a senior public servant's perception of the common good against that of the elected government?" (Keating 1995, 23).

Many public servants do not view this kind of accountability as necessarily an either/or situation, but one in which accountability to the public would be one of the factors they would consider in developing guidance for their actions. Other studies have indicated that the percentage of officials indicating this was a factor in decision making varies from system to system and even from administration to administration in the same country (Campbell 1983, 303–05). In the present study, several secretaries, when probed, agreed that other lines of accountability did exist, and that these lines included the public. For example, one secretary thought in terms of stakeholders: "Who are the principal stakeholders and how are they going to react?" (interview, October 1996). Another stated that secretaries needed to take into account the public at large, rather than leaving solely for the minister to determine how these considerations should weigh on department activities:

> Well, I think that everyone's got to take into account how the public is reacting, and it's always a real issue of how you handle public presentation of decisions. Now that's public in a narrow sense, that's interest groups. And particularly in an organization as large as ours the internal communication of decisions is critical, apart from the external. And the taxpayer in general has got an interest in the matter. So yeah, we've got a whole public relations area which tries to anticipate problems. (Interview, October 1996)

This answer indicates a sensitivity of the secretary and the department to interest groups rather than to a general interest. Later in the interview the same secretary, citing concerns similar to those noted by Secretary Michael Keating above, indicated some qualms with too direct a representation of the general interest by the public service, especially when asked to indicate his opinion of those who view the public servant acting as an agent of the people directly: "They worry me, I'd have to say. [Laughs] People who say [that] generally mean that the public servant has got the agenda. They'll manipulate groups for their own agenda. That would worry me. I don't believe that is—that ain't democracy in my terms" (interview, October 1992). Another secretary also noted the limits of his discretion by observing:

> In a matter of conscience I believe there is a broader responsibility to, if you like, good government and the people of Australia, which I'd feel if the minister was pushing a particular thing in a way that was dangerous, I would say to him, "Look, I just don't think this is

right. I don't think we ought do it this way." In the end if he directed me to do it that way, I would. I have a duty to warn and a duty to warn against going down certain routes, but in the end I don't have a separate authority to stand against the elected official. I'm not elected. I'm not—he has got the higher, superior accountability. I think it's dangerous to say you have some sort of superior, direct line to God, as a non-elected official. I understand fully the Nuremberg Doctrine and all that, but I think it's dangerous to set yourself up against an elected system. (Interview, October 1992)

Another secretary, after clearly indicating that he was accountable first and foremost to the minister, went on to list others to whom he felt accountable:

But as far I'm concerned, I believe I'm accountable certainly directly and very clearly to the government. I believe I'm also accountable in the sense of answerable to the parliament. I have to account to the parliament. I'm accountable clearly to interest groups within the public about—on various issues, but that's not strict accountability, but within that sort of general meaning of the word "accountable." All of those groups and more. (Interview, October 1992)

Although secretaries mentioned, usually when probed, several sources to which or to whom they were accountable, there is no question but that they view the minister as the sine qua non to whom they are accountable. This observation is also supported by Hyslop who found, in his study and in his work with department secretaries as an Australian public servant, that secretaries have clear lines of accountability (1993, 61–63). As well, Campbell and Halligan found that other senior executives in the Australian public service preferred the minister even over the department secretary as the primary object of accountability (1992, 212).

In recent years the accountability of department secretaries to the minister has been increased, in part by the new selection procedures discussed above. But one secretary noted that accountability has been strengthened in another way: "They've become more accountable . . . because objectives have been more clearly defined and . . . what's expected of them has been more clearly defined" (interview, October 1992).

The way in which accountability works in the Australian system hinges strongly on the relationship between the minister and the secretary. The parliamentary system does permit much direct contact, much of it informal, between department secretaries (as well as other senior executives in the department) and ministers. All secretaries had access to their ministers at any time they wanted or needed it. This permitted secretaries to develop an understanding of ministerial priorities and interests that guided them in their work. Over time the secretary and the minister develop a working relationship (Hyslop 1993, 14). Or, as former British prime minister Clement Attlee wrote, "The good civil servant studies his Minister's ways and saves him trouble" (1954, 310). Secretaries indicated how they come to know their ministers' needs and positions in several ways:

> You don't go and say, "Okay, Minister, what are you interested in here?" You observe over the first month or so of them being there what it is that emerges as their interest. I mean, you do all the right things up front by drawing their attention to the whole spectrum of activities. But you soon just work out what he's interested in, soon recognize [what] the political hot issues are, or whatever. I mean, you just observe and respond. Yeah, sometimes there's things you just have to interest him in whether he wants to be or not. And in terms of sort of spotting his interests, I think the only way you can do it is to let it emerge. (Interview, October 1992)

Another stated: "Then you see in practice that . . . he's not interested in that, he really does want to hear more about that, so you adjust to his style accordingly" (interview, October 1992). The intricacies of the way this relationship develops was explained by another secretary, who reported: "And within that, at the subordinate level, then judgments are taken and here again a system of formal, informal, spoken and nonspoken cues that are given. Then it's a case of being able to assess those and internalize them and be aware of the language that's being used, whether it's verbal or nonverbal" (interview, October 1992). Another secretary described the process in a somewhat different way:

> The trick [to developing a good relationship with a new minister] I think is . . . a combination of speaking and listening. You need to try and tell an incoming minister what his role has been. Every minister does the job in slightly different ways. Every minister's got slightly different expectations of what their role might be. So the first thing you've got to try and figure out between you is do you have a common understanding of what the role is? . . . So you need to have that dialogue. You need also to build the commonality of language, that

again, [because] depending on the background and the experience of the person that you're dealing with, terms mean different things. And it's important to have that dialogue, both the speaking and the listening, to try and make sure that you're actually using the same language. . . . Then I think it's just a case of . . . learning by doing. That it's unwise to assume that, in our briefing styles, in our personal choices . . . of the kinds of issues that they will want to get involved with are going to be the same. Now there are some things that you can anticipate, you can go and ask, "How do you like your papers?" But other things you only find out as you make mistakes and learn from them. In those circumstances, what you need is a bit of trust and a bit of willingness on both sides to do the learning. As long as you can do that it's OK. If there's a breakdown in the communication flows, though, you may not learn. And the relationship then becomes quite difficult. (Interview, October 1996)

As might be expected, some ministers and their staffs do a better job than others of communicating, whether it be specific instructions or general goals and objectives. The importance of ministers' communicating their positions effectively was noted by one secretary: "I think the main way of getting political direction is to have ministers who know what they want and can explain what they want" (interview, October 1992). This gets at an important component of responsibility noted in an earlier chapter. For accountability to be effective in a democracy, elected officials must define as clearly as possible the responsibilities of non-elected officials. Having elected officials who "know what they want and can explain what they want" is a key component in the accountability-responsibility mix.

In the end the relationship described by the department secretaries fosters a situation in which the department secretary can anticipate what the minister wants and how a given decision situation affects the minister. And this has a powerful impact on what a department secretary does:

I would do what I think the minister would do in this situation. And by and large, on discretion matters, I would follow that. That doesn't mean that I would follow that in giving advice to the minister, because that's a separate issue. But if we're talking about . . . a policy path like if . . . a pressure group has asked me to do something, . . . I think . . . perhaps my first principle—I would never do something that would embarrass the minister. And secondly I would try to do more or less what I think the minister would want me to do. That isn't true of necessarily the things that are in my discretion by legislation, which, of course, are very few. . . . There I feel I exercise my judgment. . . . But if I'm dealing with issues . . . then I think that I go down that path of . . . (a) not doing anything illegal or improper, (b) not embarrassing the minister, (c) doing what I think the minister would be likely to approve of, and (d) if I have discretion within that, erring towards the side of social equity. (Interview, October 1992)

This sentiment provides a good example of the internal checks on discretion, which are provided by the secretary anticipating what the minister, whose positions on various matters he or she has come to know, would want him to do. Within this context there is room for discretion. One minister commented:

Well, I think they should have plenty of discretion. Really, you're about administering the policy that the government sets down. And provided that they understand that they're not setting the policy, then there's no reason why they shouldn't have plenty of discretion. And actually discretion has increased quite a bit in the course of the last few years, and I think that's a good thing. I'm not an enemy of the public service; I'm not . . . taking that position. I think, the three secretaries I served with, as I said, I think they're terrific people. They're all very bright and very committed. I'm happy to give them as much discretion as you can on that basis. (Interview, November 1992)

A final insight on accountability was offered by one department secretary, who observed:

Now, you know, when you talk about accountability, if a government wants the status quo, there's no problem about the public service delivering it. So, in a sense . . . it's really only when the government wants to change things that the real problems of accountability arise. And I think that the public service is now readier to change and do things than it was twenty years ago. (Interview, October 1992)

This suggests that questions of accountability are especially important when those responsible for political direction want change.

The Department Secretary

The department secretary plays a pivotal role both in providing input into ministerial decisions and actions and in relating ministerial preferences to the bureaucracy. One secretary, discussing the working relationship with the minister, stated: "And it doesn't take very long, I think, for relations to—or methods of operating—to emerge which are satisfactory to all concerned. If that doesn't happen, then you've got a real problem" (interview, October 1992).

Ministers and secretaries need each other to succeed. For the most part, both the secretaries and the ministers recognize this key fact and put into place what is necessary to make it work. One secretary summarized the components of the relationship between departments and ministers that are likely to be most successful:

> A minister who is open, about his or her and the government's objectives, including where they really didn't have them but knew that they needed them. A minister that was prepared to take advice on face value, . . . to understand it, to if necessary seek sources of contesting advice, but to effectively give it [the department's advice] due consideration. A minister who's an effective advocate within the government, in the parliament, and in the public for his position, for the government's position, and the portfolio's position. I don't mean for the department's position. I mean for the position that you develop together. A minister that is personally proper and who isn't lazy, who has a degree of energy, vigor. It's obviously better if the minister is intelligent, capable of understanding . . . issues, and clearly better if he's a reasonable politician, has some sense of what the odds are. (Interview, October 1996)

Likewise, the relationship between ministers and department heads can break down. To some extent when that occurs it is because the analogue of what it takes to fashion good relations happens instead. A department head noted:

> It can break down a number of different ways. Some ministers become or are lazy or intellectually not up to the job. Very seldom that would be the case for a cabinet minister, but occasionally it occurs with junior ministers. . . . They can break down when ministers become, well, if ministers come to the department with a suspicion, an overwhelming sense of suspicion, that the department's not to be

trusted. And that [suspicion] . . . can be the result from the minister's own perceptions. . . . Or it can result from unprofessional behavior on the part of the department. So a department that leaks, tries to advance its own agenda as distinct from the minister's agenda, is one that won't keep the minister's trust very long. . . . Sometimes it breaks down because departments tend to place a greater emphasis perhaps on logic than policy objectives. (Interview, October 1996)

The department secretary thus plays a key role in relating politics and administration to each other in the Australian Commonwealth government. By engaging in the primary responsibilities of administering the department, providing policy advice, coordinating the portfolio among ministers and perhaps a parliamentary secretary, and providing other information to the ministers, the department head links ministers to the department and the department to the ministers. The department head brings to this relationship with ministers a mixture of expertise, an adherence to professional and legal norms, and a responsiveness to the political preferences of ministers. As noted, the relationship between department heads and ministers varies in the effectiveness with which it works. For the bureaucracy to be responsive to political preferences also requires appropriate performances by those who are on the politics side of the relationship, which in this case includes both ministers and their staff members. The part that ministerial staff play in this connection between politics and administration will be examined next.

4

The Ministerial
Staff

The ministerial staff in Australian Commonwealth government stand astride the relationship between the department secretary and the minister. One attempt to achieve greater responsiveness from the Australian Commonwealth bureaucracy has been to provide more staff resources to ministers (see chapter 1; also Campbell and Halligan 1992, 202–03; Halligan and Power 1992, 75–76, 81–84; Walter 1986, 52–59). Thus, much of the political direction of the department from the minister's office comes through the staff. In addition, the ministerial staff facilitates the work of the minister with other ministers, the cabinet, and the prime minister. Finally, the staff work to assist the minister in planning trips and in managing his or her time.

Although ministers have had some staff for many years, as noted earlier the number of staff has grown since the early 1970s and the importance of their position has increased. Even now, the staff size is modest compared with similar staffs in the United States. By the end of the Labor government in 1996, the typical cabinet minister had from ten to twelve staff members with policy-related responsibilities, listed under such titles as Principal Adviser, Senior Adviser, Adviser, Assistant Adviser, Consultant, Department Liaison Officer, Media Adviser, and so on (*Ministerial Directory* October 1995). Noncabinet ministers generally utilized from five to seven individuals in these categories while parliamentary secretaries had from two to four. This was generally rounded out with two or three secretarial-administrative staff for both kinds of ministers, one for parliamentary secretaries, and usually about three electoral office staff members for both ministers and parliamentary secretaries. The total ministerial staff at the end of the Labor period was 481 (*Ministerial Directory* October 1995). The Coalition government headed by John Howard continued heavy staffing, although the total number decreased to 423 (*Ministerial Directory* July 1996). In general, each ministerial and parliamentary secretary office in the new government contained one or two fewer staff members in the policy-related categories, compared with their Labor counterparts at the end of their thirteen years in power.

In examining ministers' staff we shall consider the following questions: What do they do? How do they assist ministers in achieving greater political responsiveness from Commonwealth departments? What other part do they play relative to the departments in policy development in the Commonwealth government?

The Mixture of Ministerial Staff

The ministerial staff in the typical office is generally a combination of generalists and specialists, with some ministers leaning more toward one or the other. One minister explained: "I believe in all-rounders rather than specialists. I especially think that is true in [this portfolio] because I can't replicate the [department] functions here with specialists because I don't have enough breadth, etc." (interview, November 1992). At the opposite end of the continuum, one minister relies heavily on specialists, usually on leave to the office from the department. One staff member explained:

> [The minister] prefers to have policy advisers from the departments that he's heading, partly because he believes that they ... have a ... good grasp of the substantive issues, and partly because they know the work systems and they've got the personal networks in those departments that facilitate the efficient handling of government business. (Interview, November 1992)

The typical ministerial office has advisers with both kinds of background. A study of Australian ministerial staff in the early to mid-1980s found this practice then (Walter 1986, 120–21). Another study found it also a practice in some other countries (Suleiman 1974, 257). This mixture does mark a departure from practices several decades ago, when ministerial staff was composed primarily of departmental officers (Smith 1977, 134). Today, part of the staff is usually viewed as "political" staff, and the other part as more specialized, and usually coming on leave (or on secondment, as it is known in Australia) from the department of the portfolio. This mix has been evident since ministerial staff started to assume its present-day status beginning with the Whitlam government (Forward 1977, 159).

Ministers may distinguish between the two kinds of staff members and what is expected as a result. One minister, for example, in explaining the different expectations of the two kinds of staff members, stated that he expected "political loyalty" from his political staff. He went on:

> They have to be on your side. They have to be prepared to die for you. I mean, they certainly have to be prepared to die for your cause, and it's preferable if they are prepared to die for you as well. . . . And, you can't expect that from public servants. . . . As liaison officers they're there to give you advice and to help, but . . . you don't own them. (Interview, November 1992)

Still, it would be a mistake to assume too much of a distance between the minister and staff members whose primary background had been in a department. The latter group of staff members works closely with the minister and other staff members. Another minister, whose role in parliament was perhaps less partisan than the one quoted above, provided an illustration of the close working relationships that develop between ministers and staff members whose primary background has been in departments: "I've been fortunate, . . . I've got two departmental liaison officers here who are so good, I mean, they're just so motivated, that the roles now are just so blurred that they're indistinguishable from my personal staff" (interview, December 1992).

A primary advantage of having staff with backgrounds in the department is that they provide institutional memory and knowledge of how policy is implemented. One minister explained: "Some of the people that I've had were technically very good and they could tell you what the technical solutions were, but also when you had in mind a policy shift, having departmental people in your office means they can often tell you what the practical difficulties of implementing that shift are" (interview, November 1992). Another indicated the practical usefulness of advice from staff with departmental backgrounds:

There's no question at all that there are some senior bureaucrats in departments that have got their own agendas. And I don't say that in the critical sense. . . . And as a new minister, there's no doubt that you get some of those agendas recycled on you that have failed. And it's for that reason very useful for a minister to have on his staff departmental liaison officers who are prepared to take, I guess, an independent view of the department and to provide you with advice about where some of the bodies are buried and I've been fortunate in having that advice. (Interview, December 1992)

The ministers interviewed thus placed great emphasis on the value of those serving in their offices who were on leave from their departments. Since the office and the department may have different objectives from time to time, the department officer serving on a minister's staff may be placed in a conflicting situation. One minister noted:

And I think obviously sometimes they have a bit of an ambivalence because their future inevitably lies with the department rather than with the minister. But, again I've found, [during] the period they're working in the minister's office, that their loyalties have been over-whelmingly to the minister and not to the department, though I can understand that there might be some tension there. (Interview, November 1992)

A risk associated with such assignments is that those who hold them may develop the reputation of being political, thus jeopardizing their future when the opposition returns to power. One adviser noted:

There are those officers who themselves are very political, and very ready and willing and able to assist the minister on domestic politi-cal issues. And, I think, some of those officers who've made no secret of their political allegiances . . . have become identified with the par-ticular party and to that extent have at times even become targets of opposition interest in parliament or in Senate committees, whatever. Now, it is possible that when—if and when—an opposition does get into power, that those people might find that their careers suffer. (Interview, November 1992)

One way that departmental officers guard against building a reputation for partisan politics is to make certain that they avoid overtly political tasks. As explained by a department secretary:

I think you'll find that ministers will also say to you if you push them that there are some tasks in an office that a public servant can't do—the hard-core political punch. I think public servants rightly sort of try, even when they are working within a ministerial office they will be careful not to become, even though they are working in a political context, not to become overtly political players. (Interview, October 1996)

Still, Australian public servants do take assignments in minister's offices, and such assignments are often viewed as career enhancing. One adviser, on secondment from a department, explained:

I think . . . it's a useful phase in a career to spend some time in a minister's office, because you get that perspective on the whole . . . policy process . . . , you get to understand . . . interaction with other ministers' offices, with domestic lobby groups, different constituencies, the media, political pressures. . . . So I personally happen to believe it's very useful for any officer to spend time in a minister's office, and you don't, in my view, have to become particularly identified in a political sense. (Interview, November 1992)

Campbell and Halligan note from their extensive study of Australian government that, regarding the prime minister's staff, this latter respondent is right. These public servants have found such service to be career enhancing (1992, 66).

Ministerial Staff Functions and the Departments

Ministerial staff functions extend across the range of the minister's interactions with the department. The staff provides analysis of department work, assists in overseeing the department, and provides information to assist the department's interaction with the minister. How do staff members to ministers perform these functions?

The title of Adviser is frequently used for ministerial staff in Australia, and when ministers and staff members are asked about the adviser's responsibilities, inevitably the first response includes the responsibility of providing advice, as noted by one staff member: "You can't help but . . . be involved in day-to-day policy advice. It's just part of the job" (interview, December 1992). This finding parallels that of Walter, who found that staff gave advising the highest priority (1986, 133). But what is this advice? What occurs as a part of providing advice to the minister?

Evaluation of Department Work

Ministerial staff evaluate briefs or briefing material sent by the department to the minister, drafts of submissions to cabinet, policy proposals, drafts of speeches, or any matter prepared by the department for the minister. At one level, some ministers assign their staffs the responsibility of establishing priority among the many briefs, indicating which are more important. One staff member explained: "It means going through the briefs that come from the department to advise on, work out which ones are the important ones, and make sure the minister gets the opportunity to read more carefully" (interview, October 1996).

Beyond this task, ministerial staff routinely engage in the basic role of evaluation. A minister stressed this responsibility: "I don't believe in directly second-guessing the bureaucracy. Sure, we'll evaluate anything they bring over. But we don't try to be an alternative policy-making body" (interview, November 1992). A minister, commenting on the role of his staff, stated: "But in the office there are about five people who have policy responsibilities. What that means is really overseeing all of the departmental material in that area of policy, giving me advice on ideas coming forth from the department, working with me on the ideas that are going to go back to . . . the department" (interview, November 1992). The reliance on staff evaluation was noted by another minister: "The advisers are here as filters, to . . . deal with the stuff coming to me from the department. And . . . telling me whether it's good, bad, or indifferent, or responsive to questions I've asked, if I've asked for something. Or whether it's . . . sensible and sound in terms of . . . what objective we're trying to pursue" (interview, December 1992).

In preparing advice for ministers, staff members may use a number of criteria. Some seem to emphasize the quality of what goes to the minister from the department, particularly written briefs or submissions that the department has prepared. One staff member explained:

> I think . . . our prime responsibility [is] to make sure that what goes to the minister is [as] comprehensive and correct as it can be, so that he has the available information. You know, it's not really a lot of making decisions at this level. There's making recommendations and looking at something and saying, "This is a lot of garbage," and sending it back to the department, or . . . saying to the minister, "I don't think this is very worthwhile for XYZ reason." (Interview, November 1992)

This respondent indicated that a ministerial adviser might examine a proposal, "to see whether factually it stands up. Whether . . . the detail that they provide actually leads you . . . to the same conclusion and recommendation that they had. And then . . . you might follow that through and find out more information" (interview, November 1992).

The most routine advice centers around commenting on submissions or briefs from the department to the minister. Advisers may offer comment on them, or even send them back for more work before submitting them to the minister. One staff member observed: "We would often . . . write back to the department and say, . . . 'This is not what we wanted,' or 'We want you to explain this or expand this,' or that sort of thing" (interview, November 1992). In some ways, staff see their role as providing quality control, which encompasses a broad meaning of the term, including whether the advice meets the political test of the office, as well as whether its general quality will hold up under wider scrutiny. One staff member explained:

> I work in the interest of my minister, which may at times not be how the department perceives its own longer-term interest, I suppose. From me, I think my minister expects political advice, and sort of a filtering system to assess departmental work in a way that can say to the minister that I think this is a very shoddy piece of work or I think we need to think about other areas. So I would call that quality control in the sense a sort of a second, independent source of advice and commentary on what his larger department is doing. (Interview, October 1996)

Another criterion used in evaluation and subsequent advice from ministerial staff relates political considerations to the department activities under evaluation. One adviser explained his role, in comparison with the department, as follows: "The difference between what I do and what the department might do can be seen in speech writing. The department might prepare the speech. I would look it over and provide the political thrust of the speech" (interview, December 1992). Another adviser also indicated that staff members were concerned with the political implications of department action:

> I think most advisers here would see their role in terms of filtering advice from the department but also occasionally involving policy formulation in the office on certain issues, and . . . more importantly

... from the government's perspective, or sheer political perspective, making sure that what is coming up, what is being discussed and settled by government with reference to specific application to your portfolio, that politically those decisions are sustainable. (Interview, December 1992)

Still another staff member stressed the differences in the perspectives of staff and department personnel: "In the case of the department, there's an expectation that policy advice is framed from the point of view of good policy, of the interests of the department . . . whereas we really are quite inseparable from the minister's role and the minister's interests" (interview, October 1996).

A department secretary indicated the important vantage point that ministerial staff bring to evaluating department activity, as well as the strengths each side brings to developing policy:

[The department does] the detailed policy development work. Their [the ministerial staff's] role in relation to that is to look at it from a much more personal viewpoint—that is to say, departmental officers, while they're politically sensitive and not stupid, don't know all of the details of the political life of the minister like his personal staff do. And the personal staff are sometimes able to point out political traps or political benefits in the broader sense. I don't mean just party political point-scoring, but you know, "Well, if you do this, remember that you've promised . . . such and such," or whatever it may be. (Interview, October 1992)

Directing the Department

A key task of ministerial staff consists of assisting the minister in directing the department. The staff become, in this sense, extensions of the minister, in providing directions to the department, feedback from the minister, and interpretations of what the minister wants. One staff member explained:

Well, a lot of [the staff's task] involves conveying to the department the minister's views on particular issues. And often he'll annotate submissions, and the views go back that way, and when his views are clearly expressed in that way our role is merely just transliterating his handwriting. But at other times he will ask for certain views of his to be conveyed to the department, or he'll give some extra background supplementing what he's written, and either because we're

asked or because we think it makes sense we convey those additional
thoughts to the department to help guide their implementation and
formulation of policy. (Interview, November 1992)

This task can extend beyond the paperwork that routinely passes from
the department to the minister to include monitoring the department's
faithful implementation of the government's position. One staffer indicated how this function worked when a senior public servant was negoti-
ating an agreement on behalf of the government. In explaining the staff
role, the adviser stated:

> The individual who was negotiating . . . [from] the department . . .
> kept referring to their position as the government position. . . . But at
> no stage in that week had he conferred with the government. Right?
> So they were his views, his decisions about the conduct of the dis-
> pute. Now, even if it's only that you come back for ratification, you
> must confer. . . . But it was an early thing that I had to do when I got
> here, which was basically just get onto this person and say, "I'm
> sorry, . . . we were basically embarrassed. We will just entirely repu-
> diate you as a negotiator if you don't basically get back in here now
> and talk this through with the minister and follow instructions."
> And that experience was not . . . something that this person had
> expected. (Interview, November 1992)

These specific needs for intervention may appear while a staff member is
monitoring more general departmental policy implementation, particularly of new initiatives that have come from government. One minister
explained:

> There are people who will seek to undermine the process just as there
> are those who will seek to support it and to kick it along. And so, it's
> very much for my closest advisers, senior advisers in this office, to
> monitor each particular sphere of responsibility and be involved with
> them very, very closely to make sure that government policy is being
> pursued, government priorities are being recognized, and that the
> practical considerations for implementation are paramount in people's
> awareness of how we actually go about putting in place our pro-
> grams. (Interview, October 1996)

The need for staff intervention may include also periods of policy
development, when the policy advice coming from the department may

differ from what the minister wants to do. In such cases, the adviser oversees policy development in a way that coincides with what the minister wants. This kind of attention from advisers is most likely to occur when there are disagreements between the department and the minister. As one adviser explained: "There have been occasions where we have had fairly strong disagreements over direction, policy direction. And you may have had to say a thing or two to make sure that they understood exactly what you meant. But there are . . . not too many instances of that" (interview, October 1996).

Another area that calls for staff attention occurs when controversy breaks out over a department action or mistake. In such instances staff members may communicate with a department in a way that assists the department in formulating its recommendation to the minister. One staff member, relating an incident where the department had provoked a controversy, indicated that the department's initial reaction was unacceptable:

> My strong gut reaction was that [the minister] needed to do more than that, that it wasn't simply good enough to say that "We're very sorry. It doesn't happen very often. We've taken action to make sure that it doesn't happen again." It was my view that we needed to . . . show that he wanted to do something to ensure independently that it didn't happen [again]. (Interview, November 1992)

The adviser recommended the minister refer the matter to an independent investigation and that the department personally apologize to those affected by its mistake. The staff member related the reaction to this advice:

> I told the secretary that that was what I was going to suggest to the minister. It is fair to say he was very unhappy. But in the end, after I spoke to the minister, the secretary and the minister spoke, and they actually agreed on that position. . . . In fact, after disagreeing with me at length, he thought about it [and] decided it was better to agree rather than have that imposed on him. (Interview, November 1992)

The question of when to intervene is often a judgment call and may vary among ministerial staff in accordance with the desires of the minister, the culture of the department, and how important given areas of the department's responsibilities are to the minister. This is illustrated by one staff member's comments. He was referring directly to his minister, but his comment also captures the subtle judgments that staff members must make when acting on behalf of ministers:

When you're a minister you're there to be a minister, not to run a department as such. That is the responsibility of the executive of the department, not the minister. But nevertheless there are matters for the public interest or public policy which the minister needs to be aware of. And some things on which a minister ought to give directions. There are fine judgments in those sorts of things, and generally, I think, [the minister] with his long experience . . . [is] a very successful minister indeed—both in policy terms and in administrative terms, . . . having good, good sense about when to intervene and when not to, and [in] the matter of intervention, the form of his intervention. (Interview, December 1992)

Facilitating Department-Minister Interaction

Ministerial staff also work to facilitate the department's contact with the minister. Part of the role of the staff member is to provide information about a minister's response to a department activity, or otherwise to clarify the minister's position on a given matter. One department secretary said:

They know the minister's mind much better than most of the department does, so when he writes on something, "I don't agree with this, please do such and such," the officer in the department can ring the ministerial staff member and say, "Well, why did he say this?" And they can explain the background, or . . . if the meaning isn't clear, they can ring up and say, "Well, do you know what this means? Do I have to go back to him?" "No, no. You don't have to go back to him; I can tell you that this is this or that." (Interview, October 1992)

A staff member explained this interaction from the perspective of the ministerial staff: "The department will contact the office and say, 'Look, we're not quite sure how to play this—whether we should just run in this way or whether [the minister] would like to consider it as an issue. What do you think?'" (interview, October 1996). Another staff member provided more detail on how this kind of interaction might work:

The head of the department . . . will quite often seek my view, saying, "Would it be a good idea to put this to the minister or not?" And I'll sometimes say, "I don't think this would be a good week to do it." Or, "I don't think it would be a good idea at all." Or, "It might need to be put another way." It's a useful sort of thing from that point of view that the department can use me as a sounding board in that respect to just test the waters and see, how far should we go with that in this form or is there another form that is going to be a bit more acceptable, or he'll get a better hearing on it if it's in another form, or so forth. (Interview, October 1996)

The department's use of ministerial staff to ascertain the minister's likely reaction to the department's activity also extends to correspondence. One staff member related: "They [the department] might have a letter from someone, and they're thinking this is the line that they want to adopt, and they would ring you up and say, 'What do you think of that?' first, before they actually submit it. So there is that tick-tacking" (interview, November 1992). The interaction between staff members and the department (and, for at least some staff members, the bulk of that interaction) consists of the department seeking information on how to produce a document that will meet the approval of the minister. One staff member stated: "So I would say that probably three-quarters, maybe half, half to three-quarters, of the contact is in that—'Can you give me a sort of a steer of how the minister will react if we say this?'" (interview, October 1996).

The interpretation of ministerial preferences to the department may also come at the initiation of the staff. Ministerial staff may independently assess departmental work and send it back for more work before it goes to the minister. One staff member stated:

They [the staff] will then take the department's recommendations, look at them at our perspective, the perspective of the policy maker. Do these recommendations accord with the intention of the policy? And we'll quite often say, "Well, look, this is not what was in mind when the government set down this policy direction, this policy path." Sometimes that means it will go straight back to the department. You say, "I'm sorry, start again." I've just done that with one last week. I said, "Look this is not at all what the minister was seeking. He's given you a very firm and clear direction as to the path he wants to go down. You're setting him off on a different path. You're ignoring a policy decision that's already been made. So please take that into account at the outset and come back with recommendations that relate to that decision." (Interview, October 1996)

In addition to this kind of feedback, ministerial staff may also ask the department for clarification, the provision of more information, the resolution of seemingly contradictory information, or other matters in a way designed to improve the quality of what eventually goes to the minister.

This facilitative role works to keep the relationship between public servants and ministerial staff from becoming adversarial. One adviser explained the usefulness of the staff for the department by commenting: "It works for the bureaucracy too because they use us as a sounding board before putting things up to the minister. You can save enormous amounts of time" (interview, November 1992).

That the staff works closely with the minister places them in a good position to know the minister's position well enough to provide this kind of feedback to the department. One staffer reported the process by which staff get to know the minister's preferences and outlook on policy related to the portfolio:

> Well, I guess I was fortunate in that I'd had quite a bit of opportunity to gain an appreciation of his views. [When I was in the department . . . I was assigned] to assist him and one or two senior officers in putting together what he regarded as a major paper on [a policy area of the portfolio]. So, as part of that creative process, discussing what he wanted, and writing, and then seeing what he wanted rewritten, and debating it, and so on, I got, I guess, quite a good understanding of his perspective on [the policy issues]. . . . And so, I don't think it was in complete ignorance of the man and his approach to [the policy of the portfolio] that I came to the office. . . . But then, of course, just working with him, seeing his reactions to papers, participating in meetings, discussions, traveling with him, one inevitably learns a great deal about his approach. (Interview, November 1992)

The frequent contact that staff members have with ministers provides them with great opportunity to learn the minister's views, likely reactions, and plans. One staff member stated:

> Well, we have a meeting with him every morning that he's here; . . . he tells us how he feels about everything. . . . But I think also that, after working for a minister for a fairly long time, that you have a pretty good sense of how they're going to react. And because of the nature of the beast, you wouldn't really be working for them in these jobs unless there was a certain simpatico. (Interview, November 1992)

A good part of the interaction between ministers and their staffs is informal but still provides the opportunity for learning the minister's preferences. One staff member indicated:

In sitting periods, when the parliament is in session, he works in that office over there, and our doors are open, so we're constantly sort of talking to each other. We would probably talk twenty or thirty times a day and maybe every day you'd have perhaps half an hour or more to have sort of a more lengthy sort of brainstorming session about what . . . we are doing. (Interview, October 1996)

The net result of this close interaction is usually a sophisticated understanding of the minister and his or her preferences, even how the minister is likely to think about or view a variety of situations. One staff member stated: "I find that you develop a sort of, almost an ESP-type relationship where you try to anticipate what they think and most times you get it right" (interview, October 1996). Another staff member explained: "There is an intuitive element in a relationship that has been as close as that for as long as that" (interview, October 1996).

With this kind of knowledge, it should be no surprise that the ministerial staff can be important in maintaining a productive relationship between the office and the department. One department secretary noted:

One of the most important connections that needs to be made, in my opinion, by me, is with the minister's principal [adviser], so that if there are any difficulties anywhere in the relationship up or down the line, if I have a secure relationship, it can be talked through and resolved. I think I have been able to do that with successive people in that position. If that's not the case, this whole arrangement becomes more difficult to manage. (Interview, October 1992)

The Division of Labor Between Staff and Departments

Although ministerial staff analyze, evaluate, and supplement the advice the minister receives from the department, no one sees the role of staff as developing policy independently. One adviser explained: "It's very rare that we sit down and develop policy, and, although we do generate quite a lot of ideas, we always turn to the department and ask them to develop them" (interview, November 1992). This suggests a division of labor between the ministerial staff and department personnel, where each brings a different set of strengths to their common work. A department secretary in describing the division of labor between the department and the ministerial staff indicated that the latter "do none of the sort of heavy detailed policy. They don't write papers on how we should respond to . . . [an]

initiative or what we should do in relation to some new development, or
what our policy should be on . . . whatever it may be. We do all of that—
. . . the detailed policy development work" (interview, October 1992).

But the staff will evaluate the output that departments provide, and
in this context may have considerable influence, as one department secretary noted:

> They clearly have the ear of the minister, and that sense of personal
> trust, and being attuned to his political philosophies, his values. . . .
> And that will certainly go to political tactics, and the minister's pub-
> lic face. But it will also go to . . . the overall implementation of gov-
> ernment programs, the future policy direction of that sector. (Inter-
> view, October 1992)

The secretary then indicated that the ministerial staff would have a
"sharper" knowledge of the "hot political issues" associated with the department, because of the staffer's closer contact with political knowledge,
especially from lobby groups. The public servant, on the other hand, may
have a deeper understanding of the policy issues (interview, October 1992).
Another secretary explained:

> The concept would be that the minister's staff handles the political
> side of business and the department handles the administrative side
> of business. Now, when it comes to the policy development, the two
> interact quite strongly and it is a matter of working it out on a case-
> by-case basis. What actually happens depends in part on numbers,
> and numbers are now large enough in ministers' offices [that they]
> become involved in—at least on a case-by-case basis—quite detailed
> administrative [matters] and also the detail of policy development
> [to] quite a considerable extent. What actually happens also depends
> on the capability on both sides and the minister's office, although
> they're now [larger than they were] they are relatively small, and the
> capacity of the individuals and the inclination of individuals in the
> ministers' offices are very important determining factors on the course
> of events. (Interview, October 1992)

One secretary indicated his appreciation for the division of labor between the department and the ministerial staff by describing some of the
ministerial staff's tasks best left to them rather than to the department:

> For example, if you've got an ALP [Labor] government, dealing with

the factions through the caucus system . . . [it] is very difficult for a departmental officer. . . . It's really much better if there is somebody there who is personally chosen by the minister and who is closely associated with the minister to be able to handle that sort of situation; . . . in addition to that, because of the situation we have in the Senate where the government doesn't control the Senate, there are a lot of negotiations that have to be undertaken with the opposition—with the Democrats in particular, and with some of the Independents—to ensure that you get your legislation through the Senate. And again, except on matters of fact and technical detail, that is something that's much, I think, more suitably done by nondepartmental people. (Interview, October 1992)

The Department–Ministerial Staff Relationship

Ministerial advisers thus constitute a primary way that ministers enhance the political responsiveness of the Australian Commonwealth government. What do those interviewed for this study think about the relationship and how it works? Generally, they believe it works well, and they hold this view for several reasons.

One reason the relationship works as well as it does is the recognition on the part of both department secretaries and ministerial advisers that the roles of each are complementary. As one minister's adviser put it: "There's no way that you could actually commission the work or, you know, achieve your goals if you had to actually do it entirely within the minister's office. So it is a complementary role" (interview, November 1992). A new Coalition minister, discussing the policy development for the reform agenda for the portfolio, remarked: "Well, [person's name] is the principal policy adviser, and he's been a key policy person in the government's reform agenda. But that's not to say we haven't had very substantial input and advice and second opinion from the department on many of the major issues" (interview, October 1996).

For their part, the department secretaries recognize and have come to accept the increased importance of the ministerial staff since the beginning of the Hawke government in 1983. The concerns still appear at times, though not often, in the interviews with department secretaries. For example, one stated:

And I guess I've also been a bit skeptical about the role of ministerial staff. . . . My sort of Westminster traditionalist soul says that the departments are actually the minister's staff; . . . so the world's moved on. I understand that. Both in 1972 and 1983, [the Labor Party] came to office immensely suspicious of the bureaucracy, with an assumption that bureaucracy was basically out to get them. So in a sense the staffers were set up to protect the minister from his department. And that's not a very good recipe for successful administration. . . . You have a body of people who are neither elected nor merit-selected through due process playing an enormously influential role in the public life of the country. I think it's pretty bad actually. I've found, just to bring us up to the present now, I have found the staff of the ministers that we have [now] playing a pretty constructive role, not running an agenda of their own, not conflicting with or competing with the department, and hence, [being] pretty facilitative of the department's interactions with the minister. (Interview, October 1996)

Nevertheless, almost all secretaries interviewed for the study report that ministerial staff are more helpful than not, and some even believe that the growth of ministerial staff has brought advantages to the public service. One department secretary noted:

In fact, I think the great advantage of having political advisers is [that,] rather than increasing the politicization of the public service, it reduces the politicization. That is not a popular view that you'd get among my colleagues. But it is my view very strongly that the ministerial staff has helped divert some of the political [heat] from the department. (Interview, October 1992)

Another department secretary indicated that the growth in ministerial staffs "has been a buffer that has removed . . . pressure towards politicizing the senior levels of the public service" (interview, October 1992). Campbell and Halligan also advance this position in their study of Australian government (1992, 202–03). It is interesting that a department secretary, looking back on the Labor period of government, indicated that a chief contribution of the Hawke and Keating years to the relationship between departments and ministers had been the augmenting of the ministerial staff. The secretary stated: "The system [of ministerial advisers] has worked well. So I think the idea that there's a single source of advice is dead. And there's nothing wrong with that at all, when sensible people realize that governments will get advice from wherever. Ergo, I think that's one [change in the Labor era] that has worked well" (interview, October 1996).

For the relationship to work well, both department secretaries and ministerial advisers emphasized the importance of building good relationships and establishing good communication between departments and ministers' offices. One secretary related:

> You know, there are people who are very worried about the increases in the size of ministers' staffs and who see that as really . . . reducing the influence of the public service on the minister. But I think if you've got good relations with the members of the minister's staff and productive and cooperative relations, in fact, that can work extremely well. . . . And it doesn't take very long . . . for . . . methods of operating to emerge that are satisfactory to all concerned. If that doesn't happen, then you've got a real problem. And usually . . . something happens to the secretary rather than to other people around the place. (Interview, October 1992)

Another secretary indicated the importance, particularly, of the minister's chief staff assistant or policy adviser in the relationship between departments and ministers:

> Our ministers' key staffers in private offices who worked productively with the department and minister . . . would absolutely guarantee that it would work well. If, on the other hand, there are some people who for their own reasons have distrust . . . given they're, on the whole, handpicked and trusted by the minister, that will very much poison the well. I can give you some tragic examples for both of those things that happened: where you have a good head of an office [that] has helped or enforced the good relationship; and the head of an office who's leading other agendas or mistrusts the department [and] has poisoned or kept poisoned the relationship. (Interview, October 1996)

The importance of good communication between department and ministerial staff was emphasized by another secretary:

> Realistically the staff in the office are the last point of advice. I mean, they can second-guess anything we say to [the minister]. It's important that they feel free to talk to us about things, that they tell us when they disagree with us and tell us where they don't . . . so a good open relationship with staff is important. And, I think by and large we've maintained it. (Interview, November 1992)

This secretary added that there are some frictions that develop: "I think that the present [minister] has more staff than I think any of his predecessors [had], to tell the truth. I think that creates difficulties for us because they're all competing for his attention" (interview, November 1992).

But this kind of criticism from a secretary was rare among those interviewed. Another staff member indicated that department understanding of the needs of a minister's office was critical:

> There's always going to be friction to some degree. I mean, the minister is never going to agree with everything the department wants, nor is he going to be satisfied with some of the advice that he gets. So there is always going to be some degree of difficulty, but it's a question of how you deal with that, I think, that makes things operate smoothly. . . . If the department knows that when we ask for something and we want it *now* we want it now for a good reason rather than, "Oh, that's the bloody minister's office again wanting something in two minutes flat that is unnecessary"—all these sorts of things, I think, have a big bearing on how the process itself works. (Interview, November 1992)

The relationship between the department secretaries and the ministerial staff is also buttressed by a belief in a politics-administration dichotomy, that is especially noticeable with department secretaries. To be sure, this is a definition that includes provision of policy advice as a responsibility of administration, but it is a definition that partitions some areas that are better left to the ministerial staff, other areas that are better left to the department, and others that they engage in jointly. The staff—though they do not voice the dichotomy doctrine as often as department secretaries, or perhaps as clearly—still recognize that there are limits to what they can ask of the departments, especially in areas of partisan politics, and they seem to behave in accordance with that recognition. Secretaries do often report relations with the ministerial office that are based on a recognition of a dichotomy as expressed by one secretary:

> Where it [the relationship between ministerial staff and department] works well, it works well indeed. And it should be complementary. The department and the office have different roles. And they have to respect each other's roles. There should be times when they disagree because it's effectively their obligation to disagree. What is then im-

portant is that the minister gets both the civil service advice and advice that is more attuned politically to the adviser's perceptions of the minister's or the government's concerns and objectives. The [minister's] office should be a warning point for the minister on the politics. I mean obviously we ought to understand the politics as well. But it really ought to be able to pick up for him any breaks in the grass that the department hasn't. It ought to be aware of the intra-party politics and of the parliamentary politics, those options. The department should be analytically strong, assemble the information, produce public policy options in understandable ways—the sort of differences that you expect between a political office and a department of state. (Interview, October 1996)

Because of these common beliefs in mutual responsibilities that recognize a politics-administration dichotomy, the division of labor between ministerial staff and the departments does seem to be better defined and more accepted by both sides than is the case in some countries. Suleiman and Thiébault found that in France, for example, ministerial offices and departments struggle with each other for influence (Suleiman 1974, 211; Thiébault 1994, 142). In Australia, the relationship between ministerial staff and the public service was more compatible in the final years of the Hawke and Keating governments than was the case at least when ministerial staff was first augmented in the early 1970s. The earlier period was marked by friction (Smith 1977, 150–51). Though it was early in the new Howard government when the second round of interviews was conducted for this study, the general pattern of relationships between ministerial staff and high-level department personnel was very similar to that of the Hawke-Keating era.

Ministers' Staff Functions with
Other Ministers and Parliament

The full role of ministers' political direction of departments also requires, since the 1987 reorganization of departments, the coordination of the ministerial portfolio as well as the ministers' representation of the portfolio in cabinet and in parliament. Ministers' staff also assist ministers in these responsibilities. Examining staff functions in this area provides better understanding of how ministerial advisers fit in the overall policy process. Providing information about these additional functions also provides more understanding of what the minister expects from office staff as compared with his or her expectations of the department.

Brokering Policy Positions

A key role that the staff plays is in brokering positions among ministerial offices, a function of ministerial staff in other democracies as well (Suleiman 1974, 212). The relative importance of this task was noted by one staff member: "And so, on any given day, one of the most intense workloads will be (a) just making sure that the oil is in the machine vis-à-vis other ministerial offices, that . . . ministers are talking if they need to be talking, or advisers talking" (interview, October 1996). According to one veteran department secretary, this is a relatively recent development:

> But the new thing that has developed . . . over the last seven or eight years is that ministerial staff have also become intra-governmental fixers; . . . if there's a difference or dispute between ministers, . . . normally . . . you've got to write a letter saying, "My Dear Minister and blah-blah-blah," and . . . it all goes over to the other depart-ment, the department drafts up a reply, and on it goes. Well, now, what the men and women in the ministerial staff can do is—they're a network—they ring each other up and say, "Look, there's a problem arising about this. You know, your guy says this, my guy says that, . . . does he really mean that, or is just the department getting to him, could we fix it like this?" . . . And so there's now, after ten years of the one government that we hadn't previously had under this minis-terial staff system, there's a real network there that oils the wheels of government—sometimes in a way that . . . departments mightn't like, in a sense that deals are done [about] which we would have liked to have been able to say, "Well look, this carries the following risks," or whatever. But still it oils the wheels of government in a way that I think ministers find very satisfactory. (Interview, October 1992)

The need to "oil the wheels" in this manner derives from several fac-tors. One is that policy issues overlap departments. In Australia, for ex-ample, logging on federal lands is an issue in the jurisdiction of both the minister for Art, Sports, and Environment (as the department was orga-nized in 1992) and the minister for Primary Industries. Many additional examples could be cited. Another consideration is that policy conflict, especially in a predominantly two-party cabinet system of govenment, occurs more within cabinet, and perhaps caucus, depending on the influence of the caucus relative to the cabinet. In either case, policy cannot be changed without cabinet approval. One staff member explained this condition:

> Well, it's a bit of a rash generalization, but in our federal system, you would spend more time squabbling, fighting, and dealing with other ministers' offices than you would the opposition. I mean, in a sense, [in] the process of government here once you're elected, the opposition is almost irrelevant until election time. I spend more time fighting and arguing with [another ministerial office] than I do anybody else. (Interview, November 1992)

It is thus no surprise that before taking a matter to cabinet, to the extent possible, ministers like to have agreement among those ministers with direct stakes in the issue as well as among the ministers representing the three central control departments, Treasury, Finance, and Prime Minister and Cabinet. As one minister put it: "And your staff play a very important role in liaison with the other ministers you have to work with, at staff level, in basically keeping that sort of stuff under control and providing a reasonable working environment for a cabinet to work in, and sorting problems out before they start" (interview, December 1992).

Staff function to negotiate and broker positions among departments and ministers. Staff recognize this as a key responsibility. One staff member noted:

> I suppose inasmuch as . . . [the] specialist advisers [in the office] deal more with the department, part of my role as well has been talking to other offices. Because . . . what you're trying to do is broker a government position, a cabinet position, or a caucus position. . . . And that means . . . you don't want to put ministers up into cabinet or wherever there may be adversaries within the sort of main political structures. It's just very exhausting and very time-consuming for them. So, again, what you try and do is broker a position amongst us. Now obviously, if you can't come to some position, then they have to go in and [go] head-to-head, sort it out themselves [in a cabinet meeting]. But what you are doing is you have a brief from your own minister . . . , and other advisers will have a brief from theirs, and you try and sort it out. (Interview, November 1992)

The importance of this staff responsibility can be gleaned from a comment by one staff member:

> There's sometimes things where you will want and the minister will want it dealt with at the adviser's level rather than ministerial level so that, if your teasing something out, just seeing how the land lies, in another portfolio, this will almost invariably be done by the adviser before you get to the point where there's a ministerial thumbprint been put on it. And you may want to revise your options in the light of that teasing out. (Interview, October 1996)

A department secretary provided additional insight on the importance of this work:

> The coordination within the government between ministers and between ministers' offices is as important for getting some of the work that we do done as the formal processes that occur in the cabinet room. To be able to engage the minister's office in dialogue, and have them engage another minister's office in dialogue to head a problem off, or to find a solution to a problem that you know is optimal (or least worse, depending on your viewpoint of the issue) has been useful many, many, many times. (Interview, October 1996)

The contact that advisers make in pursuing this responsibility can also include ministers, as well as ministers' staff. One adviser indicated, "You have constant dialogues with other ministers" (interview, December 1992). This dialogue—either with staff members or with ministers themselves—can move beyond negotiation to persuasion when there is a difference of opinion between ministers, each of whom has some jurisdiction over the policy matter in question. One adviser explained: "And what we were trying to do was persuade them [of] the wisdom of our course as opposed to that [the other minister] was taking, which was a totally different one" (interview, December 1992). The goal is to resolve differences, insofar as possible, before taking an issue to cabinet.

This role of staff members does seem to depart markedly from the findings of Walter, who, in an earlier study of ministerial staff in Australia, found that few staffers in the Hawke government reported "extensive working contact with the staff of other ministers" (1986, 134–35). This difference may be a product of several factors. Earlier, a department secretary noted this role as having become especially noticeable in the last seven or eight years, so that this may be a growing expectation ministers have of their staffs. The second round of interviews of this study confirms this expectation, as ministerial staff in the Howard government are also engaging in brokering activity. A second possibility for the difference in this and the Walter study is that, as the Labor government has extended in office, staff members have become better acquainted with each other and developed more extensive working relationships.

This was a factor in the extensiveness of the brokering responsibility in the new Howard government as well, with staff members with more Canberra experience tending to include such activities in their responsibilities more often than staff members with less extensive Canberra experience. There is little doubt that, with time, this function will be as prominent a part of the responsibilities of ministerial staff in the Howard government as it was during the Hawke-Keating era. Finally, Walter's study focused on the entire staff, whereas this study focused on ministers' principal staff members. The principal staff members might be more likely to engage in such negotiations than other staff members.

Coordinating the Portfolio

The Hawke government's reorganization of departments in 1987 created portfolios with more than one minister, and the coordinating task in some cases also includes the parliamentary secretary if the portfolio has one. Some of this coordination occurs in formal ways. One way is the periodic meeting, as described by one ministerial staff member:

> We have a weekly meeting between the two offices—the senior staff members of the offices, and any other advisory staff who were relevant to the issues that were up and running at the time. . . . And so you know, in that sense, it was a formal arrangement at the same time each week, midweek, which just ensured that you didn't accidentally let things slip. The exchanges weren't confined to that meeting. (Interview, October 1996)

A second formal device is the organization of paperwork between offices so that each knows what the other is doing. A staff member noted: "Copies of everything that go to the minister go to the parliamentary secretary, and vice versa, so that this office is aware of everything that is going to him and he's aware of everything that's coming from this office" (interview, October 1996). This paper flow usually includes, where it is practiced, briefs or other written information from the department. Of course, staff must read and analyze this information, and determine whether their principal needs to see it.

A third way to coordinate the portfolio through a formal arrange-

ment is to outline as concisely as possible the division of labor between
the cabinet minister and any parliamentary secretary or other ministers in
the portfolio. This can be a time-consuming task, as noted by one staff
member:

> In the early days of the government . . . perhaps 20 percent of our
> time was spent . . . working out precise areas of demarcation within
> the portfolio to make sure there was no danger, or limited danger, of
> different attitudes being taken towards the same area. I speak to the
> junior minister's advisers pretty regularly, maybe twice or three times
> a day. So it's tailed off since the early days. We make sure that
> everyone's singing from the same sheet of music by that type of coor-
> dination. (Interview, October 1996)

The latter part of this comment indicates reliance on informal means of
coordination, which may include some facets of the brokering responsibility discussed above. Staff members' comments indicate that the formal
mechanisms are not usually enough to provide the kind of coordination
that is needed. One staff member observed: "We have, on a several-times-
a-day basis, liaison with the [other minister's] office, for instance. Because
there are many issues it's very difficult to sort of draw the line between
[the parts of the portfolio]. . . . I spend a proportion of my time doing that
every day" (interview, October 1996).

In addition to potential difficulty in determining which side of a line
of responsibility a given area falls, another problem is that areas assigned
to different ministers in a department will overlap. A staff member reported:

> The department will talk to both offices about particular issues when
> they overlap. But more important, I think, is that the offices talk to
> each other. . . . I talk to the [other minister's] office many times a day.
> A lot of issues are fairly straight forward, we have clear-cut policies
> that we've brought in from the election—so it's not a problem, it's a
> matter of just confirming that. But at the same time, there's some-
> times examples where the ministers do have different views. And
> they also have very different perspectives. . . . So we do quite a lot of
> work at the staff level. I talk to my counterpart in the [other minister's]
> office to negotiate through a position that is acceptable to both min-
> isters. Now, you know, if there are particular issues where there are

significant policy implications, the ministers talk. And that's necessary for them to decide on their common viewpoint. But . . . there are
not often issues where there are differences of view. (Interview, October 1996)

Even if these differences of view do not occur often, it is important that
ministers and their staffs become aware when they are likely to occur to
forestall the development of breaches that might develop as well as to
indicate to the department as clearly as possible the direction the government wants to take on a given matter.

Question Time

Question time constitutes an important activity for ministerial staff in
Australia. Both the House of Representatives and the Senate have a one-
hour question time each day when parliament is in session. The minister
must be prepared for question time. Moreover, there is another coordinating task for staff derived from the practice of holding question time in
both houses. If the minister is from a given house, he or she is responsible
for answering on behalf of the portfolio in that house. A member of the
other house is designated to speak for the portfolio in that house. This
might or might not be another minister in the portfolio. In some cases all
members of the ministry in a given portfolio are from one house. At any
rate, question time requires some of the same coordinating—and at times
brokering—tasks that have been previously described.

Staff members spend a good amount of time preparing their ministers
for the question period. One staff member explained:

The other major function is looking after question time and ensuring
that he has adequate briefs, rewriting briefs. We . . . request briefs
from the department on particular issues that we think may come
up. Generally, we get . . . [newspaper] clips, we go through them,
obviously read the papers, and listen to the radio. But we would seek
briefs of them on issues that we think may be hot, and then we would,
again, review them and maybe rewrite them or go back to the department for further information before they get to [the minister].
(Interview, November 1992)

Another element of question time is preparing questions that enable the
minister to provide good news, enhance his or her personal image, publi-

cize success, or put a positive spin on government action in a department (Bradshaw and Pring 1972, 366). In Australia these kinds of questions are known as "Dorothy Dixes" and are a featured part of question time. Ministerial staff prepare these questions and arrange normally with backbenchers to have them posed at the appropriate point during question time.

The coordinating task of question time contributes to the hectic pace of staff work in Australian national government. For some staff members, a large part of the workday focuses on question time, and a significant part of that includes coordinating with other ministers who are also responsible for fielding questions related to the portfolio. One staff member explained:

> Well, when parliament is sitting, virtually on and off the entire day until question time is over will be directed at question time. In terms of staff effort, we start in the mornings by reading the papers to pick out any topical issues. We request briefing from the department on the basis of that or any other issue we might think is topical or might . . . become so. We also make assessments as to whether we want to have any Dorothy Dix questions, which our own side asks. . . . I should start by saying that after we have read the papers we have a joint meeting with [the other minister's office] at about nine o'clock in the morning to work out what we jointly think the topical issues are in [the area covered by the portfolio] and to facilitate communication between the two. The department prepares briefing [material]. At twelve o'clock I attend a meeting in [the other minister's] office, which is specifically on question time, where basically [the other minister] is briefed on [portfolio] issues. I am there if we need [input from my minister's area of responsibility]. Also, this facilitates communication, so we both know what is going on in each office. I come back down here. . . . We have a forty-five-minute meeting with [our minister] prior to question time where we brief him on the likely [portfolio] topics that may well come up, . . . He goes into question time. I watch question time to see what the issues are. So, it's three o'clock, so that's my day. Taken up from when I arrive really until three o'clock. So I put a lot of effort into it. (Interview, October 1996)

Thus, question time consumes time for both ministers and their staffs.

And it provides another opportunity for coordinating the portfolio on policy questions to the extent such coordination is needed.

Other Services to Ministers

Many of the duties that staff members perform relate to ministers' relationships with departments and with cabinet and parliamentary colleagues. But another important set of duties focuses more inside the office and relates to the personal needs of the ministers. The most important of these are managing the minister's time and providing information about informal activities within parliament.

The ministerial adviser is important in managing the minister's time. Part of this service is performing tasks that the minister would have to do if the staff were not available. But staff members, including the advisers, actually organize a minister's time and help him or her deal with the extensive time burdens placed upon ministers.

This particular function cannot really be separated from other functions served by staff members. Part of it involves making certain that the right kind of information is provided and available when the minister needs it, whether that information comes from the department or elsewhere. One staff member, after recounting a typical day where he interacted extensively with the department, with interest groups, and with staff of other ministers, explained: "It's a kind of a vetting process, to make sure that if the minister is traveling or having meetings or going to cabinets or making speeches or giving Dorothy Dixes in parliament that [the minister] has been given the right sort of information at the right time to deal with it" (interview, November 1992). A minister indicated that setting priorities for his time was a major function of his office and that the staff was important in this task:

> They're important in the task of prioritization; . . . life in this sort of business is all about . . . prioritizing, understanding what's more or less important. . . . You can't anticipate what your substantive response is going to be in everything. But you need to at least know what you need to devote to getting right and what you can assume . . . works out for itself. (Interview, December 1992)

In this instance the staff organized the minister's paperwork and time in a way that he found helpful by establishing the most important matters for his attention, and distinguishing these from what was not so important.

Ministers operate in a collective decision-making environment in which knowledge about how others are viewing them may be very useful. One minister illustrated the way his staff keeps him informed of his political environment:

> Everybody that's in this business is fundamentally in competition with you. It's a very competitive business, and particularly . . . when you're on the front bench, . . . your colleagues will grab your job the second there's an opportunity to get it. And other ministers, of course, in the pecking order in cabinet will never hesitate to stick the knife in when they get an opportunity. And that goes on around this building all the time. And your staff, your personal staff, are your eyes and ears in that respect. (Interview, December 1992)

One staff member indicated that he had provided a personal evaluation of his minister's performance to his minister:

> I have, on one occasion, gone to my minister and indicated that he needed to track issues more closely because he was being run over by the department. When we were in public meetings with bureaucrats from the department, they would often bring up things there that he would agree to, because they knew that if they submitted them to him on paper, he would not agree to it because his staff would see it and advise him about the background and cause him to oppose the policy. However, it was difficult for the staff in a public meeting to provide the same kind of advice. We could have told him what the motives were, what the background of the issue was, and why it was being proposed. We could also have given him a better idea about the consequences of a given policy. Some thought that I would be sacked for bringing this up to him, but his reaction was one of agreeing with me, and he has done somewhat better since then. (Interview, December 1992)

How often this takes place is unknown and undoubtedly varies by the minister and staff member. At least one minister attested to the value of such evaluation: "But again, it's bloody important for any politician, I think, to have staff who will never hesitate to tell you when they think you're doing something wrong. And that often, I know, is very difficult" (interview, December 1992).

The Minister, the Ministerial Staff, and Accountability

The staff speak in the name of the minister, carry out duties that the minister delegates either directly or indirectly, and answer questions interpreting what the minister wants. This provides potential power to the staffer. Yet, the staff, like department personnel, are indeed not elected and this raises the question as to whether they are also properly accountable. The findings of this study indicate that ministerial staff discretion is tempered by variants of both the internal controls advocated by Friedrich (1978) and the external controls advanced by Finer (1978). First, the staff members interviewed seemed appropriately sensitive to this question. One commented:

> My view is that we are not the democratically elected representatives, the ministers are. And that's where their burden comes from. They're ultimately accountable, but I never am. I mean, I'm accountable to my minister. But in the sense of what a minister's there to do, ministers are there to be in the business of government, and be the government, and they're elected or kicked out according to their performance. So I'm very careful about how I actually portray my role, and essentially, as I said, it's more [a] facilitative and negotiating one. (Interview, November 1992)

Another staff member, in discussing the regular interaction between ministerial staff and the department, with the staff often being asked to indicate what the minister wants, or how he or she might react to given situations, explained:

> And that role is a bit tricky at times, because I believe [the minister] believes that it's not the job of ministerial staff to make policy decisions. He, the minister, is the one who makes policy decisions. . . . That said, one is obliged to provide guidance on policy and how it's implemented, and that's probably a bit of a gray area as to when an issue is something that's more related to the implementation of policy or how the department should approach an issue . . . in a forthcoming submission. [There's a] fine line between that sort of guidance, and actually taking policy decisions yourself. But . . . let's acknowledge it's a gray area, an area of some ambiguity. (Interview, November 1992)

There are several keys to the ministerial staff members' exercising their discretion in a way that is appropriate to strengthening the responsiveness of administration to the preferences of elected officials. One is to have an understanding of what the staff member has the approval of the minister in doing, and where he or she does not have it. Key ministerial staff have frequent interactions with their ministers, and this provides the opportunity for them to understand their principals' preferences, a key element of the external control advocated by Finer (1978). Also, if staff work has been done that the minister does not like, it can be changed and in the process provide cues on future expectations. This kind of interaction led one adviser to say, "You don't . . . make unilateral decisions. . . . I can be pretty sure of what he's likely to be comfortable with or not" (interview, December 1992). And in any case in which a ministerial staff member did not know the view of the minister, as explained by one staff member: "I don't always know [the minister's views] and if I don't know them, I will ask him" (interview, October 1996).

There are also other guides to the discretion exercised by staff members. One staff member explained:

> Well, I think you have to work fairly carefully within what has been defined previously in terms of government decisions . . . on the particular issue you may be working. There . . . is a certain amount of latitude. I wouldn't like to overplay that, though. I mean, obviously, you have to work closely in concert with the department, and you do have to consult. I talk about discretion, yes. But it's discretion within reasonable bounds. And . . . anybody who's been in this job a while gets a sense of what's politically possible and what's not. And if you're thinking of going right outside the established ground rules, well obviously that's not a matter that you can take into your own hands. It's a matter for ministerial decision. . . . Depending on the nature of the issue and if there are ready solutions in sight, I think generally the minister expects you to conclude them successfully. But if . . . very substantial differences emerge, well, quite obviously that is a matter that you take up further with your minister and with your department. But . . . there's no sort of generalized view of the world that one could paint which said, "This is how an adviser in an office [or] this is how a senior adviser manages his affairs." (Interview, December 1992)

Despite the disclaimer at the end of this quotation, it is clear that this staff member has an understanding of what needs to be affirmed with the minister and what does not.

Here, there is a blurring of external and internal controls. In a real sense, as staff work in a ministerial office, they acquire knowledge of norms and expectations that govern their behavior and in that sense develop an internal guide to direct their action. Australian ministerial staff manage discretion also through conventions that they follow in performing their duties. One set of conventions concerns how staff members relate to other offices, and another focuses on the department of the minister. One adviser explained:

> I think one of the conventions that's particularly important in this business is that ministers' offices should only deal with other ministers' offices and the department of their own minister. . . . So, I conceive of it as . . . each office should either deal horizontally to other ministers' officers or vertically to its own department, and there shouldn't be any diagonal contacts because in my experience that gets very, very confused, because you end up, perhaps, trying to influence another department contrary to the view of that department's minister or that minister's office. (Interview, November 1992)

This adviser did allow that he might on occasion break this convention:

> And so, on very, very rare occasions, if you can't get hold of anybody relevant in another minister's office and it's top urgent and perhaps your own departmental people aren't available or they've failed or something like this, then on very, very rare occasions I might do that, but otherwise know that on those occasions that I am breaking what I believe to be a sound convention. (Interview, November 1992)

Even this exception is noted by the staff member recognizing that there must be objective extenuating circumstances before violating this convention. Another staff member after being asked if he contacted other departments, responded: "We wouldn't go direct to the department. . . . I hadn't really thought about it until you asked but I would have thought that was a bit sort of improper because we have no real relationship with them [other departments]" (interview, October 1996). Other studies confirm this norm (Campbell and Halligan 1992, 70).

A stronger convention relates to what is and is not appropriate for a minister's office to ask from a department. The working relationship is a close one, as noted by a minister:

> There's scarcely any piece of paper that circulates around the office,
> or speech for that matter, which isn't an amalgam of material initi-
> ated here, developed further in the department, reported back . . . ,
> that sort of thing. . . . What happens here is it gets, if you like, politi-
> cally pruned and packaged. And, that's in terms of the end product.
> And at the beginning . . . broad parameters [are] set [in this office] as
> it circulates into the department. (Interview, November 1992)

This convention can be best noted by the practice of not asking the department to handle work that could be described as political. One staff
member explained:

> There are quite firm guidelines on that. . . . There are a range of
> things that one does not ask the department for advice on. Particu-
> larly in the lead-up period to an election, when you may be doing a
> number of functions involving Labor candidates or thinking about
> policies for an election agenda—all of that sort of thing. We tend to
> be fairly strict about observing the guidelines, which means the de-
> partment only handles government business and doesn't handle La-
> bor Party business. And they're well aware of the rules in that re-
> spect, and if people do seek to get help from the department on [or]
> for something that's purely a political exercise, the department gen-
> erally responds negatively. (Interview, December 1992)

Another staff member indicated:

> We would seek factual information from [the department]. You know,
> they provide factual information, or if it's a press release on some-
> thing and some issue, no matter what it would be, we might get them
> to do a draft, or provide a brief that has the facts in it. And if there's
> politicization, if we want to make a big issue out of it, then that's
> done here. We would never ask them to do that. (Interview, Novem-
> ber 1992)

There are occasions when it appears that departments could be somewhat more politically attuned than they are. Two of the ministerial staff
members related incidents where departments had released freedom of
information requests to individuals, including the opposition, about politically sensitive matters without informing the minister or the ministerial
staff about the request or the release. One staff member explained that
this practice was "indicative to some extent of the arm's-length relation-

ship on some of these things" (interview, December 1992). The staff member indicated that to avoid such incidents he had in the past requested a list of outstanding freedom of information requests, but this was not something he was currently monitoring. He related another example from another department in which thousands of pages were released to the shadow minister without informing the minister. His reaction: "They [the department] just stuffed up [made a major mistake] in a way that they ought not to" (interview, December 1992). But these kinds of differences in expectations are likely to occur because, "There are completely different focuses and time lines, so I'm involved in a ministerial office as opposed to a department. A ministerial office is overtly . . . political; the department isn't" (interview, December 1992).

The increasing part that ministerial staff play in Australian government will require more attention to the appropriate political direction for ministerial staff. Jack Waterford, editor of the daily newspaper in the nation's capital, the *Canberra Times,* delivered a lecture in which he detailed several instances where staff members made major mistakes during the Hawke and Keating Labor governments (Waterford 1996). Some of these mistakes were products of ministerial failure to adequately direct staff members, and in some instances the mistakes were the product of staff members' engaging in conduct for which they were not authorized. In one instance, the mistake led to the resignation of a minister, but in the others, the minister "wore" the mistake (as they say in Australia, meaning that he suffered embarrassment) but remained in the ministry. Waterford's examples provide evidence that those who are concerned about accountability and responsibility in Australia will continue to focus on the relatively new phenomenon of powerful staff members in the Australian ministry.

The findings of this study with respect to the functions of ministerial staff in Australia also do not differ appreciably from earlier studies (Smith 1977, 146–47; Walter 1986, 146–50). There can be little doubt that ministerial staff in Australia extend the influence of ministers and assist them in important ways in increasing the political responsiveness of the Commonwealth bureaucracy to the government of the day. From the beginning of the augmenting of this staff in the early 1970s, the staff has provided ministers with policy advice, as noted by previous studies. In more recent years the staff's reach has extended to other areas. Ministerial advisers in many offices are more active than they once were in providing oversight for implementation of policy by departments. They are also more active in brokering positions with other ministers' offices in developing policy for consideration by caucus and cabinet. The reorganization of Australian departments in 1987 created the need for assistance in coordinating portfolios among members of the ministry. The Australian Commonwealth ministerial staff in the Hawke and Keating governments provided strong assistance to the elected executive for exercising political direction of departments, and in facilitating the communication between departments and ministers (Keating 1995, 23).

For the most part relations between ministerial staff and departments are cooperative, and the relationships of the staff conform with the symbiotic relationship described by department secretaries earlier in the study. Moreover, the relationships of staff members to the departments—as described by staff members and department secretaries in this study—conform with the findings of Hyslop's study of department secretaries (1993, 25–31). Because of the ways that ministerial staff assist the departments and the ministers in interacting with each other, they facilitate the mix of the strengths that bureaucrats and politicians can bring to policy making in a democracy (see also Halligan and Power 1992, 82). The ability of ministerial staff to enhance the mix of strengths is facilitated by departments' adjustment to the emerging role of the ministerial staff. It is also assisted by the staff remaining appropriately accountable to ministers in most cases.

The importance of the increased role for ministerial staff is further affirmed by actions of the new Howard government after the Labor government lost power in March 1996. Without missing a beat, the new government continued the utilization of ministerial staff with very much the same expectations of staff participation in the functioning of ministerial offices and a continuance of their relationships with departments, other ministers, and parliament in general, as had been the case in the previous Labor governments. There was very much a sense of déjà vu when these relationships were discussed with ministers and ministerial staff in 1996 as they had been in the interviews conducted four years earlier.

5

The Minister

Ministers are the focal point for exercising political direction of administration in a parliamentary system. And the Hawke government that came to power in 1983, where the Labor ministers interviewed originally began their tenure as ministers, emphasized increasing the influence of politicians and the party over the bureaucracy (Campbell and Halligan 1992, 60). Moreover, Campbell and Halligan conclude that ministers in the Hawke government established greater political control over Australian government than was true for prior governments (204). The early signs of the new Coalition government led by John Howard that was elected in March 1996 indicate that Australian elected leaders will continue the quest to exert control over the bureaucracy. The potential impact of a minister on departmental action was forcefully stated by one staff member:

> [My minister] is quite a good example of . . . a minister who's broken new ground in a portfolio; . . . he demonstrated not just an ability to administer effectively a big department of state, but I think he very ably demonstrated an ability to fashion policy, strategy, in ways which had very far-reaching consequences and in ways which were often not in harmony with the thinking of the departmental advice. (Interview, December 1992)

Let us now examine the perspective of ministers as to how responsive they have found the bureaucracy and what they have done to exercise political direction over it.

Ministerial Direction of Departments

An important test of how well mechanisms designed to increase political responsiveness of the public servants work must be the evaluation by elected officials of the relationship between themselves and the bureaucracy. By this measure, Australian Commonwealth ministers appear to be reasonably satisfied, although they (as their staff members noted in the previous chapter) can point to times of resistance that required persistence on their part to win the day with the bureaucracy. One minister related in general terms the overall expectation of the public service in Australia:

> What we seek out of departments is loyalty to the government, but not [to] the party in government. And that's . . . the key to our relationship with the public service. I expect that if my party should go out of government that they would give the incoming government exactly the same loyalty and service. I think that's the trick to making our system work. (Interview, November 1992)

A newly minted Coalition minister voiced similar expectations: "Well, I think it's as simple as [this:] the department is there to serve the government of the day in a professional way, exercising at all times loyalty, not entering at any time into politics" (interview, October 1996).

In establishing expectations for the department, most ministers clearly expect that the department secretary will be responsible for administrative decisions related to the department. One minister related:

> My secretary, and this might sound self-evident but I don't think it is, I actually expect him to administer the department. And the reverse of that is that that means I don't administer the department, I keep out of it. . . . I can't hold him accountable for administering his department if I stick my fingers in it. I, actively, stay out of it. Then, he is fully responsible, for the good and the bad. So I've taken that conscious decision. (Interview, October 1996)

This minister's reported practice comports well with the view of Woodrow Wilson, who stated: "And let me say that large powers and unhampered discretion seem to me the indispensable conditions of responsibility. Public attention must be easily directed, in each case of good or bad adminis-tration, to just the man deserving of praise or blame" (1992, 20). Some ministers intervene more directly in administrative details, but not many do. Ministers establish expectations that assign certain responsibilities to the minister, other responsibilities to the department, and some to both. In the latter category ministers expect active assistance from the depart-ment in developing policy. One minister noted:

> Theoretically, I would say that essentially the minister is responsible for policy direction to the department and also for the political di-rection—that is, when not so much policy issues but problems arise that have very clear political implications, then, direction comes from the minister. On the other hand, it does not really always work like that in practice in the sense that the department plays an enormous policy-making role because it has resources that neither the minister nor the party has. So while I think it would be true to say, at least in two of the three departments that I have been in charge of, the gen-eral policy directions are determined by the minister, . . . a lot of the development of significant parts of the policy very much come from the department. And, also, the minister's intentions in policy are of-ten much moderated as a result of interchange between the minister and his office and the department. (Interview, November 1992)

Just what the information is that "moderates" the ministers' intentions no doubt varies. It may be practical administrative implications for new policy thrusts (Young and Sloman 1982, 30–31). It may be an indication of how policy might impact another portfolio. Or it may be an explana-tion from the institutional memory of the bureaucracy. Whatever it is, this "moderation" process suggests a working method that emphasizes a blend-ing of the perspectives of the ministers and the departments. The minister obviously must bring the preferences and reality that is defined by politics (Blondel 1991, 7).

The bureaucracy, however, must also participate in policy develop-ment. To do this, Australian department personnel actively engage in de-veloping policy and presenting advice on policy. This raises the question of just how aggressive the department should be. Does the department's action that "moderates" a minister's point of view infringe upon legiti-mate political influence that should be exercised by the minister, or is this action fulfilling the responsibility of the public service to provide the best advice possible as policy is formulated? Does this sometimes mean that ministers rely too heavily on their departments? The line between elected officials' perception that the bureaucracy is obstinate and overly resistant and the perception that their caution is helpful can be a very thin line indeed. The rationale for caution is substantial. Public servants have a responsibility to protect a minister from an action that will be subsequently regretted, perhaps by the minister, and perhaps by the department after the minister has moved elsewhere (Rose 1984, 158). The interview evidence suggests that modern Australian ministers adopt operating methods that encourage departments to indicate their objections to a proposed course of action. One minister voiced the view of most ministers, both Labor and Coalition, when he stated:

> What I'd normally do on this or any other issue is to ask the department for a brief. Maybe give them some idea where my thinking was. But I'd often say to them, "If you have a different view, bring it back. I want to see what you come up with." And then if their position and my position differ, we'd get in a room and argue it out. . . . And I guess in that sense I'm looking to them to make me aware of problems that I might not be across. And they've done that a couple of times. A lot more than a couple of times. It's been very helpful. (Interview, October 1996)

By and large, ministers indicated that they wanted input and debate as policy was being considered, but once a decision was made, the public service had a responsibility to carry out the policy. One minister, for example, said of the interchange between the department and the minister that produces a change in the minister's policy stance: "Well, I think it often is useful in the sense that they've had a long-term association with many of these areas, which the ministers have not had, and it's usually a modification of mostly in the sort of fine-tuning areas" (interview, November 1992). Another minister presented this view:

> We have a system essentially where, for the most part, public servants obey the ministers. . . . No one comes in here and tells me that they're not going to do something. They may make good reasons for why they shouldn't do it, and I listen. There's no obstruction of orders by the public servant. It's fairly much a democratic-centralist command system in this process. (Interview, November 1992)

A third minister clearly prefers policy advice, but more in other ways than by advancing a position: "Well, I never see the department's job is to make policy. That's the politician's job. Certainly they can give advice on different alternative means of achieving, or hopefully achieving, the same objectives. And in putting a range of options" (interview, November 1992). In formulating their input to ministers, departments also work in the context of prior knowledge of the minister's position on given matters, guidance from the minister's staff (see chapter 4), and awareness of the government's general policy stances on a given policy question. Ministers expect departments to take this kind of knowledge into consideration as departments formulate their input. The most typical attitude toward the department's role in policy formulation was expressed by a minister:

> They know the direction . . . the government would be coming from. And for that reason, the majority of the advice you get is advice that you have no difficulty with. But, as I said, they don't hesitate to try it on. And I think that's a good thing, personally, because my view is that . . . at least you get people that are strongly motivated about the portfolio and have got a view on it and, . . . providing you then learn to recognize what that bias is, you know that people are constantly going to be coming from a particular direction. And if you disagree with it you can discount the advice to that end and then get to a stage where you just agree to disagree with bureaucrats that have that view and tell them precisely what it is you want. That's not a problem. (Interview, December 1992)

The usefulness of the experience of the bureaucracy to a minister was noted by another minister and explains why most ministers want reactions and advice strongly put by public servants. When asked if he changed his views as a result of input by public service personnel, the minister responded:

> Oh, absolutely. And, in fact, it's a case of not just sensible public policy making. I think it's good political sense. It's a good way of protecting your own ass because, I mean, the last thing I think any minister wants is a bunch of bureaucrats that are constantly kissing your ass and trying to tell you what you want to hear. I've on numerous occasions had advice given to me pointing out the difficulties that would occur if a particular course of action that I had—I was advocating—was pursued; . . . it took me twelve months just to get a working knowledge of the individuals that I was dealing with in particular organizations whereas the bureaucrats that I was working

with had had a decade of experience with these people. . . . I do have enormous respect particularly for individuals in the department. You know that you can rely on their advice. They'll give you good advice. They will say to me, "Oh, look, the reason that so-and-so said that to you or wants you to do this is because of this and this and this, which happened five years ago or because of his relationship with X, Y, or Z. And although on the surface of it, Minister, it makes sense to do this, if you do it it means that there will be these consequences." That has happened quite often in my portfolio. And yes, I think I would honestly say that I have changed my view on many occasions because of advice I've got from departmental officers. (Interview, November 1992)

The melding together of various perspectives was viewed by ministers as a goal of the present system of minister-department relationships and as being frequently achieved, and several ministers emphasized the collaborative nature of the relationship with the departments. One minister stated:

But you tend to find that the Australian public service is such that there is a fair amount of respect for dissent and diverse views. I mean, I find that if I sit down with a group of bureaucrats, they don't all single-mindedly parrot the views of the secretary. They all have different views, and you get a reasonable debate going. So there's a sense of self-confidence amongst at least underlings at this level (probably isn't further down, but at least at this level there is), so you can get them second-guessing the department without real detriment to their careers, I think. I do have a few suspicions about some elements of that; by and large that's true. . . . And they tend to both educate you, and also educate your other advisers [staff]. The blend of the two strains in your office will tend to keep things on track. Virtually all elements of the political process associated with your portfolio really then start to meld into the office, and the bureaucrats who are in your office and your own senior advisers then constantly see the departmental big picture, probably even more broadly than does the secretary of the department. (Interview, November 1992)

One minister, who was at times in the interview critical of the resistance he had sometimes experienced from departments, was nevertheless definitely positive about the collaborative effort between him and the department in formulating a new policy:

So I tended to have my own views, which were not that much different from the department's, but also a concern that we massaged through the policy so that we actually achieved an effective outcome. And plus I added to it . . . an element (that I think is terribly important) of political reality, in terms of the legislative processes that departments are not well across, so that you could do things in appropriate timing in a way that gets it through [the House and Senate]. (Interview, December 1992)

This is another reflection of the mixing of perspectives that collaborative policy making provides. Another, noted by former British prime minister Clement Attlee is similar: "The Minister is more in touch with the ordinary man and woman than the civil servant. . . . It is the business of the Minister to bring in the common touch" (1954, 313). Attlee also noted that strong ministers would argue with policy advisers but, after a reasonable period of discussion, would say, "Well, this is my policy, I don't want to argue it any more. Now let us consider how best to implement it" (309). The modern Australian minister would agree. One minister after describing a process in which he would request alternate viewpoints and argue difference with department personnel stated, "the ultimate decision is mine" (interview, October 1996). Another stated:

I've said I want to be told the pros and cons of anything, so I don't go out and live in a fool's paradise. After all, I've got to defend whatever decision I make. And if I don't know the negatives then I'm not prepared to answer them. I may decide to go ahead regardless of the negatives, but I need to know what they are . . . Sometimes I choose to go my own way. Other times, I'll take their advice. It depends on how committed I am to what it was I was being briefed on . . . it might have been something that was in our policy for the election. I can think of an example right now, where it's not proving easy to finalize it for implementation. It's a question of cost and also complexity. We're trying to work through those issues now. But I've said, "That is our commitment to the people. We have to find a way through. Go back and work at it again." (Interview, October 1996)

Overall, ministers expressed high regard for department personnel and this was not surprising. Even in the United States, where bureaucrat bashing is commonplace, those who work with civil servants generally come to respect them. In other countries the same is true. In Great Britain, a BBC report on the civil service summarized the regard that British ministers held for bureaucrats: "Academics, journalists and backbench MPs may castigate the bureaucracy, doubt its competence, question its energy, jealously observe its pretensions to power, but ministers give little hint of this. They tend to marvel at civil servants' industry, integrity and sheer availability" (Young and Sloman 1982, 94).

Resistance from the Bureaucracy

Even in the context of collaboration, ministers can recall instances of resistance from departments. The fine line between the need that most ministers feel for a department to present policy advice in a vigorous way without becoming too resistant to political direction is indicated by the following minister:

> I would have thought for all appropriate purposes there is a fair degree of democratic control if the minister wishes to exercise it. This doesn't mean that . . . a particular ministerial view might [not] be modified as a result of debate with the people in the department who are expert in this area. I can remember in the early days [of his career as a minister] one particular issue where a powerful public servant had particular views that disagreed with mine. And it was a very painful process, because you would find that what you wanted changed was changed only marginally. And it was a series of operations through a number of trenches; . . . if a minister wants to do something that really is running against what a department wants to do, . . . then it is a much more costly process in time and effort than when what the minister wants is roughly in accord with what the department wants. But most of . . . the leading departmental figures see themselves as basically working [for] the minister, but bringing their own expertise. And that's where the sort of debate that I would put it, in nearly all cases, that's a productive and creative situation. Like I say, I can remember one very clearly which wasn't, but . . . those things are perhaps inevitable. (Interview, November 1992)

Given the length of time this minister had served, the one instance he remembered is interesting because the report indicates such a situation is contrary to the usual case. Another minister related his experience in two departments when he advanced major policy changes:

There were Labor Party firm policy commitments and/or my own firm policy commitments of which the department did not approve. . . . But, the department realized that it was firm Labor Party policy whether we politicians liked it or not, either. They were stuck with it. So there was never any serious attempt to subvert or anything like that. The other fairly major policy issue was [a taxation issue]. We did introduce a . . . tax, and I had a strong personal commitment to that, . . . The department view was that they didn't need it, that they could keep adjusting the [existing tax] in a rather arbitrary way, rather than a formula-driven way, and that was good enough. Well, I mean, I didn't agree with that nor did the cabinet agree with it. . . . But, once the department realized that I was personally strongly committed to that, there was again no attempt at subversion. And, indeed, they worked very well to implement what I think turned out to be a pretty good policy. (Interview, November 1992)

A third minister explained how resistance was sometimes manifested:

There are individual offices [within a department] and indeed some entire sections that deal with a particular subject that have got a particular bias and particular agenda, which they will never, ever, ever hesitate to take up an opportunity to re-present. And quite often, and this has happened, too,—if they don't do it . . . by way of departmental briefs, they will often try to do it in terms of draft speeches that are prepared for ministers to [give]. In just a paragraph or a line . . . something will be slipped in that will say that . . . the government will place an emphasis on this or whatever. And I've blue-penciled a lot of that stuff out, and I've actually had to say, and you obviously do it in a reasonable way if you want to maintain a relationship in the end, . . . make a joke out of it sometimes. But I have on a couple of occasions actually said to department officers, "Come on. Stop trying it on, you know. I keep on taking it out and you people keep putting it in. That's the end of it." So that goes on. I've got to say this: In the main, at least the departments I have worked with . . . very professional, highly qualified people usually. Very expert in what they do. Hard-working. Available as they need to be twenty-four hours a day, literally. . . . You want them, they're here. And it's absolutely a case that if the draft—if the briefing that they're giving—is specific and precise, they will deliver on it right whether

. . . it totally disagrees with their point of view or not. So at the end of the day, I mean, there's no argument. They will give you their advice freely and fearlessly, thank God, and disagree with you and say, "Look, we think your decision's wrong for all these reasons." But at the end of the day you simply say to them, "Look, this is what I'm going to take to cabinet. This is the particular bias that I want to put in it. This is how I want it argued from this perspective." (Interview, December 1992)

Though the points of resistance are real, one measure of responsiveness may be the judgment of the ministers of the new Coalition government led by John Howard that was elected in March 1996 after thirteen years in opposition. Lengthy periods of opposition tend to produce higherthan-usual suspicions by political leaders of bureaucrats who have loyally served their political opponents for a long period of time. Certainly that was the observation of many at the beginning of the Howard government, as it was thirteen years earlier when the Hawke Labor government assumed power. Some of that suspicion still persists. One minister discussing the relationship between ministers and their departments related:

I think it varies from minister to minister in terms of their relationships with their department and the extent to which those departments might share the philosophy of the government or resist the philosophy of the government. We're a new government in town after thirteen or fourteen years. It is quite apparent that some departments contain within their ranks people who are not too sympathetic to our approach. (Interview, October 1996)

But when discussing their own departments, four of the five new ministers interviewed for the study reported that they had found their departments responsive. The minister quoted above reported in the case of the portfolio department: "I've not had that experience. . . . I am fortunate enough to have been one of those who inherited a department that is very largely focused on outcomes rather than on processes and political objectives, and the pursuit of ideology" (interview, October 1996). In fact, several ministers reported that they had found their departments more responsive than they had anticipated. One minister indicated:

And what strikes me, coming in as a new minister—and I have a department that people would generally consider as a difficult department in that they tend to run their own agendas. This is the public perception. Also, this is the political perception. They run their own agenda. They wait out ministers who are difficult. That's not really been my experience. My experience is that they have been extraordinarily keen to try and please me and do what I want. . . . I found [this] interesting because I wasn't quite expecting that. So they try very much to read the tea leaves and look at every nuance of what I say or do. (Interview, October 1996)

Another minister relating experience with the portfolio department from the first seven months of office reported: "Well, that's one of the great surprises to me. And that's why I say I think they are very professional. . . . And I was very surprised at just how responsive, how quick they could produce work that was very reliable. And it wasn't me driving it, it was cooperative teamwork" (interview, October 1996). A minister pursuing a reform agenda indicated: "The relationship with the department has gone amazingly well. We had a major reform agenda. They were not a department that were viewed as being sympathetic to this agenda. But I treated them like professionals, and they have acted like professionals and have really not resisted this in the way that I thought that they might" (interview, October 1996).

The view of the new Coalition ministers may not be surprising to at least some department heads. One secretary related: "The department will instinctively serve the minister. It's ingrained in the culture of this place" (interview, October 1996). The resistance experienced from the bureaucracy may also be a function of continuing to view the policy area from the same perspective as was the case with the previous government, not out of desire to oppose the new government but derived from the tendency to continue patterns of behavior once they are established.

In fact, this is one of the strengths of bureaucracy: it institutionalizes patterns of behavior that governments desire to persist over time. One new minister, for example, related: "We have a very big program in [an area of the department], that I've just sort of had to bludgeon the department into. I think the common thread is not that they're not trying, but what they're trying to do is do things the way they have always done things. . . . I don't think this is conscious. I think they're trying to help" (interview, October 1996). Another minister related: "I've found some very staid ways. Very rigid. . . . I've found that they are to a large extent process-oriented. I'm not sure that they are terribly interested in the practical outcomes of what government service delivery is about or that they seek to apply that practical outcome to all that they do" (interview, October 1996). This kind of concern was perhaps best elaborated by a ministerial staff member reporting the general responsiveness of the department:

> Generally [it's been] responsive. We came into power with quite a defined set of policy priorities. There did appear to be quite a bit of effort by the department to be looking at those priorities. However, having said that, there is, I find, still a sense that "we've always done it this way" or "we've done [it] this way for the last ten years and why would you be wanting to change it?" So I would say there is a slowness in response that I didn't expect. . . . And it's been variable. Different areas of the department have been more responsive and more proactive than other areas. So there isn't a consistency across it. Some areas have been very responsive. I couldn't complain about it. Others not so. So I would say slower than I expected. But then I haven't worked for a minister's office before. I don't have anything to compare against. (Interview, October 1996)

Despite these concerns, the consensus among those interviewed in the new coalition government, as well as department secretaries, is that the expectations about the relationship between top politicians and departments in Australia, as well as the working relationships between them, remain very much the same in the new Coalition government as prevailed in the previous thirteen years of Labor government.

What emerges from this discussion is that a key skill of high-level civil servants is to assist ministers as they sort through conflicts that arise between what is politically desirable and administratively possible (Rose 1980, 333). From the viewpoint of the public servant, departments have the responsibility to warn ministers of the possible adverse consequences of given policy options or program directions. The fine line that a top public servant must walk is noted by Campbell and Wilson: "Too little determination in emphasizing the difficulties of ministers' favourite but unworkable projects may mean those ministers will stumble into disaster; too much determination shades into obstructionism, which ministers may believe reflects a political hostility to their policies" (1995, 23–24).

The positive side of this duty of the top public servant is that it will indeed save the government from embarrassment. The negative side centers on unelected officials who are not responsive, as illustrated in the BBC's *Yes, Minister* series by the fictional Sir Arnold, the cabinet secretary who, as he planned early retirement, explained to the fictional Sir

Humphrey, a department head: "My successor, Humphrey, has to be someone who can be firm with our political masters" (Lynn and Jay 1988, 18). In situations deriving from this kind of attitude, weak ministers may opt not to counter the resistance when they should, leaving in place policies or directions that should be changed to better reflect the present political preferences of the larger polity.

Assuring Appropriate Responsiveness

Although political officials expect their bureaucratic policy advisers to point out problems and may even find it exasperating at times, their testimony is that usually the system works. The picture that emerges here is one of occasional resistance, and of a sensitivity on the part of the minister which recognizes that such episodes will occasionally take place. The hapless fictional British minister in *Yes, Minister* exclaimed: "Those civil servants can talk you in or out of anything. I just don't seem to know my own mind any more" (Lynn and Jay 1987, 87). Can ministers only function in this way, or do they have a shot at translating political preference into government action?

The ministers interviewed indicated that there were several tactics they could use to achieve appropriate responsiveness from the departments. The first and most basic device to assure departmental responsiveness is, in the first place, to increase control of the appointment of the department secretary and to fix the term of the appointment. This has made department secretaries more sensitive and responsive than they might otherwise be. One minister discussing the new appointment process indicated: "I think that helps to establish a good relationship between most ministers and the head of their department" (interview, November 1992). This was intensified in the 1987 department reorganization by the Hawke government. The impact of this reorganization was explained by one minister:

> And [former Prime Minister] Hawke did a huge shake-up in 1987. What he did, what tended to happen in all of those departments, is [that] highly energetic and innovative bureaucrats got placed in charge of them, and not just in charge of them, but down the line at the deputy secretary and first assistant secretary level. And they were frequently quite devoted to the idea of change, now, so you wouldn't have said you had a problem there of bureaucratic inertia. (Interview, November 1992)

In these cases, the department secretary made the appointments lower in the hierarchy but generally took into account the ability of persons in those positions to work well with the minister—a practice in place even prior to the greater involvement of ministers in the appointment of the department secretary (Hyslop 1993, 82). Also, these individuals almost always came from the ranks of career public servants.

One department secretary put a historical perspective on the increased responsiveness over time of the Australian public service. Of the service when the Labor Party returned to power in the early 1970s, and the changes since then, he said:

> It was a public service in which security of tenure was virtually absolute, in which security of tenure of department heads was absolute, in which the only people in the service were the ones who had joined at the bottom and gradually worked their way up to the top. There'd been one government for twenty-three years, and therefore there was a certain satisfaction with the status quo. And the public service was seen or perceived to be an obstacle to rapid change. . . .
>
> [Now,] security of tenure has at the senior levels in effect gone, and people are much, much more accountable in the sense that there is greater scrutiny from ministers and ministers' offices. . . . A lot of them have come up through the public service quite rapidly; they haven't yet acquired the stodginess of thirty-five years in the one job. . . . And all of that has changed the nature of the public service and has made, I think, the public service as a brake on change . . . much less of a problem. (Interview, October 1992)

Another secretary describing that era (during which he joined the public service) indicated: "And they were just major fiefdoms at that time where walls would continue between departments. For decades people wouldn't speak to each other" (interview, October 1996). The reform of department head selection coupled with the traditional ministerial responsibility in Westminster systems fosters a very real belief among Australian public servants that they indeed do work for the ministers, similar to that found by Campbell and Wilson in Great Britain (1995, 250–51).

A second device used by ministers to assure departmental responsiveness has been to utilize expertise outside the bureaucracy, to either counter the bureaucracy or dilute the policy advice the ministers receive. One minister observed: "There is nevertheless a view usually that, amongst some ministers, that they like to have an area of development of policy . . . which sits outside the public service and ultimately feeds into it" (interview, November 1992). Another minister explained how utilizing external sources of expertise could be effective in developing changes in policy or organization to conform with the government's intent:

> And we've also made considerable use of inquiries, advisory bodies, so as to really have—one of the concerns I think that all ministers have is to have—other sources of top-notch information and policy advice, so that in this department, for instance, my predecessors or my predecessor made great use of . . . the biggest inquiry into [the policy of the department] since the Second World War, and that was run very much by outside experts, university people, and things like that. In addition, we have an Advisory Council, which is not a departmental body but a body of a mixture of academics and people with expertise in the [policy of the department], which advises the minister directly on policy issues. All the time [we] make use of private consultancies and university consultancies for particular policy operations. So, the minister seeks to balance the expertise and weight of the department both through his own personal staff, through advisory bodies attached to ministers, and through specific task forces of various kinds, mainly built up by people outside the department. (Interview, November 1992)

Another minister lauded the public service on preparing detailed analysis of party platforms during elections, indicating in detail "what it would take to implement any of the particular proposals that they put down" (interview, November 1992). This practice has apparently come to be emphasized more, beginning in the 1980s, than had previously been the case (Hyslop 1993, 22). The minister just quoted indicated that he found these analyses very useful, but that he relied on advice from outside the department when he wanted to develop a major reform in the department. He explained:

> I picked a fellow that was basically out of the department but had been in the academic community some time, a fellow who's now a professor over at the ANU [Australian National University], to essentially resolve one of those binds that departments eventually get themselves into, to break loose, if you like, and find ways in which that sort of bureaucratic log-jam can be overcome in processes that

can't necessarily be activated simply by the normal day-to-day relationship between the ministers and heads of departments. (Interview,
November 1992)

This minister four years later observed that utilizing such outside expertise in a successful way is unusual because the number of individuals who
can serve effectively in such a capacity is not great, largely because expertise in the policy area as well as expertise in the bureaucracy is relatively
rare, at least in Australia, and perhaps elsewhere as well. The minister
explained: "But I was lucky there. By and large, . . . you would not auto-
matically expect to find people who could do the job for you. And, I mean
this was not a job that any old person could do. And I just happened to be
lucky in . . . having him around. [He was] relatively trusted by both sides"
(interview, October 1996). Still, there is a rationale for relying on study
and recommendations by those outside a given department to produce
reform within a department. A staff member explained the rationale:

> In simple terms you cannot rely on organizations to reform them-
> selves; . . . it was impossible to ask the department to look at funda-
> mental changes in policy direction, or fundamental changes in struc-
> ture, because you're asking people to change the policies that they
> have been the architects of for the last decade, or else to abolish
> areas that they are the controllers of. So we've gone the path of [ap-
> pointing a review team], . . . and you aren't constrained by being
> identified with past policy areas. We can use them to spur the more
> able and forward-thinking people in the organization to come up
> with some changes that senior management would tend to argue
> against. So the review process is a mechanism to speed up change
> and to force change in areas where, if we left it to the department,
> inertia would prevail. (Interview, October 1996)

A third way that ministers interact with departments is to be proactive and make certain that departments follow their direction, especially
when changes occur that might differ from departmental preferences.
Campbell and Halligan found in their extensive interviews of Australian
public service personnel that ministers in the Hawke government were
much more likely than their predecessors to take the initiative in policy
formulation and to indicate what they wanted from their departments
(Campbell and Halligan 1992, 61–62). The key in this tactic is to develop
clear policy objectives and to communicate them effectively to the depart-

ment in the context of firm resolve. One minister explained: "I do think it's very important that a minister establish the political lines. What I mean by that, I don't mean the partisan ones, but a minister lets the department know the minister is boss and that's it. I have the sort of personality that I can do that very quickly" (interview, October 1996). Several ministers considered this tactic the best way to achieve compliance to political direction. One stated:

> Well, I suppose I get the best out of people by being very demanding. You've probably heard that, in the few months you've been here. But I know pretty much what I want and how I want to get it, and I demand extremely high-quality work. But . . . I do try and give constant feedback, both in terms of hopefully identifying with some precision what it is I want—not leaving people floundering around without guidance or with mixed messages, that's important—and secondly, if I don't like something . . . telling people why I don't like it rather than just, "I don't like it, do it again." And, I think people by and large feel pretty stretched by this, but also they're professional and pretty responsive if they can see the point. And [the trick is] making people see the point of what you're doing, and seeing how it fits together, and . . . the larger picture you're trying to paint. (Interview, December 1992)

Another gave his view of how a minister could be effective in achieving the compliance of a department:

> Well, it is the capacity to just tell the departments they're wrong. To say, "That is not what we're going to do." And to insist that whatever you want to be done, I mean, this is after a proper analysis. . . . I'm assuming here a minister who has analyzed the situation and believes firmly that the department's tack is wrong. Then the good minister is the one who will tell them it's wrong; he'll insist that the tack be reversed, and he will insist that there will be no undermining of the new tack. (Interview, November 1992)

This minister indicated that he was very satisfied with his relationship with the departments over which he had served as minister:

> I don't think that I ever got undermined. I can't think of a time when someone set out to undermine me by leaking documents or whatever, so I didn't experience that. I think you've got to make it clear to

departments when you take on the job that you won't be dropping it, but if [they undermine you] . . . you'll deal with it severely and swiftly. You've got to make them know that you mean business. So that actually never happened to me. In terms of resisting, as I said, the good secretaries are the ones who will challenge you, if you like, and I was fortunate in having three departmental secretaries who did that regularly, but who would all accept the decision once made. Now there—I was very close with the caliber of the people with whom I dealt. And I'm a fan of the public service man. I think by and large we've got a lot of good people. But you do have to be prepared to say no. (Interview, November 1992)

Another minister put it rather colorfully:

And there are areas where my department has dragged its feet, and I've said, "I mean it! We will go this way!" Now, it's not that there's advice to the contrary. It's just that they have—it's like a horse that wants to go over and eat the oats over here instead of staying on the road. I have a road up there, and occasionally there are times that they think that maybe that's a better road down there. But I enjoy the opportunity to say, "No, this is what this government is going to do. I'm afraid you're going to have to get on with it." (Interview, October 1996)

The provision of clear direction guides the bureaucracy in each particular situation. But it is important in another way as well. Such directives communicate ministerial preferences that department secretaries, and others in the department, may apply in similar cases in the future. "Ministers' influence is . . . indirectly increased by officials' anticipations of their reactions. Politicians often 'decide' unknowingly by virtue of the anticipations they have created in officials" (Heclo and Wildavsky 1981, 132).

Several department heads emphasized the imperative of clear communication from the minister in order to assure responsiveness from the department. One secretary said, "I think that the only way you can really succeed is to talk a lot" (interview, October 1996). Even if the minister does not know his or her policy objectives at a given point, department heads emphasized the utility of feedback to let the department know it is on the right track. One department head stated: "If you don't agree with our advice, tell us. If you don't like the quality of it, tell us. If it's not what you need, tell us" (interview, October 1996).

The provision of clear communication of political preferences does not always occur. It is easier to prescribe than to fulfill the requirement. Elected leaders do not always provide political direction, which can constitute the major failure in creating politically responsive actions by the bureaucracy. Consider the following, which appeared in a news story nearly four months after the new Coalition government assumed power:

> However 100 days of Coalition government have come and gone with McLachlan [the Defense minister] on the bridge at Defence and the engine-room watch is becoming irritable at the inactivity. "We are in the engine-room down below but nothing much is coming down on the telegraph," says one senior officer. "We are all watching the pointer, but it just doesn't move." (*Sydney Morning Herald*, June 25, 1996)

This minister subsequently appointed a study committee to examine the Australian Defence Department, which will report in 1997. It is possible that the "engine-room" will receive its signals after that point. But this is not unusual. One department secretary reported:

> There's one minister I had where . . . there was an underlying lack of trust, but it was more a failure to articulate clearly the vision that he had. The department struggled to know what the hell he wanted. I'd have to admit that, [in] many in the department (and I'd have to include myself in that), there was a feeling that if he wanted what we think he wanted it didn't make sense. . . . It wasn't a very productive relationship. I think on both sides that it didn't work very well. . . . Now that was again due to the nature of the individual. He wasn't a great communicator. But I guess we failed in not trying to be as up-front with him as we might have been. . . . We sort of groped through, trying to work out what he wanted rather than having an up-front discussion about it. Well, there were a couple of attempts to have up-front discussions with [him]. It didn't lead to anything very clear because it all led to him sort of saying, "You people aren't capable of delivering what I want. Now get in someone else who can." They couldn't deliver either. (Interview, October 1996)

Another department secretary explained the difficulty of ministers sending clear signals to the bureaucracy: "Frequently it's because ministers don't know what they want until they see it. And they need something to rub up against, respond to" (interview, October 1996). This suggests that the department must, in many cases, make guesses about what the minister wants and through trial and error come up with proposals or actions that meet the minister's approval. In such situations the department may propose in small increments to get reactions that they can use to go on to the next step. Inevitably there will be times when the development of a position takes two steps forward and one back (or vice versa), which could be frustrating to both sides.

Another difficulty in rendering political directives is that not only may ministers not know what they want, they may want to steer clear of undesirable consequences that result from implementing given decisions. Many want to take credit for successes but deny responsibility for failures. Although high risks may offer the potential for high gains, mistakes can also lead to punishment at the ballot box, in the cabinet room, or at the meeting of the party caucus.

Another problem is that elected governments may support conflicting objectives as they attempt to be responsive to competing interests. Such conflicts across department lines readily appear. In the United States the simultaneous support of tobacco farmers and promoting less smoking for health reasons is often given as a prime example. Conflicts within departments may also take place, with competition for a given limit of resources often being the battleground on which such conflicts appear. Finally, even if ministers do not know exactly what they want, departments can utilize feedback that indicates what is working well and what is not working well from the minister's perspective. Department heads prefer regular meetings where that can occur. They also report that ministerial influence increases when ministers engage the department directly, usually at several levels from the secretary on down. But ministers have busy schedules, and providing direction for the department is only one item. Some ministers simply prefer to emphasize other aspects of their position. As one department head explained: "You might think it's a terrific idea to meet once a week, which we in the office think would be great. The minister puts it in his diary [calendar], and then we find he's in central Australia, or . . . somewhere else, . . . not here. He's not a guy whose diary you fill up with that sort of thing" (interview, October 1996). In this kind of case, the department attempts to compensate and can certainly utilize the ministerial staff to help ascertain the preferences and evaluation of the minister. But the minister who forgoes engaging the department forgoes exercising the kind of influence that he or she could otherwise exercise over department activities. And as a consequence, political direction of the bureaucracy is diminished.

Another key part of the policy process is implementation of policy decisions once they have been made. In Australia, ministers and their staff members readily assign the primary responsibility for this phase of policy making to the departments. Ministerial direction continues in this phase in several ways. If a department makes an error that leads to negative political consequences or bad publicity, ministers are likely to intervene. One minister, discussing the way that public servants could properly exercise discretion, explained:

> The general rule that I run is that they have to make a judgment as to whether there will be political consequences, that is, unfavorable publicity, questioning of what's been done. If they think it is likely to have those consequences, then, I think, anything like that they would talk to their immediate superiors, go ahead and make the decision, whether it is something that needs to be brought to my attention or whether it is something they can handle themselves, recognizing that if they handle it themselves and the thing blows up then they bear the consequences of that. . . . I think that it would be true to say that most of the department would certainly not want to do something that would cause difficulties for the minister. I think they are mostly motivated like that. So right through the department that tends to be the kind of way to look at it: Is it something which as far as they can see is likely to have political implications? In this department, because the regulations are extraordinarily detailed, I don't think we have very much of a problem in that area. (Interview, November 1992)

In addition to this kind of intervention, ministers also assign ministerial staff to oversight the work of the department and to monitor the department's observance of the minister's and the government's preferences and actions (see chapter 4). The overall importance of staff in effective ministerial direction of departments was noted by one minister: "It was a combination of quite strong direction from here, combined with always a very strong personal office. I had no tolerance for weak links in the minister's office and ran a pretty tight and tough ship. People who weren't up to it didn't last long" (interview, October 1996). Overall, the Australian ministers interviewed would agree with the British minister who stated that sometimes encounters with public servants were "a very bruising knock-out, knock-down, drag-out fight." Nevertheless, the British minister said: "I think it's a weak minister and a weak-minded minister who is more than irked by that sort of opposition. To use that as an excuse for not doing what a minister wants to do, to use that as a reason why party policy hasn't been put into operation is really a minister looking for reasons to excuse his failure" (Young and Sloman 1982, 26–27).

Variations

It is clear that ministers can have a great impact on the department; it is equally clear that not all do. This was noted most by several ministerial staff members, who are in a front-row seat for observing ministerial behavior. One staff member reported:

> It's interesting . . . that the amount of influence a minister's office can have . . . on policy formulation can either be very, very substantial or very minimal. That depends entirely on the individual minister, and it depends to a certain extent on the minister's standing within the government, his relationship with the prime minister, and . . . on how powerful . . . the department [is in] . . . the public service and the bureaucracy. (Interview, December 1992)

There are several factors associated with how well a minister controls a department. These factors include the department's characteristics, the minister's general effectiveness, the minister's time of service in the department and knowledge about the department, the minister's tactical expertise, and the goal agreement between the department and the minister.

The Department

Departments vary in the amount of discretion that can be exercised by department personnel. In Australia, for example, the Department of Social Security (as in the United States) is highly proceduralized, with many decisions pre-formed by agency rules and regulations. Day-to-day operations provide little opportunity for public servants to exercise what little discretion they have in a way that is not in compliance with political preferences as interpreted by the minister. Other departments may have a culture where change comes slowly. The reorganization of Australian government in 1987, which established mega-departments, tended to overcome this tendency. But many believe that departments that were not re-organized in 1987 may be more likely to resist change.

The Minister

At the time of the first set of interviews for the present study, there were sixteen cabinet ministers plus the prime minister in the Labor government, and also junior ministers and parliamentary secretaries, each with certain duties of oversight of the departments. At the time of the second set of interviews, there were fourteen cabinet ministers in the Coalition government and, like the Labor government, also junior ministers and parliamentary secretaries. Some were obviously more effective than others, and this is likely to be true in any government, in Australia or elsewhere. The study did not do a survey of "most" and "least" effective ministers, although staff members, members of the press, and academics could have named obvious contenders for each category.

One obvious difference between ministers is the extent to which they have the energy and intellectual capability to actively lead a department. One minister indicated that ministers without appropriate drive and wit may rely too much on the department secretary:

> The ideal secretary is one who is sympathetic to you and what you're trying to do, both, but who is prepared to disagree with you; . . . they have to be prepared to stand up and tell you when they think you're wrong. Now, the truth is that the relationships tend to work in reverse to that. We have quite a tradition here, I think, of ministers relying upon departments too much. Which probably hasn't changed; some still do, and they do that because it's easy. If your information is power, and all the information is held by the department, then the department has really a very strong position, and with some ministers it's just easy to go along with what they recommend, and so that's what happens in a lot of cases. (Interview, November 1992)

This indicates that ministers must be both able and proactive in influencing the department. But this minister's report is probably exaggerated somewhat, especially given Campbell and Halligan's finding that ministers under Prime Minister Hawke did exert political direction over departments (1992, 61–62). We also noted that ministers have developed in their staffs alternative sources of information and advice. The capability of ministerial staff varies from office to office, but it is a source that all ministers utilize.

Time and Ministerial Knowledge

Time is obviously a factor in determining how successful a minister is in directing a department, and it works in a variety of ways. When a different party has won an election and takes over the government, a number of things can happen. Pet policy proposals favored by the department but not adopted by the previous government will be presented again to the new minister. The new minister must establish a working relationship with the department. There is always some suspicion about the loyalties of bureaucracies that have labored only recently in the service of the opposition party. One minister indicated:

> Often at that stage [when the government is new], where the public service are not overly well known to ministers . . . there was, certainly in my case, more tension . . . than later on. And I think, now, it would be true in most departments that there's a fair understanding of the government's and the minister's position amongst the top echelon of public servants, and some ministers have been within a department for a number of years. (Interview, November 1992)

One variant of the time dimension is this knowledge of the minister. In most cases, he or she would be more dependent on the expertise of the department early in assuming a portfolio. However, a minister might have expertise independent of having previously served in another portfolio. Consider the following comments:

> I started out as [minister] after being shadow [minister] for three years in opposition and had about ten years of previous activism in [the area]. And accordingly . . . I had a very detailed program, which was largely on the public record in one way or another and was really just a matter of . . . communicating that; . . . the department jumped and responded and all their professional resources were devoted to keeping up with me rather than . . . trying to set directions for me to follow. (Interview, December 1992)

> I was plunged into [a ministry] where I'd had no previous experience, no technical or professional background, and really had to learn an entire portfolio and a very technical one at that . . . from scratch. And in that environment I was really very much a creature of the department, at least until I got up a head of steam. And after that [there] was more of a two-way flow, you know, I developed

ideas myself, and particularly as we moved as a government into a [change of policy] that was unfamiliar for the department, and they were learning as much as I was, as we went along. And that was more of a backwards and forwards kind of relationship. (Interview, December 1992)

I came to this portfolio with an . . . intelligent layman's knowledge of everything, but I was very keen to . . . develop a coherent sense of [departmental policy]. . . . And, I spent a little time working myself into it. . . . I'm very keen to sort of develop patterns and shapes of responses. So . . . that's been more of a symbiotic sort of thing backwards and forwards with the department. (Interview, December 1992)

These comments indicate the varying ways that ministers may be dependent on a department more at some times than at others. That ministers are more dependent on the department for a period of time when first assuming a portfolio was noted by a ministerial staff member:

And, so often you'll find that ministers, particularly in the early years, are very dependent upon the advice they get from their secretary and their advisers . . . , so they tend not to rock the boat and they tend to go along with it. But, the longer they're in the job, the more self-confident they become, the more knowledgeable they become, and the more they'll tend to direct the department in the areas they want to see have a focus. (Interview, November 1992)

Even here there are, no doubt, differences in whether a given minister has a reform agenda when he or she assumes the portfolio, or how long it takes to develop one once there. Nevertheless, it is appropriate to assume that new ministers, and especially those who come to office when government changes from one party to another, will need to rely especially heavily on the department secretary and other department personnel for a period of time (Hyslop 1993, 38–40; Laver and Shepsle 1994, 303).

The factors of time and experience raise the question of just how often ministers served in given portfolios during the thirteen years of the Hawke and Keating governments. A key factor in diminishing political direction over bureaucracies in American national government has often been the high rate of turnover among political appointees. What is the case in Australia? The average length of service in cabinet in the Hawke and Keating years was over five years, or almost two terms of office (see

Table 5.1

Ministerial Service in Hawke and Keating Cabinets

Number of Cabinet Ministers [a]	Length of Service (months)		
	Total [b]	Average	Shortest and Longest
39	2,413	61.9	5–156

Sources: Material compiled by Laurie A. Waldron of the Australian Public Service Commission, from *Commonwealth Government Directory,* 1986–1987, 1988, 1988–1989, June and December 1989, June and December 1990, June and December 1991, August and December 1992, February, June–August,September–November 1993, March–May, June–August, September–November 1994, December 1994–February 1995, March–May, and June–August 1995; from *Parliamentary Handbook,* 1991, 1993; from the Internet, "Chronology of Recent Events Relating to the Membership of the Parliament, December 1995." In addition, other material was used as supplied by the Australian Public Service Commission.

a. Excludes one minister who only served for one month until another minister had secured election to parliament. Includes ministers without a department-based portfolio

b. Excludes the service of Robert Hawke (106 months) and Paul Keating (50 months) as prime minister.

table 5.1), since the maximum term of office for an Australian government is three years. This period is longer than the time that Heclo found that U.S. political appointees stayed in office (1977, 103–04) or even the longer period of 52.7 months found by Maranto in the Reagan administration (1993, 76–77). This period is also longer than the four-and-a-half-year average a recent study found for western European ministers between 1945 and 1984 (Bakema 1991, 74–75). It is also about six months longer than the average total service of a department head in Australia.

Since cabinet ministers could and did serve in more than one portfolio, the expectation is that on average a cabinet member served a shorter period of time in a given portfolio. And this indeed is the case (see table 5.2). The average length of service in a given portfolio was about thirty-four months, or almost three years. The average cabinet minister did serve in more than one portfolio, and some served in many (see table 5.3). Again, this mobility from post to post was greater than the average in Europe—partly because of the longer service of Australian ministers, as the same party held power for thirteen years (Bakema 1991, 90).

Ministers' service in portfolios means that most departments had three or four ministers during the thirteen-year Hawke-Keating period, with most tours as minister at a particular department lasting about three years. The average actually dips below three years because there were some portfolios where the average tour of duty was shorter. For example, in the six-

Table 5.2
Average Length of Portfolio Service,
Hawke and Keating Governments, 1983–1996

Number of Portfolios [a]	Length of Service (months)		
	Total	Average	Shortest and Longest [b]
71	2,518	34.5	5–120

Sources: Information provided by the Australian Commonwealth Government Public Service Commission as follows: "Commonwealth Government Hawke Ministry," dated March 11, May 25, July 14, November 4, 1983, January 21, April 3, 1984; "Commonwealth Government Second Hawke Ministry," dated December 13, 1984, February 16, March 13, 1987; "Commonwealth Government Third Hawke Ministry," dated July 24, September 18, 1987, January 19, 1988, February 15, 1987, September 2, 1988, April 6, May 22, 1989; "Commonwealth Government Fourth Hawke Ministry," dated April 4, May 7, 1990, February 1, 8, 19, June 3, 4, 7, December 9, 19, 1991; "Commonwealth Government Keating Ministry," dated December 20, 27, 1991, January 14, February 25, May 27, November 11, 1992; "Commonwealth Government Second Keating Ministry," dated March 24, 27, April 14, 27, July 13, December 23, 1993, January 23, 30, March 1, 25, June 1, 1994, June 20, October 20, 1995. Also *Parliamentary Handbook* 1993.
Note: Only cabinet ministers were included in this analysis. When a minister was elevated to cabinet status holding the same portfolio, the previous time serving in the portfolio was also counted. This tended to take place in the first two Hawke ministries, prior to the reorganization in 1987 that combined several smaller departments into larger departments. The time that a minister spent in cabinet without portfolio is not counted in this computation. Since reorganization occurred several times, if a minister retained the major part of a portfolio, the time count was not interrupted. The service of the two prime ministers is not included in the computation.
 a. When a minister served in a portfolio in which he or she had previously served, the time was combined.
 b. Service of two months or less was excluded. In all but one case this occurred when someone acted until a minister was named to a portfolio, or at the time of the shift from Mr. Hawke to Mr. Keating in late 1991, or the brief service of Prime Minister Hawke as treasurer after Mr. Keating left that post for the backbench.

Table 5.3
Mobility of Ministers Through Portfolios
in Western Europe, 1945–1984, and Australia, 1983–1996

	No. of Posts Held			
	One	Two	Three or More	Total
Western Europe	58.7	25.4	15.9	1798
Australia	42.1	36.8	21.0	38 [a]

Sources: Bakema 1991, 90. See also the sources for table 5.1.
Note: figures are in percentages.
 a. Some cabinet ministers did not hold a portfolio in Australia.

Table 5.4

Months Served in Portfolio in Australia, 1983–1996

	≤12	13–24	25–36	37–48	49–60	>60	Total
Number of Portfolios	9	21	26	2	3	12	73[a]
(Percent)	(12.3)	(28.8)	(35.6)	(2.7)	(4.1)	(16.4)	(99.9)[b]

Sources: See sources for table 5.1.
  a. Does not include portfolios served two months or less.
  b. Error due to rounding.

and-a-half-year life of the Department of Transport and Communications, six ministers served, with the longest period of service being twenty-one months, although departments such as Foreign Affairs and Defence tended to have long-serving ministers. Only about 25 percent of the portfolios were served by one minister for four years or more. Over 40 percent of the portfolios were served by a minister for two years or less (see table 5.4).

In shifting from one portfolio to another, a minister does not have to re-learn all facets of being a minister: the components of the position that relate to parliament, to the political party, to the cabinet, and if the portfolio is not a central agency (Treasury, Finance, and Prime Minister and Cabinet departments), relating to the central agencies, including developing the budget and expenditure controls. Still, the ministers shifting to a new portfolio must learn the new department, which is, of course, a major component of the position. And the phenomenon described above—of the diminished capacity to provide policy direction during the learning period—persists, regardless of previous experience in other departments.

There are, of course, reasons for changing ministers. Some do not show the competence necessary to continue in a portfolio. Some retire. Some are forced to resign because of breaches of behavior. The first Hawke administration served only twenty-one months, as the election was called very early in the three-year term. Several changes were made after that election, so those serving in the first Hawke administration would probably have served longer had the early election not been called so soon. And, once a vacancy occurs in one portfolio, there may be shifts that require changes in other portfolios, as in the game of musical chairs, until all are filled.

At times ministers want to move to more influential portfolios, and at times persons showing competence in one area are moved to another requiring exceptional talent because of the plans government has for that portfolio. In some cases, a minister with ability is shifted from a portfolio in which the performance has been below par into another where his or her talent may be more readily utilized. With respect to competence, one minister related: "I think continuity is very important, but it's got to be continuity combined with competence. Continuity for continuity's sake only guarantees that there may be fewer mishaps through sheer ignorance or inattention" (interview, October 1996). Another issue in turnover is the capacity for new ministers to bring in new ideas and renewed interest in directing the department. One secretary noted: "There's another issue about whether some ministers are there too long and they get too comfortable in the job and they're no longer concerned with policy issues and so on" (interview, October 1996).

For the most part most department secretaries report that the problem of ministerial turnover has not disrupted department-ministerial relationships. One department secretary noted: "I think, at the time you get worried at the high turnover. In retrospect, I don't think that it makes a huge amount of difference. Desirably you ought to have ministers there long enough so that they get on top of the portfolio and can actually be positive contributors before they move on" (interview, October 1996). The turnovers are usually facilitated by the fact that ministers often learn quickly, especially if they have previously held a portfolio. One department secretary explained:

> It depends on the minister's capabilities; . . . there are very few ministers who aren't reasonably quick at picking things up. There are some who aren't, but most of them are pretty swift. I think it takes a couple of months. But what happens each time is that the departments have very good briefing material available. . . . I think ministers that I've been associated with have adapted pretty quickly. Some, you've got to hold their hands a bit more than others, but for the most part they do read their briefs, they work hard, and if you've got the staff on side then the staff can also identify what are the issues that are likely to rise in the parliament. (Interview, October 1996)

Too rapid a turnover does weigh to the disadvantage of political direction of the bureaucracy. One department secretary remarked: "If there's sort of [a] reputation for ministers changing quickly, people will say 'Well, you know, if we wait long enough they'll go away.' That's a real problem" (interview, October 1996). And another problem is whether ministers can develop knowledge of the portfolio rapidly enough to provide effective political direction. One department secretary noted:

> But I think if you change a minister more than every couple of years it becomes counterproductive. . . . [If] ministers make mistakes and have to be removed . . . so be it. But I think there's a time after which the minister becomes in control of his department, in a way that they should be in control, that's productive, and things are being achieved. They know the players, they know the agenda, they know the lobby groups. They know what can and can't work. And on they go and get things done. (Interview, October 1996)

Tactical Skills

Ministers who know how to carry the day in cabinet—and hence parliament (at least in Australia)—are also likely to have great influence in their departments. There is little doubt that the Labor Party required ministers to be strong advocates to win in the budget Expenditure Review Committee, which must approve each department's proposed budget, and in cabinet. Graham Richardson, who served as minister in several portfolios, has written, "One of the reasons why Labor governments have been so successful for so long is that the Budget proposals of Cabinet ministers are really put through the mincer" (1994, 326). Describing a colleague who was not successful in cabinet, Richardson reported: "He is not by nature pushy or aggressive and he did not like the kind of confrontation that Cabinet debate frequently engenders, often withdrawing Cabinet submissions or retreating early when under attack" (325).

Successful ministers have the reputation of being strong fighters for their cause. Those more likely to be successful are those who are tough and persistent and who also know and can argue their case (Heclo and Wildavsky 1981, 144–45). Several ministers agreed with this observation, as one put it: "My instinct is the departments infinitely prefer strong ministers rather than weak ones because so much of their survival and effectiveness depends on the battle being waged on their behalf [by the minister]" (interview, October 1996). Those who can advance the department's interest outside the department are also likely to have more impact inside the department. It is paradoxical in some ways, but the stronger the minister the greater the department's regard for that minister and thus the greater his or her influence within the department (Larsson 1994, 177–78). Laver and Shepsle write: "It seems generally agreed that most senior civil servants prefer a strong minister who can win battles for the department in cabinet, to a weak one who can be manipulated but who cannot defend departmental interests in the outside world" (1994, 303).

Goal Agreement

The ministers and department secretaries interviewed for this study reported cooperative relationships, with each partner having well-defined expectations of the other. This was, no doubt, enhanced by broad agreement between the elected and the appointed officials in the various departments. One minister explained: "And I think what worked best was when I had a head of department with whom I had both personal and intellectual sympathy and we were in harmony in terms of identifying a problem that we wanted to solve and in terms of the broad approach for getting there" (interview, October 1996).

Labor ministers for the most part reported good relationships with their department secretaries. They indicated that there were few news leaks or other devices designed to build political support for positions contrary to that of the minister or the government. Those ministers who reported some resistance generally referenced earlier periods of the government's tenure, and these episodes generally occurred as the government planned changes of some magnitude.

The new Liberal-National Coalition government, led by John Howard, experienced more resistance in its early days after assuming power in March 1996. The Howard government's first task was to cut the budget of most departments and to do so in ways that directed the departments away from several programs emphasized by the Hawke and Keating Labor governments. The most visible resistance was leaks from departments to political reporters, obviously designed to let supporters know the direction of the new government. Much of this occurred in the context of the formulation of the government's first budget, which cut expenditures from the projections of the previous government by a considerable amount. But by the time of the second set of interviews, seven months into the term of the new government, most ministers reported finding their departments responsive, though some were still annoyed by earlier leaks.

Coordination of Portfolio

The reorganization of Australian departments in 1987 combined previous departments and incorporated more than one minister—and often

parliamentary secretaries—into a given portfolio. The basic reorganization continued through the end of the Labor Party's term in power, with
some modifications as parts of departments were sometimes shifted to
new departments. The new Howard government continued the same basic organization when it assumed power in March 1996.

Although more than one member of a given ministry might well have
been assigned to a given portfolio prior to 1987, the result of the 1987
reforms has added to the responsibilities of ministers, for, in sharing a
portfolio, they must now coordinate with each other more than in the
past. This coordination is vitally important in the relationship between
ministers and departments, because lack of coordination can potentially
cloud the lines of communication between elected officials and the bureaucracy by providing mixed signals about priorities and positions, which
may make it difficult for departments to determine how best to be responsive to political preferences.

Both Labor and Coalition ministers report that coordinating the portfolio is one of the more challenging (and often frustrating) aspects of their
position. One former Labor minister related this experience:

> Nobody could quite know what everyone else was doing. You used
> to have constant problems with the demarcation of lines that would
> have to be drawn about who was looking after what. You then had
> the . . . cabinet minister—who at the end of the day was responsible
> to cabinet—so had to intrude into other areas [under the purview of
> the junior minister], which got peoples' backs up. Who then, you
> know, sort of thought you were second-guessing them or not having
> confidence in how they were doing the job or whatever. (Interview,
> October 1996)

The situation of senior and junior ministers sharing portfolios sometimes
works well and sometimes does not. One former minister related: "An awful
lot depends on the personalities of the people . . . involved. I had the best
and the worst of those relationships" (interview, October 1996). Another
minister stated: "I always made sure that the prime ministers gave me people
I could work with. Every now and then the system breaks down if you get
two antagonistic personalities" (interview, October 1996). In general, the
ministers believed that assigning discrete areas of responsibility was the
best way to avoid conflict. But this becomes a problem in some cases,
when the lines of demarcation between discrete areas become blurred, or
when the cabinet minister feels the need to intervene. A minister described

some techniques he found useful, but even these did not always work:

> Having the staff being in reasonable contact with each other. By having files come over for our attention concerning the other minister and vice versa so that we always knew what [each other was] thinking, by probably meeting at least once a day for half an hour on particular problem areas; by taking them into my confidence when there were issues that didn't concern them that were big issues in [the portfolio], by making clear to them that they had administrative and policy-making duties that could be pursued . . . other than if it involved extra expenditure of money (then I had to be brought in). But the basic philosophy was to give your associate or junior minister a discrete area . . . they are in charge of, and not go and second-guess them. I did that a couple of times and got in strife, interfered a couple of times. They got a bit miffed but were able to sort it out. (Interview, October 1996)

The key issue appears to be turf. One minister described the relationship with a senior minister: "That was a difficult and prickly relationship mainly because he was very, very paranoid about his turf, his own involvement in his responsibility. He resented the idea of having someone put there, to . . . begin with, and was damned if he was going to give me much to do" (interview, October 1996). Another minister called the shared portfolios a "major structural failure. . . . Where the individuals were OK, it worked extremely well. When they didn't it was a disaster. In some cases, let me tell you, I use the word advisably, a disaster, a real disaster" (interview, October 1996). Apparently relationships are likely to work best when there is a junior-senior relationship that installs persons in each position for which there is some distance in rank and seniority within the party and the ministry. But one minister indicated that even same-status portfolio sharing could work, "if there's an atmosphere of mutual respect and give and take between the ministers concerned" (interview, October 1996).

The problems with shared portfolios appear to be bipartisan in nature. The new Coalition ministers are also wrestling with the best ways of handling the delicate relationships between ministers. One stated:

> Well, we work at it constantly because of the diversity of the range of issues that we have to cover; . . . [it is] one of the most difficult tasks that we have. But . . . I meet regularly with both my parliamentary

secretary and the other portfolio minister. We begin each parliamentary week, for example, by meeting together privately, prior to the meeting with our departmental heads. . . . And our staffs interact widely. My chief-of-staff would consult sometimes almost on an hourly basis when the ax is really flying with [the junior minister's and parliamentary secretary's] senior staff. (Interview, October 1996)

Some of the potential perils of the relationship can be gleaned from the tactics of another minister:

I try and be a fairly dominant minister, I guess, is how I do it, and I'm across the other two ministers' portfolios really well. And in the end I have a right to override them if I choose. They wouldn't be too happy if I did. . . . I have to take stuff to cabinet on behalf of the other ministers, so I have to be happy with the cabinet submission. . . . Now I try to give . . . good latitude. And occasionally, when I think something's going wrong, I'll interfere. (Interview, October 1996)

In another case, the minister reported no problems as yet and then added, "But anything in life with personalities and human beings can be complex, so who knows?" (interview, October 1996).

Ministers and Responsiveness of the Bureaucracy

So the picture that emerges from the interviews with ministers corroborates the picture presented in the previous chapters by department secretaries and ministerial staffs. The overall relationship between the political and the administrative in Australia is a symbiotic relationship, with each side usually recognizing the need for cooperation and good communication. There also seems to be a good deal of respect for the relative contributions that each major player can bring to the policy process. Resistance to ministerial direction does occur, but those instances do not dominate the discussion as they often do in the United States. In fact, according to those interviewed, resistance that prevents the department presenting its views in a satisfactorily aggressive way does not occur often.

The responsiveness of departments can be diminished by the relatively new practice of utilizing more than one minister within a given portfolio. This practice increases the workload of the cabinet minister, often requires deft staff and department efforts to coordinate, and sometimes leads to friction between ministers, which threatens to cloud the direction of the department. In most instances coordination does occur; in some instances it does not. Further, the threat that ministers may work at cross-purposes or fail to work together is always a possibility.

This conclusion does not deal with the broader question of whether ministers in modern-day governments can be appropriately responsible for all activities of departments. The debate in Australia certainly illustrates the pressures toward a broader accountability of departments to parliament, in addition to the traditional lines of departmental accountability to ministers (Emy and Hughes 1991, 350–51). But ministers do report, on the whole, that the direction they seek to provide to departments does have an impact.

6

Lessons for U.S. Public Administration

The picture that emerges from interviews with Australian Commonwealth ministers corroborates the picture presented by department secretaries and ministerial staffs. There are also no substantial differences between Labor and Coalition ministers in the way they report their relating to departments and their staffs. Laver and Shepsle have proposed a model to illustrate the varying ways elected and career officials relate, particularly in parliamentary settings.

The model builds on varying relationships between ministers and the cabinet, the larger legislative body, and the civil service. A "bureaucratic government" focuses the power to make and implement public policy in the permanent civil service. A "legislative government" decides all policy in the legislature, with the cabinet mechanically implementing it. In "prime-ministerial government," a powerful prime minister dominates a collective executive. In "party government," the caucus is dominant as the prime minister and ministers who form the executive part of government are subject to the discipline of a well-organized party. In "cabinet government," the collective executive does not defer to individual ministers and exerts enough power to make collective decisions that are binding on all members. Finally, in a "ministerial government" (which Laver and Shepsle prefer), the executive is powerful but individual ministers, as heads of major departments, have significant impact on policy that falls under their jurisdiction (1994, 5–8). As defined by these models, the overall relationship between the political and the administrative in Australia makes it a ministerial government.

In Australia, both elected and appointed officials recognize the need for cooperation and good communication. There also seems to be a good deal of respect for the relative contributions that each major player can bring to the policy process. Resistance to ministerial direction does occur, but these instances do not dominate the discussion as they often do in the United States. When resistance does cross the line, ministers believe they have the necessary power and influence to effectively counter such moves.

This study began with noting that a key challenge in all democratic governments is to develop appropriate bureaucratic responsiveness to political direction. As the study progressed, we noted how one democracy handles the relationship between bureaucrats and politicians. Are there any lessons in what we have learned that might be applied to this relationship in the United States?

Fostering Cooperative Relationships

One clear lesson from the synthesis of insight offered by public administration scholars and the experience of the Australian Commonwealth government is the need for the blending of the strengths of both political and administrative officials, for effective public policy in a democracy. Australian ministers seemed genuinely interested in and grateful for departmental input, while policy matters are in debate, in the earliest stages of development. In this interaction, ministers may find their views modified or influenced by the information that departments can bring to bear on a policy question. They found valuable the departments' sharing of the practical administrative implications of policy options, and the provision of knowledge that comes from department expertise and experience. They also note that advice from departments has saved them embarrassment and provided information useful to them as they formulate policy. Although ministers believe that the bureaucracy occasionally resists change, by and large they have found that department heads and their department colleagues have been responsive to the changes introduced earlier by the reform-oriented Labor government and by the new Coalition government.

In addition to input on policy direction, on which ministers clearly believe they should have the final word, departments were also involved in policy development. Ministers devoted their attention to what some called policy direction, in which the broad outlines of goals of the policy were set. The department then had the task of filling in the details, or developing the policy, with the recognition that these details were important and were expected to conform to the purpose of the overall directions of the policy. Of course, ministers could revisit the policy as it was being developed, and ministerial staff were expected to oversee the process. Ministers were most appreciative of bureaucrats who are in their corner, who attempt to help ministers achieve their objectives.

For their part, Australian department secretaries clearly relish the departments' role of providing policy advice, which ranges from delineating several options and providing the pros and cons of each to making and arguing for an explicit recommendation. The departments' contribution comes from their expertise and experience, including knowledge of how proposals will impact administrative practices in the department. The department heads know that others will be involved in providing policy advice, especially the ministers' staff members, and sometimes consultants and academic-based researchers from outside government. Further, they recognize that the ministers (and the government) decide the overall policy objectives to be pursued. Nevertheless, department heads believe that departments should and do have input into the ministerial and cabinet decisions. They believe that they should and will be called upon to offer assistance in probing options for achieving the objectives set by the minister. They also have substantial responsibility for writing the policy. There are thus several junctures where bureaucratic expertise and experience can influence the final policy.

Another way that expertise and experience contribute to policy formulation in Australia is through department staff who are on leave in the minister's office and who become a part of the minister's staff. Ministers report that these individuals are very useful in analyzing policy proposals and provide an important supplement to the advice provided directly by the department. These, and other members of the minister's staff, augment the policy input provided from departments by evaluating it, stating their reactions to it, or possibly sending it back to the department for further work, as necessary. Staff members also provide an important function in facilitating the interaction between the ministerial office and the department. Department secretaries reported that what they found especially useful was the information from staff members about the minister's reactions, communications, and needs.

The interviews with top politicians and bureaucrats in Australia indicate that each side of the politics-administration relationship brings important resources to the policy-making process. These interviews confirm that the strengths of the bureaucracy include the kinds of resources identified by Heclo and others in studies of the United States: institutional memory, professional competence, continuity, and the experience and knowledge based on the responsibilities associated with the department or agency. Resources offered by the political side of the relationship include openness, new blood, fresh ideas, and political accountability (Heclo 1987, 195). Australian ministers would add to this the knowledge of the political environment, familiarity with parliamentary processes and preferences, and a greater ability to think strategically in the larger political context. Elected officials are also potentially less isolated and insulated from the larger political environment than non-elected officials.

In contrast to the practices in at least some policy areas of some presidential administrations in the United States, the Australian government has not excluded the bureaucracy when making policy decisions. When the potential contributions from either side are excluded for any reason, the result runs a great risk of diminishing the quality of the policy. The divergent but complementary strengths of politicians and bureaucrats suggest that the relationship between them should take place in an overall climate of cooperation. And, in fact, public administration scholars have offered prescriptions arguing for a conditionally cooperative approach in the relationship between career public servants and political appointees. Heclo asserts:

> Any premise of compassionate cooperation and participatory management overlooks the bureaucracy's divided loyalties, its needs for self-protection, and its multiple sources of resistance. Unconditionally negative approaches fail to recognize the enduring character of bureaucratic power and a political leader's need to elicit the bureaucracy's help in governing. . . . [This approach] implies a kind of cooperation that is conditional on the mutual performance of the political appointees and the civil servants. It emphasizes the need of executives and bureaucrats to work at relationships that depend on the contingencies of one another's actions, not on preconceived ideas of strict supervision or harmonious goodwill. Conditional cooperation rejects any final choice between suspicion and trust, between trying to force obedience and passively hoping for compliance. (1977, 193)

To this end, Durant advocates a "creative" engagement between political and bureaucratic sides of this relationship. This can occur when appointees respect the bureaucracy's concern about management and program capacity and the bureaucracy respects the political leader's concerns about partisan policy objectives, responsiveness to legal presidential and legislative goals, and expeditious results (1992, 319).

Although other scholars use different language, it is clear that they believe a symbiotic relationship is at base necessary for the ultimate success of policy making in a democracy. Aberbach and Rockman write: "Good management, as reflected in open channels of communication, willingness to listen to advice, clear articulation of goals, and mutual respect, in fact, may also constitute good politics for [U.S.] department secretaries or their assistant secretaries" (1988a, 609). Patricia Ingraham, after reviewing three case studies in which policy success was achieved, found that it was "attributable to joint action by political executives and high-level career managers" (1991, 192). Paul Light asserts that, when the political-bureaucracy connection fails, it is difficult to fix blame on one side or the other, since the lack of skill this implies may apply to either the appointee or the careerists. It is interesting that Light finds interpersonal skills to constitute the most important predictor of political appointees' evaluations of the career service, with positive evaluations of the career service being associated with the high interpersonal skills of the evaluator (1987, 169–71).

Studies of the relationships between political officials, their appointees, and career civil servants in the United States suggest that these findings and prescriptions emphasizing cooperation to foster a symbiotic relationship are too often ignored. By contrast, this study indicates that the relationships between ministers, their offices, and the departments in the Australian Commonwealth government for the period studied do for the most part conform with the type of prescriptions proffered by the scholars noted above. Further, the relationship between elected and appointed officials in Australia enhances the ability of both groups of officials to achieve their goals in the policy process.

There are two chief problems with ministers' providing political direction of the bureaucracy in Australia. One is that, although the average service in cabinet and as minister of a given portfolio compares well with other democracies, the number of times portfolios are held for two years or less is very high. This is mitigated somewhat by the usual practice of ministers' serving in successive portfolios over time. But longer service in a given portfolio would afford the possibility of more effective political direction. A second problem hinges on portfolios with more than one minister. Ministers, their staffs, and department heads deal with this in a variety of ways, but it is one feature of Australian government that tends to diminish the clarity with which politics speaks to administration. Despite these caveats, the overall conclusion of this study agrees with the observation of Australia's former prime minister Paul Keating that the government there has achieved a good balance between the need for political direction and the need for competent public servants to provide the services of government (1991). Moreover, the expectations of ministers of the relationships between politicians and departments does not vary by party in Australia—ministers in the newly elected Coalition government voice very similar views to their counterparts in the recent Labor governments.

Implicit in this mix is the need for competency on the part of those who provide political direction. Although elected officials in the United States publicly question the competence of public servants, there is little public attention devoted to the competence of elected officials in directing the bureaucracy. Further, in thinking about effective relationships between elected and non-elected officials in democracies, scholars do not often deal with varying levels of competence of elected officials, although they have questioned in a general way the competence of some political appointees. Yet this is a factor that must be taken into account and emphasized more than it has been in the past by both scholars and others interested in the relationship between elected and appointed officials in a democracy. One of the more candid appraisals of elected officials' competencies has been provided by Arthur Tange, a former department head in Australia. He wrote, after retirement and after having worked with numerous ministers: "In my short or long experience with each of about twenty ministers or acting ministers, I found not everyone was as competent as the theorists seem to suppose at defining what the government policy was to which I should work. Some needed occasional reminders of what their own cabinet, or what the Prime Minister had been saying" (Tange 1982, 10).

The conditionally cooperative relationship requires that elected and career officials meet several standards in order for the relationship between politics and administration to work well in democratic governments. The key standards found by this study include elected officials competent enough to formulate clear objectives and communicate them effectively to public servants. It requires respect for neutral competence by both elected and non-elected officials. And the relationship is governed by a common understanding of a kind of politics-administration dichotomy that defines appropriate behavior for both elected and non-elected officials.

Establishing and Communicating Objectives

The setting of clear objectives by politicians constitutes one of the key elements in effective political direction of the bureaucracy. This is not easy in any government, where policy must often serve a variety of objectives, and it is undoubtedly more difficult in a government with separation of powers, as in the United States. Moreover, elected leaders may well want to protect their options by being flexible enough to take credit or avoid blame with the consequences of policy changes that are difficult to predict. Despite these difficulties, even in the United States, studies of successful direction of the bureaucracy stress the importance of clear objectives (Randall 1979). Campbell and Halligan found in their study of Australian public service personnel that ministers in the Hawke government were much more likely than their predecessors to take initiatives in policy formulation and to indicate what they wanted from departments (1992, 61–62).

In the present study, both ministers and department secretaries stressed the importance of clear objectives, with the ministers also stressing the will to back up their positions. The interviews with ministers noted earlier in the study emphasized providing clear direction and giving feedback to the department when the minister disagreed or did not like the department's actions. Several ministers also underscored the importance of establishing a tone in their relationship with department personnel that signaled that the minister was clearly in charge and on top of the job.

Far from reacting negatively to strong direction from ministers, department secretaries seemed to appreciate ministers who did define clear objectives and who followed through on them. The importance of ministers' communicating their positions effectively was noted by one secretary: "I think the main way of getting political direction is to have ministers who know what they want and can explain what they want" (interview, October 1992). In Australia, as in Larsson's study of Sweden, the department heads preferred strong ministers over weak ones. Strong ministers exercise more influence in the department to be sure; but they also extend the department's influence in government (Larsson 1994, 177–78; Attlee 1954, 309; Heclo and Wildavsky 1981, 144–45).

This key need for elected officials to provide clear direction is frequently overlooked in examinations of the accountability and responsibility of career officials in a democracy. Without clear direction (which may be provided both formally and informally), the risk increases that the conduct of bureaucrats will not conform with democratically based preferences. Further, without such direction there is little available against which the conduct of career officials can be measured, or taken account of. Yet elected officials are clearly variable in their ability to provide clear direction and to communicate it effectively. Heclo and Wildavsky observe that "Ministers . . . come in all types" (1981, 130). The primary responsibility for assuring that the government remains responsive to citizens rests with elected officials. Any failure on their part to enunciate properly these preferences to the bureaucracy diminishes democratic government.

A second factor facilitating the effective political direction of bureaucracies is communication. Once a government develops an objective, it is then crucial—if the democratic preferences are to be translated into government action—that the objective be communicated clearly to unelected officials. Rose writes: "A minister who has views and can articulate them clearly and consistently to his higher civil servants is much more likely to have the actions taken in his name accurately reflect the mind of the minister than a minister whose mind is unclear, inconsistent, irrelevant to departmental views, or simply blank" (1984, 156).

For effective blending of the strengths that politicians and bureaucrats bring to the policy-making process, each must communicate effectively with the other. Career officials must have knowledge of the goals of elected officials. Elected officials must know how those goals fit with the ability of bureaucrats to design programs that will implement the goals and the likely consequences that will result. But, U.S. politicians have sought to enhance political direction of the bureaucracy by creating greater numbers of political appointments that penetrate ever deeper into the organizational hierarchy of federal departments and agencies. The reason for this is clear: presidents and their entourages believe that if they appoint their own persons to positions in the bureaucracy they will be better able to control it (Hart 1987, 128–29).

There is broad agreement among students of U.S. politics that the attempt to control the bureaucracy by increasing the number of political appointments is a failed approach. It dilutes political direction, reduces the connection between department public servants and high-level political superiors, and creates a new problem: how to achieve some harmony of direction among the competing interests of presidential appointees

(Heclo 1977, 94, 97, 230–39; Heclo 1987, 213; Ingraham 1991, 191–93; Jones 1994, 57; Kaufman 1981, 185–86; Light 1987, 163–65; Pfiffner 1987, 62–63; Rose 1980, 338; Rourke 1992, 544; Wildavsky 1987, xiii). In short, it has reduced the possibilities of effective communication between U.S. politicians and bureaucrats. Whenever effective translation of political directives into bureaucratic action takes place in this country (and some scholars have found that this does indeed occur), it does so in spite of the large number of political appointees in agencies and departments, not because of it.

Thus far, Australia has avoided the temptations so readily acceded to in America for creating several layers of political appointments within departments in order to effect control of the bureaucracy. Although the new Howard government terminated a larger number of department heads than had been the case for past Commonwealth governments, those who were appointed tended to have high-level experience in the bureaucracy. Moreover, department executives who held places in the top hierarchy of the departments just below the department heads for the most part stayed in place. This turnover demonstrated that political leaders in Australia now exert more influence on choosing the heads of the Commonwealth departments than their counterparts did prior to the last decade. As well, in Australia there has been an increase in ministerial staff since the early 1970s, but thus far the growth has been constrained. The average minister in Australia manages his or her constituency services and runs the department, often as large in size as some state governments in this country, with fewer staff members than the typical U.S. senator.

Although the Australian government is smaller than the U.S. government, the utility of a smaller group involved in the interface between politics and administration is readily apparent. Top bureaucrats have direct contact with ministers and their staffs. They interact regularly with each other. The ministerial staff is relatively small and retains frequent contact with the minister. They also often facilitate the communication between the minister and the department. The interaction between the minister, the minister's staff, and the department management is frequent enough that those responsible for receiving political direction can understand the preferences, priorities, interests, and policy positions of the minister, who is the source of political direction. This increases the chances that effective communication can occur between politicians and bureaucrats, which is more likely to assure that the complementary strengths of each will be brought to bear on policy formulation.

Reducing the number of political appointments goes against the grain of American politicians looking for a solution to the problem of democratic control of administration. But it is clear that effective policy making would be served if the number of appointees were reduced. The U.S. government is indeed larger than many others in the family of democratic nations, but the ratio of department and agency personnel appointed by politicians to career public servants is also greater in this country than in others. Further, the popular reforms associated with reinventing government should focus directly on reducing the number of U.S. political appointments. In Australia, the use of career public servants on ministers' staffs offers another possibility for consideration for reducing the problem associated with too many U.S. political appointments. The assignment of career bureaucrats to some of these positions in the United States might increase the overall level of ability at that level, while bringing the accumulated bureaucratic experience to bear on policy formulation and facilitating communication of administration goals to lower levels of the agency or department.

Respect for Neutral Competence

Australian politicians respect the neutral competence of the bureaucracy. The findings in this study note the reliance of ministers on the departments for developing the details of policy, and a respect for the bureaucratic knowledge and experience that can be brought to bear on policy development. The other side of this experience emphasizes the caution that bureaucrats bring to the policy-making table. Ministers attest to how frequently this input has kept them from making mistakes they would later regret. The close interaction between ministers and departments thus permits departments to provide leadership as needed while the politicians develop new initiatives.

It also permits departments to post cautionary notices as necessary to avoid paths that might lead to mistakes. This latter benefit is sometimes noted by U.S. political appointees. James Pfiffner, for example, has noted that some recognized the good fortune to have career public servants who kept them from "bear traps" or from "shooting myself in the foot" (1987, 61). This kind of quality connection between bureaucrats and the public service, however, appears to occur only sporadically in the United States, while it is a stable, built-in protection in the Australian system.

A second important result of ministers' respect of neutral competence can be noted by their practice thus far of appointing as department heads persons who either have risen through the ranks of the bureaucracy or, if they come from outside the bureaucracy, have had in the past substantial experience in the bureaucracy in almost all cases. Some fear that this could change over time, and it could. But thus far Australian governments have resisted whatever temptation might be present to appoint as department heads those whose primary experience has been campaign, election, or party related.

The Australian respect for neutral competence contrasts with the decline of this value in the United States. Neutral competence was one of the chief values for those who successfully advanced civil service reforms in the United States beginning over a century ago. This need derived in part from the increasing complexity of government activities, which required expertise, skills, and experience to perform the tasks of government. The Progressive reforms were designed to enhance this kind of competence. Moreover, the emphasis on neutral competence that has been a part of our heritage ever since then was born of both the concern for competence and the desire to further it in the future. But the value given to neutral competence is steadily diminishing in the United States. Rourke writes: "The growing demand for responsiveness in government policy making puts the survival of a professional outlook characterized by independence of judgment and indifference to political pressures increasingly at risk in the corridors of American bureaucracy" (1992, 545).

Rourke notes that those who attack neutral competence may do so for several reasons. Presidents wanting to innovate may find neutral competence too passive; and Congress recognizes that neutral competence skews power in the bureaucracy in the direction of the executive branch. There are sources of information and expertise other than the bureaucracy that political leaders may consult (Rourke 1992, 539–44).

Public administration scholars in the United States typically see the proliferation of political appointees as one manifestation of the diminished value of neutral competence. The attacks on neutral competence derive in part from the concerns of presidents and their entourages that their own appointees are to be counted on to do the White House bidding, more than a public servant who has been promoted to a similar position in the bureaucratic hierarchy. Part of the attack, though, proceeds from a philosophical base, which finds neutral competence difficult to describe and believe. Because this is so, "Presidents and political theorists find the idea of 'neutral competence' impossible to describe. No one plausibly can lack interests; thus, all advice or discretional possibilities are skewed" (Aberbach and Rockman 1988a, 608). Garvey also points to the diminished value of neutral competence: "The Old Theory [based on Progressive principles] was an ethical theory in that it relied on the internal values of well-educated public servants to discipline the conduct of government business" (1993, 20). Garvey finds problems also with the "Old Theory," because, "We know today that neither higher education nor professional expertise can guarantee non-partisan, disinterested, or incorruptible conduct by civil servants" (34).

The obvious consequence of the diminished value of neutral competence is the belief that politicians must have their own people in positions of responsibility in agencies and departments. This belief leads to the practice of more appointments of those whose knowledge and experience are suspect; it can also cut people with that knowledge and experience out of the policy-formulation loop where this kind of input is sorely needed. This practice creates communication problems, making it difficult for politicians to provide political direction to bureaucrats and for bureaucrats to provide appropriate levels of information to politicians. Too much political direction can also thwart the "civil service's independent responsibility to uphold legally constituted institutions and procedures" (Heclo 1977, 244).

The Australians interviewed in this study place a much higher value on neutral competence than do their U.S. counterparts. Elected officials demand loyalty to the government of the day but recognize that loyalty can be switched if the outcome of the next election places the opposition in power. They also generally hold bureaucrats in high regard.

One advantage of belief in neutral competence is that it fosters respect for the professional knowledge, expertise, and experience that bureaucrats can bring to the table as policy decisions are made. It fosters the notion that this expertise and experience can serve politicians representing different political parties equally well. For these reasons, neutral competence is a value that ought to be encouraged and promoted by bureaucrats, politicians, and scholars in the United States.

With respect to politicians, the prospects for greater respect for neutral competence in the United States are mixed. The bashing of bureaucrats that has become commonplace in the United States since the early 1970s does not foster heightened respect for neutral competence. Although criticism of public servants is not unknown in Australia, the interviews for this study produced none of the hostility to bureaucrats that is often voiced in this country. Rather, the interviews indicated a respect for public servants that American scholars might find surprising. For example, one minister indicated:

> The public service respond the best when you recognize the competence that's there and find ways of drawing out and utilizing it. Not by-passing it. Not being cynical and skeptical about it. Not hiring in a mass of talent from the outside. It's there! There's a huge amount of competence in our system. Much more so than out in the private sector. Pound for pound the quality is better. And you've just got to learn how to utilize it. (Interview, October 1996)

But there is some hope for fostering greater respect for neutral competence in the United States, because paradoxically, despite the negative attitudes that give rise to bureaucrat bashing, many politicians and political appointees come to view bureaucrats in a more positive light as they acquire experience. A Reagan appointee, James Miller, found that his initial impressions were erroneous, for example:

> Some heads of government institutions assume that the career staff are by definition the enemy, that they are impossible to guide and manage, and thus must be stopped by virtually any means possible. Miller likes to say that when he became Chairman [of the Federal Trade Commission] he assumed that 20 percent of the career staff were sympathetic and 80 percent were actively opposed to the Administration's goals. . . . Miller's views about the career staff have since altered dramatically. Miller now contends that he had it exactly backward; 80 percent of the career staff are loyal employees and only about 20 percent actively opposed the goals of the Administration. (Rock 1987, 246)

The self-defeating nature of the initial attitudes toward the bureaucracy held by political appointees like Miller was noted by Rock: "Miller could have won over the career staff earlier if he had realized that the agency's low morale under his predecessor had predisposed the staff to be receptive to a positive agenda and good management" (1987, 247). The contrast with Australia is noted by ministerial staff members who reported that they knew there were those in the departments who anticipated working positively with a new government. One staff member related that a study initiated by the minister would "spur the more able and forward-thinking people in the organization to come up with some changes, which senior management would tend to argue against" (interview, October 1996). The problem in the United States is that initial negative attitudes toward bureaucrats can produce self-fulfilling prophecies. The less bureaucrats are involved in policy formulation, over time, the less they have to offer in the process (Heclo 1987, 202).

It is interesting that most scholars have found there to be little substance to the concern that U.S. political appointees often voice—that the careerists are likely to resist the appointees as the latter seek to introduce change (Aberbach and Rockman 1988a, 609; Ingraham 1991, 192–93; Ingraham 1995, 106–07; Rubin 1985, 196; Volcker 1988, 9–10; Wildavsky 1987, xii–xiv). Relations between the two generally improve over time (Pfiffner 1987, 60; Huddleston 1987, 63). But by the time this occurs, the appointees have often reached the end of their brief tenure, and it is too late to promote the cooperation needed for effective policy making (Light 1987, 157). They are replaced by newly minted appointees who begin the cycle again. Perhaps political appointees would at least hesitate in giving full play to their attitudes if more of them were aware of the observation of one British minister, who stated: "I think that a minister who complains that his civil servants are too powerful is either a weak minister or an incompetent one" (Young and Sloman 1982, 25). The Australian ministers interviewed for this study share this view.

As for scholars, especially those involved in educating future bureaucrats, there is a need to place greater emphasis on the value of neutral competence. Garvey's discussion of neutral competence emphasizes his view that it was once an important value held by public servants and assumed the position of an ethical theory. Lilla has written of the decline of the ethos of the old public administration, which stressed such values. He argues that higher education programs in public affairs and administration should stress moral education to include appropriate moral habits for someone serving in a democratic government. Although Lilla's point is well taken, he explicitly rejects the ethos of the old public administration because it is "inappropriate for most officials in government today" (1981, 16). The reason is that the old ethos does not offer appropriate guidance for the greater discretion available to public servants today.

The strength of comparative analysis appears when analyzing arguments like Lilla's. Compared with an earlier time, Australian public servants also have greater complexity in their positions and in the areas over which they have responsibility. This stems from many sources including the reorganization of many departments in 1987, which created larger departments and provided in many cases more than one minister with responsibility for the department. Moreover, it is clear that Australian public servants are not supervised as Finer would prescribe: "Elected representatives . . . are to determine the course of action of the public servants to the most minute degree that is technically feasible" (1978, 411–12). Australian department heads plainly see their role as providing policy advice, including options to achieve given objectives, as well as providing recommendations. They recognize that the minister may not agree with their advice, but that they must nevertheless offer it and make it a part of policy deliberations. Further, after general objectives have been set, the public service fills in the details to conform with those objectives, with the recognition that those details are important in setting future policy directions.

Ministers likewise accept public servants' input into the policy formulations. The reason stems from their respect for public servants' competence, and the belief that they will provide the best information possible. In other words, public servants' adherence to the value of neutral competence is the foundation that permits elected leaders to accord them a legitimate place to participate in the "political" decision of helping to formulate policy. The importance of holding firm to this value is noted by Michael Keating, head of the important Department of Prime Minister and Cabinet in the Paul Keating government, who writes:

> Good advisers are not politically naive and they are expected to be loyal to the government of the day. . . . neither should they become such protagonists on behalf of particular policies that they risk becoming embroiled in partisan political debate. . . . This does not mean that public servants have no views of their own, but it does mean that they can be sufficiently detached to advise in terms of what they understand to be the government of the day's objectives. (1995, 22)

Once neither elected nor career public servants believe in neutral competence, politicians will begin to exclude public servants from policy deliberations—as has been happening in some situations in the United States in recent years. The "new" public administration emphasizes public servants' acting on their own values, independent from those of elected officials. But even George Frederickson, a strong advocate of the "new" public administration, warned that public administrators displaying and acting on the values of the "new" public administration, risked substantial opposition from elected officials (Frederickson 1971, 329).

Far from rejecting neutral competence either as being irrelevant to modern bureaucrats or as ensuring that bureaucrats served the status quo and the establishment, educators who teach future public servants should reinforce it as one of the great values of public administration if they believe that policy processes are improved by the input of career public servants into policy formation. The importance of the expertise that bureaucrats bring in policy formulation must not be lost. Michael Keating put this challenge very well when he stated: "The public service has to be able to give advice frankly, without fear or favour. In particular, it has a responsibility to draw on its professional knowledge and accumulated experience to point out any possibly unpalatable implications of particular policies which might otherwise have remained unforeseen or been glossed over" (Keating 1995, 23). Another civil servant, from Great Britain, offered this prescription for dividing the responsibilities of elected and appointed officials: "I think the job of the civil servant is to make sure that his minister is informed; that he has all the facts; that he's made aware of all the options and that he is shown all the considerations bearing on those options. It is then for the minister to take the decision" (Young and Sloman 1982, 21).

The Politics-Administration Dichotomy

The politics-administration dichotomy, advanced most forcefully by Woodrow Wilson (1992) and Charles Goodnow (1900) holds that there are distinct responsibilities of politics and administration in government, and in its original form, stressed the differences between the two. Wilson, for example, stated, "The field of administration is a field of business. It is removed from the hurry and strife of politics. . . . Administrative questions are not political questions" (1992, 18). But this principle has long been suspect because it was difficult to neatly parse certain activities on one side or the other, and there were obvious activities in which both participated. Nevertheless, anyone who has read thus far has to be struck that both ministers and department heads in Australia consider that dichotomy, or at least a version of it, to be very much alive, and one that they use to define their relationship with each other. Their definition of the dichotomy is somewhat different from the traditional definition attributed to Wilson and Goodnow.

Australian department heads very much believe that they have responsibility for administering their departments. This includes following the law that authorizes and defines their programs as well as the management of the department. Australian ministers by and large share this view. Although ministers differ in how much they intervene into department management and administration, most do not have the time or the inclination to do so. As one minister stated: "The actual administration and structure of the department really only rarely comes before ministers unless ministers want to be really highly interventionist" (interview, November 1992). Woodrow Wilson would undoubtedly agree with this minister's operating philosophy. The minister's position coincides with Wilson's metaphor to illustrate the appropriate role for administrators: "The cook must be trusted with large discretion as to the management of the fires and the ovens" (1992, 20).

Ministers, their staffs, and the department secretaries also indicated that there was an understood division of responsibilities between the ministers' offices and the departments. And the Hawke government actually acted on this dichotomy principle when designing reforms to increase political control of the bureaucracy. The decision to increase the ministers' personal staffs rather than place more political appointees into the departments provided ministers with the staff to handle better the more political and partisan side of their responsibility. This reduced the kinds of partisan activities that ministers may have expected departments to undertake (writing partisan speeches, scoring debate points against the opposition, brokering policy positions with other ministerial offices or the party caucus, and so on). These kinds of activities have been assigned to ministerial staff. They rely on departments for information and for preparation of lengthy documents, such as cabinet submissions. They utilize this information in their work, but they do not expect the department to enter into the partisan fray.

But Australian ministers and department heads add an important new dimension to the more traditional view of the politics-administration dichotomy. They share a belief that departments should and must be involved in policy development, which was traditionally assigned solely to the politics side of the dichotomy. Department heads believe that the department should have robust input into new policy directions as they are developed by the minister. The department heads recognize that they will share with others the role of providing advice on new directions, but they expect that they will be at the table offering advice and that their advice will be respected and often, though not always, heeded.

Ministers also expect department heads to offer policy advice. They appreciate that advice and acknowledge that it has an impact on their decisions. Ministers increase their degree of comfort by eliciting advice from a number of sources, including their staff and outside sources. They have made occasional use of expertise from consultants and university faculty when they have sought to introduce policy changes. But they rely heavily on their departments to provide information crucial for their decisions. Even the reform-minded ministers in this study found the caution of the bureaucracy to be useful. Thus, both ministers and department secretaries define a large role for the bureaucracy in policy formulation in Australia.

The Australian elected and non-elected officials cited in this study operate in accordance with a modified version of the politics-administration dichotomy similar to that defined by Montjoy and Watson (1995). They argue that a major reason U.S. scholars and practitioners have rejected the politics-administration dichotomy derives from its assumption that bureaucrats do not (and should not) engage in policy advice, or in any similar activity associated with the formulation of policy directions. The Montjoy-Watson definition prefers that elected officials not meddle in administration, and this is the preference of the department heads in this study as well as most ministers most of the time. The ministers would reserve that possibility, particularly if problems developed in implementing policy, or the department made mistakes and did not provide for properly correcting them as viewed by the minister. Montjoy and Watson conclude with a definition of the dichotomy that emphasizes the difference between politics and administration on the one hand and policy and administration on the other. The former establishes clear lines between the responsibility of elected and career officials, whereas the latter permits career officials to engage in policy advice (Montjoy and Watson 1995, 231–38). The working definition of the dichotomy in Australia confirms the joint involvement of ministers and bureaucrats in policy development and the insulation of the bureaucracy from partisan political pressures and interventions, as stipulated by Montjoy and Watson. But ministers expect to intervene in administration when it is necessary to do so.

A dichotomy between politics and administration provides a firm foundation for the value of neutral competence. The tendency of U.S. public administration to reject neutral competence was based in part on the perception that it appeared stultifying and seemed to exclude values, such as equity, that some believe should be included as a basis for decision making (Frederickson 1971, 310–14). Perhaps neutral competence was tied too closely to the old politics-administration dichotomy, which denied a role for the bureaucracy even in policy formation, making it so far removed from reality that it was rejected outright, rendering any concept or value associated with it suspect as well. For whatever reason, bureaucrats and scholars—in rejecting neutral competence as being irrelevant, in order that career public servants could become more relevant to important decisions made by government—have paradoxically run the grave risk of becoming more irrelevant to policy making. Public servants' adherence to the value of neutral competence was the basis upon which politicians were willing to admit them to the policy-making table in the first place. Former Australian prime minister Malcolm Fraser wrote of his preference for public servants to be politically detached and nonpartisan: "Unless this is the case with the career official, the stability and the professionalism of the public service will also be subject to severe strain" (1978, 7). Perhaps the rejection of the value of neutral competence by U.S. elected officials was based on their perception that public servants had ceased adhering to it as well.

All of this suggests the need in the United States for a reexamination of neutral competence within the context of a redefined definition of the politics-administration dichotomy. The lesson from this comparative study suggests that a reinvigoration of neutral competence may be necessary for the bureaucracy to take its proper place in policy formulation in a democracy. It also suggests that when the relationship between bureaucrats and elected officials is out of balance, the reason may lie with bureaucrats as well as with elected officials, something that public administration scholars sometimes do not emphasize. This suggests that public servants must recognize that the broad directions of public policy must be set by elected political leaders. This further suggests that, ultimately, those directions are the prerogative of elected officials. The policy advice and input from bureaucrats should focus on development, consequences, and evaluation of options within the legal framework that should bind behavior of both bureaucrats and elected officials.

This role for career officials is not an easy one in the U.S. system of government. Norton Long has argued that agencies and departments must build their political power if they hope to achieve their objectives (1949). Ronald Sanders has found that career officials often testify before congressional committees and engage in other policy advocacy to build support for programs (1994, 222–23). The multiple sources of political power in a separation-of-powers system invites end runs, and a playing of one power center against another. It is within this context that neutrality must be rebuilt, perhaps over a period of time. It will have a different flavor than the neutrality practiced in Australian government. The need is great to rebuild high regard for neutral competence if the U.S. government is to restore the bureaucracy to a fuller role in policy formulation as well as to avoid errors and illegalities that have marked several recent administrations (Aberbach and Rockman 1988a, 610). The road map provided by the experience in Australia suggests the direction that should be traveled.

Accountability and Responsibility

The study noted in chapter 2 that the concepts of accountability and responsibility define the relationship between non-elected and elected officials in a democracy to translate public preferences into policy. Accountability emphasizes answerability for one's behavior or actions. Responsibility emphasizes empowerment to engage in action or activities. The person acting upon the grant of power must be answerable or accountable for the use of that power. This study provides an opportunity to examine these concepts as they apply to a top group of public officials in one of the world's leading democracies. Both the department secretaries and the ministerial staff included in this study are not elected. They hold influential positions. What observations and conclusions can be offered about these concepts from the findings of this study?

A key finding of this study is the importance of elected officials defining clearly the responsibilities of the bureaucracy, or what they want the bureaucracy to do. This is basic if the bureaucracy is to be responsive to the preferences of the people, as defined by elected officials. It is also a necessary precondition to accountability because the definition of responsibility establishes the basis upon which non-elected officials must answer for their actions. The picture of responsibility that emerges from this study is that it combines both the external and internal direction of non-elected officials advanced by Friedrich and Finer more than a half century ago. Finer's external directions are important to department secretaries and ministerial staff. They not only recognize that the minister has the last word, but that he or she provides much guidance along the way. One department secretary spoke of their minister's communication through "formal, informal, spoken, and nonspoken cues that are given" as important for guiding their work. The staff spoke of their awareness of the minister's position and emphasize that their role is to facilitate the minister's preferences, not to take up an independent position. Both groups learn from interaction with the minister as well as from following the course of policy development and communication between the minister and the department. Both groups of non-elected officials seem to have finely adjusted antennas, tuned into the minister's preferences on issues.

Another keen example of Finer's external definition of responsibility stems from the formal positions laid out by the government and by the law. Both department secretaries and ministerial staff referenced the overall policies laid down by government as a source of guidance for their actions. Secretaries explicitly mentioned their obligation to carry out the law that applied to their department. Staff members were more likely to mention the general positions associated with the government.

A final example of the external direction of non-elected officials preferred by Finer consists of the eagerness with which the ministerial staff (as one might expect) as well as the department secretaries follow the desires of the ministers. Both department heads and ministers stressed the responsiveness of the bureaucracy to ministerial direction. In fact, new members of the Coalition government in Australia have found the Australian bureaucracy to be much more responsive than they had anticipated, and some ministers indicated that their trust in the professionalism of the service had been reciprocated by the departments' acting in a highly professional way. Further, key ministerial staff members indicated that they spent a lot of time discussing with department personnel the likely reaction of their ministers, on matters resulting from queries initiated by the departments, which again indicates that departments in Australia are keen to follow direction by ministers.

But as critics have pointed out in the past, the external controls advanced by Finer are not enough, because they inevitably do not provide guidance that is minute enough to cover all the situations in which non-elected officials might find themselves. There were numerous examples in the exercise of discretion, noted by those interviewed, that illustrate the importance of internal definitions of responsibility.

First, several department secretaries indicated that, ideally, the minister and parliament would provide policy direction, but once that direction had been established they believed they were responsible for the way the policy was administered. They admitted that even in such situations, some ministers did get into management details. But they preferred this not to be the case, and in most instances ministers do leave the details to the departments. In such situations the actions of the departments would be guided by Friedrich's internal definitions of responsibility, especially as they relate to actions based on professional knowledge and judgment. The department secretary is thus responsible for how a law is adminis-tered, but is then accountable to the minister for the results of carrying out that responsibility.

Second, the department secretaries and ministerial staff are also guided by their anticipations of what their elected superiors want, an important component of internal definition of responsibility advanced by Friedrich. In such situations the non-elected official tries to do what he or she thinks the minister would want done. The calculation of anticipated reaction may include information provided as a part of the external controls noted above. But in the end, it is often up to the non-elected official to apply what is learned, and that judgment is based on an anticipated reaction based on knowledge previously acquired in a variety of ways.

Third, the ministerial staff interviewed overwhelmingly viewed their responsibility as being to facilitate the minister in his or her work. They reported that they learned what the minister wanted and then applied it. Although there are lapses in a few cases, as described by Waterford (1996), in almost all situations ministerial staff members act within the delegation given by the minister. The direction from the minister was not always specific, but rather derived from the staff's anticipation of what the minis-ter wanted or what the minister's reaction would be to certain situations. Heclo and Wildavsky point out that such anticipation increases the minister's influence (1981, 132). Both the external and the internal definition of responsibility that impacts the behavior of department secretaries and ministerial staff are facilitated by the factors of communication and clear objectives (noted above). Both groups of non-elected officials indicated on several occasions the value of the regular interaction with ministers for learning what they were expected to do. Both external and internal direc-tion are important in establishing the responsibility of non-elected officials. Though some direction comes from each, the two combine to reinforce each other. Non-elected officials learn to anticipate (internal direction), for example, by information that is provided them directly by elected officials (external direction).

Finally, it is important to note that bureaucrats in Australia have, as one of their responsibilities as defined by elected officials, the responsibil-ity of participating in formulating the directions for policy that they will ultimately be responsible for implementing. Ministers in the study, as noted, expect strong participation by departments in the formulation of policy proposals. To the extent that advice is accepted by the ministers, the departments in effect take part in defining their responsibility to the minister. Further, even if the advice is not taken, their close participation at this stage of policy formation provides high quality information that they can use to fine tune the definition of their responsibility when they must implement the policy. It will also enhance their ability to anticipate how their actions in implementation will likely be taken into account at a later time by the minister. Thus, the Australian ministers' respect for neutral competence, and the modified definition of the politics-administration dichotomy that guides interaction between ministers and departments constitute important components of defining responsibility for the departments in Australia.

Any assessment of responsibility is incomplete without considering how elected officials view the viability of the system that is in place. Are non-elected officials responsive to the responsibilities defined by elected officials? In the United States, there is general disgruntlement among elected officials about the way bureaucrats carry out their work. But the Australian ministers interviewed for this study were generally satisfied with the responsiveness of the Australian public service. They believed they had ample opportunity to provide direction, and that the direction they provided worked. Although the ministers may not be the most objective observers of their own performance, their perceptions are important, because any successful system of accountability should meet the test of being approved by the elected officials who are a key component in that system.

Accountability in a democracy requires that non-elected officials give an account of their actions and activities to elected officials. In Australia, as we have noted, that requires departments to account to the minister responsible for the department, and through that person, to the cabinet and parliament. Both department secretaries and ministerial staff are keenly aware of this accountability. Department secretaries in recent years have worked to keep the accountability lines to ministers as clear as possible. Accountability enforces responsibility, because as non-elected officials carry out their responsibilities, whether externally or internally defined, they know that they are accountable for their actions to elected officials.

Ministers do believe that their ability to enforce accountability and elicit the appropriate behavior of bureaucrats has been enhanced by reforms adopted by the Hawke and Keating governments. Ministers believe that their greater control over the tenure of department secretaries has made the department heads, and consequently their departments, more responsive than they otherwise would be. Ministers rely on the secretary to make sure that the their views prevail in the department. The greater role by elected officials in selecting department secretaries (as compared with the earlier method) has also made it more likely that secretaries are in place who share the policy goals of the government. Thus, the limited extension of political appointments into the bureaucracy has been an important component in achieving a more accountable bureaucracy.

The mechanisms of accountability and responsibility work somewhat differently in a parliamentary system than they do in a government system that emphasizes separation of powers as in the United States. Nevertheless, there are some fundamentals that suggest paths whereby the relationship between elected and unelected officials in the U.S. government might improve. These fundamentals have been elaborated earlier. They include a definition of accountability and responsibility marked by an appreciation for a modified definition of the politics-administration dichotomy; a respect for neutral competence; an emphasis on political leaders' defining goals as clearly as possible to set the boundaries of responsibility for public servants; robust participation by departments in policy formulation; and deference to the political direction set by elected officials within the legal framework that departments and agencies must work. These fundamentals are applicable to other members of the family of democratic nations, including the United States.

The application of these fundamentals to the United States does require some adjustments. Charles Jones writes: "The Founders were not ignorant of the potential advantages of accountability or responsible government, but they found greater advantages in another system" (1994, 147). The U.S. system makes fine lines of accountability difficult to establish and results in multiple definitions of responsibility. Nevertheless, it is important in democratic societies to develop ways for members of the bureaucracy to account for their behavior to duly elected officials. The fact that this may be difficult does not mean that citizens, politicians, or bureaucrats should give up trying to arrive at appropriate methods of accountability. In the first place, the findings of this study about accountability do have direct application for the U.S. executive branch. Second, any system of responsibility and accountability in the United States must also take into account the legislative branch. In order to explore this aspect of accountability in the United States, let us consider Congress directly.

Appreciating the Role of Congress

Those who have examined the political direction of the U.S. bureaucracy, especially in detail, have noted the great impact of legislature on departments and agencies. Kaufman's exhaustive study of bureau chiefs, for example, concluded that Congress clearly had the upper hand in influencing the bureaus (1981, 161). Abney and Lauth's study of administration in the fifty states found that more than one-third of the agency heads that the governor had some say in appointing ranked the state legislature ahead of the governor in the amount of influence brought to bear on state policy making. For those agency heads who had been selected without the governor's involvement, more than 60 percent chose the legislature over the governor as the entity that exercised the most influence (1986, 64–67). Despite these findings, public administration scholars often neglect the legislative branch when examining the relationship between politics and administration. Perhaps the primary reason for this is that many public administration scholars are modern-day heirs of the Progressive tradition when it comes to examining the relationship between politics and administration. Heclo notes:

> Progressive reformers were basically executive-oriented and usually ended up assuming that the president stood at the top of an executive hierarchy. But as a practical matter it was impossible to deny that Congress is also part of the government of the day, and in its several parts—parts that are not under the control of any presidential party—capable of exerting greater influence over departmental work than any president. (1987, 204)

Jones cautions that the presidential-centered perspective can lead to inattention to the larger and more permanent government, in which a president must find his own place (1994, 284). And one group of scholars points to the necessity of considering the legislative branch, asserting: "The closer one looks at the way agencies behave and the problems they produce, the more their behavior seems the product of congressional action" (DiIulio, Garvey, and Kettl 1993, 21).

In Australia, although the terminology is different, the struggle between the legislature and the executive for control of the bureaucracy is similar to that waged in this country. The Management Advisory Board in Australia has attempted to preserve the Westminster model of department accountability, where the department leaders are accountable for their actions primarily to their minister, and the minister is accountable to parliament (MAB 1993). But backbenchers, the opposition, and members of the Senate would like more influence than they currently have. At present the battle in Australia has not encroached on neutral competence as much as has occurred in this country, but department secretaries, backed by their ministers, have resisted opening accountability lines to parliamentary committees. They recognize that it is easier to accommodate one power center, their minister, than the multiplicity of power centers that would result.

The necessity of the bureaucracy in this country to respond to a multiplicity of power centers (and the president or governor may not even be first among equals in relative standing, among these power centers) and the existence of divided government (with one party controlling the presidency and the other at least one house of the legislature) necessarily complicate efforts to reform the politics-administration relationship in the United States. The proliferation of personal, committee, and institutional staffs in the U.S. Congress in the last twenty-five years introduces another element into the equation. Although the Republican leadership of Congress has promised to reduce the size of staffs, it is not clear how far this reduction will go or how long it will last. What is clear is that the new congressional leadership will likely push strongly and energetically for congressional prerogatives in overseeing the bureaucracy. This likelihood (which would be present in varying concentrations regardless of which party controls Congress) calls into question the support for reforms of the bureaucracy that would deregulate it or reinvent it. Perhaps the best that might be hoped for is the kind of attention and discussion that would focus on (1) the appropriate balance between politics and administration, between Congress and the bureaucracy, and (2) the adoption of a conditional cooperative relationship that would blend in policy making the strengths of political and bureaucracy institutions. These developments would be as desirable for the legislative branch as they would be for the elected and politically appointed officials in the executive branch. Then there might be appropriate attention to the condition noted by Gormley: "The deeper tragedy is that legislative pressure serves so often to narrow rather than to broaden the bureaucracy's perspective" (1989, 221).

In the end, U.S. bureaucrats must look both to Congress and to the president to establish their responsibilities, and they must be accountable to both. This makes the position of those in leadership posts in agencies and departments a difficult one. It suggests that the internal definition of responsibility advanced by Friedrich is more important in the United States than in Australia, simply because the external definition of responsibility advanced by Finer is more difficult to fashion in our system of government.

Reforming the U.S. Bureaucracy

In the last decade there has been great emphasis on reform of government in this country. Through the lens of a comparative perspective, the relationships between elected and non-elected officials in Australia do provide a basis for evaluating some of these reforms. The most comprehensive reform proposals have been the Volcker Commission in the late 1980s, and the more recent National Performance Review led by Vice President Al Gore at the national level (Volcker Commission Report 1989; NPR 1993). An effort led by former Mississippi governor William Winter focused on the state level, and to some extent, the local level of government (Winter Commission Report 1993). The National Performance Review and the Winter Commission report were heavily influenced by the now well known work by David Osborne and Ted Gaebler, *Reinventing Government* (1992).

Of these reports, only the Volcker Commission emphasized the need to examine the proliferation of political appointees, and its impact on effective policy making. The National Performance Review (1993), often called the Gore report, recommends cutting White House staff and middle-level managers in agencies and departments, although it is not clear how many of the targeted managers are political appointees and how many are career civil servants. Neither the National Performance Review nor the Winter Commission report focus as centrally as would be desirable on ways to make the political-bureaucracy interface more effective: by fostering an appropriately cooperative relationship between them, by reducing the number of political appointments, by introducing appropriate training programs for new appointees, and by reducing the denigrating of bureaucrats that has been all too prevalent in recent decades. By and large, the reforms also neglect the important structural features of American government and pay far too little attention to the legislative branch in their prescriptions for the future. The lessons of Australia, and other democratic countries, should encourage future reformers to tackle these issues as well.

Reform of the relationship between politicians and bureaucrats in this country cannot occur without some attention to accountability and responsibility. At the outset of this consideration, these concepts pose difficult dilemmas in this country of shared authority and separation of powers, which characterize the national, state, and many local governments. The reform proposals that have been considered in recent years have not devoted much attention to accountability; to the extent they have, they have widely missed the mark. Wilson observes that the Gore report's most striking feature is its "near absence of any reference to democratic accountability" (1994, 668). To the extent that the Winter Commission report and the Gore report focus on accountability they do so through the emphasis on treating citizens as customers. Osborne and Gaebler indicate that "customer-driven systems force service providers to be accountable to their customers" (1992, 181). Wilson notes some of the practical problems with this position, namely that government agencies do not have the same economic incentives as private companies do for employees to treat citizens as customers. He also states that some government agency relationships with citizens and firms are coercive rather than voluntary (Wilson 1994, 670–71).

The concept also denigrates the notion of citizenship, which posits a higher plane for the relationship between citizens and government than that connoted by a customer metaphor. Still the Gore report does avoid one problem posed by previous commissions to reform national government: although it does not deal well with accountability, at least it does not pose an accountability model that is presidentially centered. Wilson indicates that the principle of democratic accountability can no longer be associated with presidential power because of the size and scope of government activities (1994, 671). There is also another reason: the U.S. government system posits multiple lines of accountability. These reform proposals neglect accountability to legislative bodies, and for that reason are incomplete.

But overall, these reform proposals' lack of emphasis on accountability and the related concept of responsibility suggests a need to increase the focus on these concepts, as the United States continues the quest to better define the relationship of politicians and bureaucrats. The public discussion of these principles in Australia stands in stark contrast to the paucity of the same in the reform discussions in the United States. A part of the need here is to focus attention and begin discussion of what these principles mean in a separated system of government where authority is widely shared.

Less comprehensive reforms have been proposed by several scholars, and the Australian experience generally lends support to several of these ideas and proposals. The need for longer tenure for political appointees has been a persistent theme of several studies, beginning with Heclo (1977). Heclo has more recently argued that there is a need to emphasize middle-range tenure, which will still bring new ideas and vitality but will permit some continuity at the levels of political appointees (1987, 213).

The Australian situation is a studied contrast. The department secretaries, although appointed by politicians, can be considered careerists since almost all have had extensive experience in the bureaucracy. In this system it is up to the ministers and their staffs to provide the vitality and new ideas, although departments can also contribute. To a large extent the political side of the relationship meets this need, and at times ministers hire outside consultants to conduct studies that produce reform agendas. Though ministers often move from one portfolio to another (and in some cases too often), their length of service in the cabinet is on average much greater than in comparable situations in the United States. In the Labor governments, both sides of the relationship in Australia brought long tenure (although ministers often moved to new portfolios), which assures that it is not a government of strangers but a government of people who have worked together for many years, at least until Labor lost in the 1996 election. This is probably easier in the smaller Australian government than it would be in the larger U.S. national government. But it does suggest that Heclo's desire for longer tenure could in reality provide benefits to the U.S. system.

Achieving middle-range tenure poses a challenge. Perhaps seeking a commitment from potential appointees would make some difference. Further, if some future administration had the courage to reduce the number of political appointees, the result would elevate the influence and effectiveness of those who were appointed, making a longer tenure more attractive, although tenure in these positions was short even when there were fewer of them. However longer tenure is achieved, it is a factor that future administrations (and Congress) should emphasize more in the recruitment and appointment process.

The rapid turnover of political appointees in the United States makes it more difficult for norms of appropriate behavior to develop. The multiplicity of elected officials who are set against each other in the U.S. separation-of-powers system and checks and balances constitutes another source of variegated notions of appropriate relationships between politics and administration. The Australian experience suggests the viability of at least two reforms suggested by American scholars. Heclo's middle-range tenure proposal would also provide an antidote to the problem of weak norms. Ingraham's findings suggested a second need: most political appointees are not well trained for the positions to which they are appointed, so there is dire need for better-developed in-service training programs. Newly elected members of the U.S. Congress, as well as of many state legislatures, receive at least a few days of orientation training prior to assuming their positions. Similar sessions would be useful for political appointees. Part of the curriculum of these programs (for both newly elected members of Congress and political appointees) should include attention to the appropriate norms that govern relationships between politics and administration. The concerns of Heclo and Ingraham could also be addressed by either appointing or assigning more career civil servants to many present political appointee positions. Their tenure would likely be longer than is typically the case nowadays and their experience level would permit them to acquire the knowledge necessary to perform the duties of the position much more quickly.

Perhaps in the end, the greatest likelihood for change in the relationship between elected officials and the bureaucracy may come from the bureaucrats. By emphasizing the fundamentals of accountability and responsibility in performing their duties, public servants might encourage elected officials to do likewise. The failure of the formulas utilized by elected officials over many years should also encourage them to try a different approach. The ultimate result will not, can not, and should not be to duplicate the mix of the political and bureaucratic that is found in Australia. But trying to achieve some of the practices suggested by the fundamentals identified in this study will likely make the relationship between top elected leaders and the bureaucracy in the United States a far better relationship than it is today—or will likely become if no one tries at all.

Bibliography

Interviews

The Australian public officials interviewed were promised that their names would not appear with any quotations associated with their interviews and that specific identifying language would be deleted. The interviews are noted by the month and year in which they were conducted. All interviews were conducted face-to-face in Canberra, the Australian capital city; they were tape-recorded and later transcribed. The interviews with ministers and their staff members were conducted in their offices in Parliament House. The interviews with the department secretaries were conducted in their departmental offices, located throughout Canberra.

In the 1992 round of interviews, the original plan was to interview the cabinet minister, the minister's chief staff member, and the department secretary of half the eighteen departments. The department secretaries and staff members were generally available because they were located full-time in Canberra. The ministers were more difficult to schedule. Ministers have the usual kinds of duties associated with holding important executive positions. In addition, they have the duties normally associated with legislative membership—roll call votes and constituency services and duties. In the Labor government, Australian parliament generally sat for two weeks and adjourned for two weeks. Ministers, along with their legislative colleagues, almost always leave Canberra when parliament is not in session, including the weekend between the two weeks that parliament is in session. Thus, ministers are very busy when they are in Canberra, and then they leave, which makes them difficult to reach. At the midpoint of the study, the decision was made to interview two former ministers and one minister who was not among the eight identified at the outset. As it turned out, most ministers had been responsible for more than one department during their ministerial career, and many of the department secretaries and ministers had worked with each other at least in the past if not at the time of the interview.

The second set of interviews, conducted in October 1996, seven months after the new Coalition government assumed office, provided an opportunity to look ahead as well as back. Interviews were requested with the fourteen cabinet ministers, and five agreed to be interviewed. Four top staff members were interviewed in the remaining nine cabinet ministers' offices. Four former Labor cabinet ministers were interviewed. All of them had previously been interviewed in the first set of interviews. The department secretaries interviewed included some who had been terminated, some who had been interviewed previously, and some who had not been interviewed previously. All interviews occurred in Canberra, were tape-recorded, and later transcribed.

Books and Articles

Aberbach, Joel D. 1990. *Keeping a Watchful Eye*. Washington, D.C.: Brookings Institution.

Aberbach, Joel, and Bert A. Rockman. 1988a. "Mandates or Mandarins? Control and Discretion in the Modern Administrative State." *Public Administration Review* 48.2 (March–April): 606–12.

Aberbach, Joel, and Bert A. Rockman. 1988b. "Political and Bureaucratic Roles in Public Service Reorganization." In *Organizing Governance Governing Organizations*, ed. Colin Campbell and B. Guy Peters. Pittsburgh: University of Pittsburgh Press.

Aberbach, Joel D., Robert D. Putnam, and Bert A. Rockman. 1981. *Bureaucrats and Politicians in Western Democracies*. Cambridge, Mass.: Harvard University Press.

Abney, Glenn, and Thomas P. Lauth. 1986. *The Politics of State and City Administration*. Albany: State University of New York Press.

Attlee, Clement R. 1954. "Civil Servants, Ministers, Parliament, and the Public." *Political Quarterly* 25.4 (October–December): 308–15.

Bakema, Wilma E. 1991. "The Ministerial Career." In *The Profession of Government Minister in Western Europe,* ed. Jean Blondel and Jean-Louis Thiébault. New York: St. Martin's Press.

Banfield, Edward C. 1975. "Corruption as a Feature of Governmental Organizations." *Journal of Law and Economics* 18 (December): 587–605.

Barzelay, Michael. 1992. *Breaking Through Bureaucracy*. Berkeley and Los Angeles, Calif.: University of California Press.

Bernstein, LeaAnne. 1987. "Permanent Guerrilla Government: Legal Services Corporation." In *Steering the Elephant: How Washington Works,* ed. Robert Rector and Michael Sanera. New York: Universe Books.

Blondel, Jean. 1991. "Cabinet Government and Cabinet Ministers." In *The Profession of Government Minister in Western Europe,* ed. Jean Blondel and Jean-Louis Thiébault. New York: St. Martin's Press.

Bradshaw, Kenneth, and David Pring. 1972. *Parliament and Congress.* London: Quarter Books.

Brauer, Carl. 1987. "Tenure, Turnover, and Postgovernment Employment Trends of Presidential Appointees." In *The In-and-Outers,* ed. G. Calvin Mackenzie. Baltimore: Johns Hopkins University Press.

Brudney, Jeffrey L., and F. Ted Hebert. 1987. "State Agencies and Their Environments: Examining the Influence of Important External Actors." *Journal of Politics* 49.1 (February): 186–206.

Burke, John P. 1986. *Bureaucratic Responsibility.* Baltimore: Johns Hopkins University Press.

Caiden, Gerald E. 1988. "The Problem of Ensuring the Public Accountability of Public Officials." In *Public Service Accountability,* ed. Joseph G. Jabbra and O. P. Dwivedi. West Hartford, Conn.: Kumarian Press.

Campbell, Colin. 1983. *Governments Under Stress.* Toronto: University of Toronto Press.

———. 1986. *Managing the Presidency.* Pittsburgh: University of Pittsburgh Press.

———. 1993. "Public Service and Democratic Accountability." In *Ethics in Public Service,* ed. R. A. Chapman. Edinburgh: Edinburgh University Press.

Campbell, Colin, and J. Halligan. 1992. *Political Leadership in an Age of Constraint.* Pittsburgh: University of Pittsburgh Press.

Campbell, Colin, and Graham K. Wilson. 1995. *The End of Whitehall: Death of a Paradigm?* Cambridge, Mass.: Blackwell.

Campbell, Colin, and Margaret Jane Wyszomirski, eds. 1991. *Executive Leadership in Anglo-American Systems.* Pittsburgh: University of Pittsburgh Press.

Castles, Francis G., ed. 1989. *The Comparative History of Public Policy.* New York: Oxford University Press.

Castles, Francis G., ed.. 1991. *Australia Compared: People, Policies, Politics.* Sydney: Allen and Unwin.

Cohen, Jeffrey E. 1985. "Presidential Control of Independent Regulatory Commissions Through Appointment: The Case of the ICC." *Administration and Society* 17.1 (May): 61–70.

Commonwealth Government Directory. Canberra: Australian Government Publishing Service (AGPS). August 1992, December 1995–February 1996, June 1996.

Crenson, Mathew A., and Francis E. Rourke. 1987. "By Way of Conclusion: American Bureaucracy Since World War II." In *The New American State,* ed. Louis Galambos. Baltimore: Johns Hopkins University Press.

DiIulio, John D., Jr. 1994. "Principled Agents: The Cultural Bases of Behavior in a Federal Government Bureaucracy." *Journal of Public Administration Research and Theory* 4.3 (July): 277–318.

DiIulio, John J., Jr., Gerald Garvey, and Donald F. Kettl. 1993. *Improving Government Performance.* Washington, D.C.: Brookings Institution.

Durant, Robert. 1992. *The Administrative Presidency Revisited.* Albany: State University of New York Press.

Dwivedi, O. P. 1985. "Ethics and Values of Public Responsibility and Accountability." *International Journal of Administrative Sciences* 51.1: 61–66.

Dwivedi, O. P., and Joseph G. Jabbra. 1988. "Public Service Responsibility and Accountability." In *Public Service Accountability: A Comparative Perspective,* ed. Joseph G. Jabbra and O. P. Dwivedi. West Hartford, Conn.: Kumarian Press.

Eisner, Marc Allen, and Kenneth J. Meier. 1990. "Presidential Control Versus Bureaucratic Power: Explaining the Reagan Revolution in Antitrust." *American Journal of Political Science* 34.1 (February): 269–87.

Emy, Hugh V., and Owen E. Hughes. 1991. *Australian Politics: Realities in Conflict.* 2nd ed. South Melbourne, Australia: Macmillan.

Etzioni-Halevy, Eva. 1983. *Bureaucracy and Democracy: A Political Dilemma.* London: Routledge.

Evans, M. Stanton. 1987. "Steering the Elephant." In *Steering the Elephant: How Washington Works,* ed. Robert Rector and Michael Sanera. New York: Universe Books.

Fesler, James W. 1984. "The Higher Civil Service in Europe and the United States." In *The Higher Civil Service in Europe and Canada: Lessons for the United States,* ed. Bruce L. R. Smith. Washington, D.C.: Brookings Institution.

Finer, Herman. 1978. "Administrative Responsibility in Democratic Government." In *Bureaucratic Power in National Politics,* ed. Francis Rourke. 3rd ed. Boston: Little, Brown.

Forward, Roy. 1977. "Ministerial Staff Under Whitlam and Fraser." *Australian Journal of Public Administration* 36.2 (June): 159–67.

Fraser, J. M. 1978. "Responsibility in Government." *Australian Journal of Public Administration* 37.1 (March): 1–11.

Frederickson, H. George. 1971. "Toward a New Public Administration." In *Toward a New Public Administration,* ed. Frank Marini. Scranton, Pa.: Chandler Publishing Company.

Freund, Ludwig. 1960. "Responsibility—Definitions, Distinctions, and Applications in Various Contexts." In *Responsibility,* ed. Carl J. Friedrich. New York: Liberal Arts Press.

Friedrich, Carl J. 1950. *Constitutional Government and Democracy.* Boston: Ginn and Company.

———. 1960. "The Dilemma of Administrative Responsibility." In *Responsibility,* ed. Carl J. Friedrich. New York: Liberal Arts Press.

———. 1978. "Public Policy and the Nature of Administrative Responsibility." In *Bureaucratic Power in National Politics,* ed. Francis E. Rourke. 3rd ed. Boston: Little, Brown.

Garvey, Gerald. 1993. *Facing the Bureaucracy: Living and Dying in a Public Agency*. San Francisco, Calif.: Jossey-Bass.

Gaus, John. 1936. *The Frontiers of Public Administration*. Chicago: University of Chicago Press.

Gilmour, Robert S., and Alexis A. Halley. 1994. "Co-managing Policy and Program Development." In *Who Makes Public Policy?* ed. Robert S. Gilmour and Alexis A. Halley. Chatham, N.J.: Chatham House.

Goodnow, Frank J. 1900. *Politics and Administration*. New York: Macmillan.

Gormley, William T., Jr. 1989. *Taming the Bureaucracy*. Princeton: Princeton University Press.

Grafstein, Robert. 1992. *Institutional Realism: The Social and Political Constraints on Rational Actors*. New Haven: Yale University Press.

Halligan, John, and John Power. 1992. *Political Management in the 1990s*. Melbourne: Oxford University Press.

Hart, John. 1987. *The Presidential Branch*. New York: Pergamon Press.

Hawke, R. J. L. 1989. "Challenges in Public Administration." *Australian Journal of Public Administration* 48.1 (March): 7–16.

Heclo, Hugh. 1977. *A Government of Strangers: Executive Politics in Washington*. Washington, D.C.: Brookings Institution.

———. 1984. "A Comment on the Future of the U.S. Civil Service." In *The Higher Civil Service in Europe and Canada: Lessons for the United States*, ed. Bruce L. R. Smith. Washington, D.C.: Brookings Institution.

———. 1987. "The In-and-Outer System: A Critical Assessment." In *The In-and-Outers*, ed. G. Calvin Mackenzie. Baltimore: Johns Hopkins University Press.

Heclo, Hugh, and Aaron Wildavsky. 1981. *The Private Government of Public Money*. 2nd ed. London: Macmillan.

Hedge, David M., Donald C. Menzel, and Mark A. Krause. 1989. "The Intergovernmental Milieu and Street-Level Implementation." *Social Science Quarterly* 70.2 (June): 285–99.

Hedge, David M., Michael J. Scicchitano, and Patricia Metz. 1991. "The Principal-Agent Model and Regulatory Federalism." *Western Political Quarterly* 44.4 (December): 1055–80.

HRSCFPA (House of Representatives Standing Committee on Finance and Public Administration). 1990. *Not Dollars Alone: Review of the Financial Management Improvement Program*. Canberra: Australian Government Publishing Service.

Huddleston, Mark W. 1987. "Background Paper, Twentieth-Century Fund Task Force on the Senior Executive Service." In *The Government's Managers*. New York: Priority Press.

Hyneman, Charles S. 1950. *Bureaucracy in a Democracy*. New York: Harper and Brothers.

Hyslop, Robert. 1993. *Australian Mandarins: Perceptions of the Role of Departmental Secretaries*. Canberra: Australian Government Publishing Service.

Ingraham, Patricia W. 1991. "Political Direction and Policy Change in Three

Federal Departments." In *The Managerial Presidency,* ed. James P. Pfiffner. Pacific Grove, Calif.: Brooks/Cole.

———. 1995. *The Foundation of Merit.* Baltimore: Johns Hopkins University Press.

Jones, Charles O. 1994. *The Presidency in a Separated System.* Washington, D.C.: Brookings Institution.

Kaufman, Herbert. 1981. *The Administrative Behavior of Federal Bureau Chiefs.* Washington, D.C.: Brookings Institution.

Keating, Michael. 1995. "Public Service Values." *Australian Quarterly* 67.4 (summer): 15–25.

Keating, Paul. 1991. "The Challenge of Public Policy in Australia." *Canberra Bulletin of Public Administration* 65: 16–20.

Kelly, Paul. 1992. *The End of Certainty: The Story of the 1980s.* St. Leonards, Australia: Allen and Unwin.

Kernaghan, Kenneth, and John W. Langford. 1990. *The Responsible Public Servant.* Halifax: The Institute for Research on Public Policy.

Kettl, Donald F. 1992. "Micromanagement: Congressional Control and Bureaucratic Risk." In *Agenda for Excellence,* ed. Patricia W. Ingraham and Donald F. Kettl. Chatham, N.J.: Chatham House.

Khademian, Anne M. 1995. "The New Dynamics of Legislating and the Implications for Delegating: What's to Be Expected on the Receiving End?" *Journal of Public Administration Research and Theory* 5.1 (January): 19–44.

Kiewiet, D. Roderick, and Mathew D. McCubbins. 1991. *The Logic of Delegation.* Chicago: University of Chicago Press.

Krislov, Samuel, and David Rosenbloom. 1981. *Representative Bureaucracy and the American Political System.* New York: Praeger.

Larsson, Torbjörn. 1994. "Cabinet Ministers and Parliamentary Government in Sweden." In *Cabinet Ministers and Parliamentary Government,* ed. Michael Laver and Kenneth A. Shepsle. New York: Cambridge University Press.

Lauth, Thomas P. 1989. "Responding to Elected and Appointed Officials." In *Handbook of Public Administration,* ed. James L. Perry. San Francisco: Jossey-Bass.

Laver, Michael, and Kenneth A. Shepsle. 1994. "Cabinet Ministers and Government Formation in Parliamentary Democracies." In *Cabinet Ministers and Parliamentary Government,* ed. Michael Laver and Kenneth A. Shepsle. New York: Cambridge University Press.

Light, Paul C. 1987. "When Worlds Collide: The Political-Career Nexus." In *The In-and-Outers,* ed. G. Calvin Mackenzie. Baltimore: Johns Hopkins University Press.

———. 1995. *Thickening Government.* Washington, D.C.: Brookings Institution.

Lijphart, Arend, ed. 1992. *Parliamentary Versus Presidential Government.* Oxford: Oxford University Press.

Lilla, Mark T. 1981. "Ethos, 'Ethics,' and Public Service." *Public Interest* 63 (spring): 3–17.

Long, Norton E. 1949. "Power and Administration." *Public Administration*

Review 9.4 (autumn): 257–64.

Lowi, Theodore J. 1993. "Legitimizing Public Administration." *Public Administration Review* 53.3 (May–June): 261–64.

———. 1995. "Lowi Responds." *Public Administration Review* 55.5 (September–October): 490–94.

Lucas, J. R. 1993. *Responsibility*. Oxford: Clarendon Press.

Lucy, Richard. 1993. *The Australian Form of Government*. 2nd ed. Melbourne: Macmillan Education Australia.

Lynn, Jonathan, and Antony Jay, eds. 1987. *The Complete Yes Minister: The Diaries of a Cabinet Minister by the Right Hon. James Hacker, MP*. Topsfield, Mass.: Salem House.

———. 1988. *Yes, Prime Minister: Diaries of the Right Hon. James Hacker*. Topsfield, Mass.: Salem House.

Lynn, Laurence E. 1981. *Managing the Public's Business: The Job of the Government Executive*. New York: Basic Books.

MAB (Management Advisory Board). 1991. *Accountability in the Commonwealth Public Sector: An Exposure Draft*. Canberra: Australian Government Publishing Service.

———. 1993. *Accountability in the Commonwealth Public Sector*. Canberra: Australian Government Publishing Service.

Maranto, Robert. 1993. *Politics and Bureaucracy in the Modern Presidency*. Westport, Conn.: Greenwood Press.

March, G. James, and John P. Olsen. 1984. "The New Institutionalism: Organizational Factors in Political Life." *American Political Science Review* 78.3 (September): 734–49.

Marx, Fritz Morstein. 1957. *The Administrative State*. Chicago: University of Chicago Press.

Mascarenhas, R. C. 1993. "Building an Enterprise Culture in the Public Sector: Reform of the Public Sector in Australia, Britain, and New Zealand." *Public Administration Review* 53.4 (July–August): 319 28.

Mediansky, Fedor, and James Nockles. 1975. "The Prime Minister's Bureaucracy." *Public Administration* (Sydney) 34.3 (September): 202–18.

———. 1981. "Malcolm Fraser's Bureaucracy." *Australian Quarterly* 53.4 (summer): 394–418.

Michaels, Judith E. 1995. "A View from the Top: Reflections of the Bush Presidential Appointees." *Public Administration Review* 55.3 (May–June): 273–83.

Ministerial Directory. 1995. Australian Government Publishing Service. October.

———. 1996. Australian Government Publishing Service. July.

Moe, Terry M. 1982. "Regulatory Performance and Presidential Administration." *American Journal of Political Science* 26.2 (May): 197–224.

———. 1985. "Control and Feedback in Economic Regulation: The Case of the NLRB." *American Political Science Review* 19: 1094–1116.

Montjoy, Robert S., and Douglas J. Watson. 1995. "A Case for Reinterpreted Dichotomy of Politics and Administration as a Professional Standard in

Council-Manager Government." *Public Administration Review* 55.3 (May–June): 231–39.

Mosher, Frederick C. 1968. *Democracy and the Public Service*. New York: Oxford University Press.

Nalbanian, John. 1994. "Reflections of a 'Pracademic' on the Logic of Politics and Administration." *Public Administration Review* 54.6 (November–December): 531–36.

Neustadt, Richard. 1980. "Foreword." In *Presidents and Prime Ministers,* ed. Richard Rose and Ezra N. Suleiman. Washington, D.C.: American Enterprise Institute for Public Policy Research.

NPR (National Performance Review). 1993. *From Redtape to Results: Creating a Government That Works Better and Costs Less*. Washington, D.C.: GPO.

Osborne, David, and Ted Gaebler. 1992. *Reinventing Government*. New York: Plume.

Parliamentary Handbook. 1991. Canberra: Australian Government Publishing Service.

Pennock, J. Roland. 1960. "The Problem of Responsibility." In *Responsibility,* ed. Carl J. Friedrich. New York: Liberal Arts Press.

———. 1979. *Democratic Political Theory*. Princeton: Princeton University Press.

Peters, B. Guy. 1978. *The Politics of Bureaucracy*. New York: Longman.

———. 1988. *Comparing Public Bureaucracies*. Tuscaloosa: University of Alabama Press.

Pfiffner, James P. 1987. "Political Appointees and Career Executives: The Democracy-Bureaucracy Nexus in the Third Century." *Public Administration Review* 47.1 (January–February): 57–65.

Rainey, Hal G. 1991. *Understanding and Managing Public Organizations*. San Francisco: Jossey-Bass.

Randall, Ronald. 1979. "Presidential Power Versus Bureaucratic Intransigence: The Influence of the Nixon Administration on Welfare Policy." *American Political Science Review* 73.3 (September): 795–810.

Reith, Peter. 1996. "Towards a Best Practice Australian Public Service." Discussion paper issued by the minister for Industrial Relations and the minister assisting the prime minister for the Public Service. (November).

Richardson, Graham. 1994. *Whatever It Takes*. Sydney: Bantam Books.

Rock, Emily. 1987. "Commerce and the Public Interest: James C. Miller at the Federal Trade Commission." In *Steering the Elephant: How Washington Works,* ed. Robert Rector and Michael Sanera. New York: Universe Books.

Romzek, Barbara, and Melvin Dubnick. 1987. "Accountability in the Public Sector: Lessons from the Challenger Tragedy." *Public Administration Review* 47.3 (May–June): 227–38.

Rose, Richard. 1980. "Government Against Sub-governments: A European Perspective on Washington." In *Presidents and Prime Ministers,* ed. Richard Rose and Ezra N. Suleiman. Washington, D.C.: American Enterprise Institute.

———. 1984. "The Political Status of Higher Civil Servants in Britain." In

Bureaucrats and Policy Making: A Comparative Overview, ed. Ezra N. Suleiman. New York: Holmes and Meier.

———. 1987a. "Steering the Ship of State: One Tiller but Two Pairs of Hands." *British Journal of Political Science* 17: 409–33.

———. 1987b. "Giving Direction to Permanent Officials: Signals from the Electorate, the Market, Laws and Expertise." In *Bureaucracy and Public Choice,* ed. Jan-Erik Lane. Newbury Park, Calif.: Sage.

Rose, Richard, and Ezra N. Suleiman. 1980. *Presidents and Prime Ministers.* Washington, D.C.: American Enterprise Institute.

Rourke, Francis E. 1991. "American Bureaucracy in a Changing Political Setting." *Journal of Public Administration Research and Theory* 1.2 (April): 111–29.

———. 1992. "Responsiveness and Neutral Competence in American Bureaucracy." *Public Administration Review* 52.6 (November–December): 539–46.

———. 1993. "Whose Bureaucracy Is This Anyway? Congress, the President, and Public Administration." *PS: Political Science and Politics* 26.4 (December): 687–91.

Rubin, Irene S. 1985. *Shrinking the Federal Government: The Effect of Cutbacks on Five Federal Agencies.* White Plains, N.Y.: Longman.

Sanders, Ronald P. 1994. "Reinventing the Senior Executive Service." In *New Paradigms for Government,* ed. Patricia W. Ingraham and Barbara S. Romzek. San Francisco: Jossey-Bass.

Scholz, John T., and Feng Heng Wei. 1986. "Regulatory Enforcement in a Federalist System." *American Political Science Review* 80.4 (December): 1249–70.

Scholz, John T., Jim Twombly, and Barbara Headrick. 1991. "Street-Level Political Controls over Federal Bureaucracy." *American Political Science Review* 85.3 (September): 829–50.

Smith, R. F. I. 1977. "Ministerial Advisers: The Experience of the Whitlam Government." *Australian Journal of Public Administration* 36.2 (June): 133–58.

Stein, Lana. 1991. *Holding Bureaucrats Accountable.* Tuscaloosa: University of Alabama Press.

Stillman, Richard J. II. 1987. *The American Bureaucracy.* Chicago: Nelson-Hall.

Suleiman, Ezra N. 1974. *Politics, Power, and Bureaucracy in France.* Princeton: Princeton University Press.

Suleiman, Ezra N., ed. 1984. *Bureaucrats and Policy Making: A Comparative Overview.* New York: Holmes and Meier.

Sundquist, James L. 1995. "The Concept of Governmental Management: Or, What's Missing in the Gore Report?" *Public Administration Review* 55.4 (July–August): 398–99.

Sydney Morning Herald. 1996. "Sabre Rattling in Russell," by David Lague. June 25. Internet version.

Tange, Arthur. 1982. "The Focus of Reform in Commonwealth Government Administration." *Australian Journal of Public Administration* 41.1 (March): 1–14.

Terry, Larry D. 1995. *Leadership of Public Bureaucracies.* Thousand Oaks: Sage.

Thelen, Kathleen, and Sven Steinmo. 1992. "Historical Institutionalism in Comparative Politics." In *Structuring Politics: Historical Institutionalism in Comparative Analysis,* ed. Sven Steinmo, Kathleen Thelen, and Frank Longstreth. Victoria, Australia: Cambridge University Press.

Thiébault, Jean-Louis. 1994. "The Political Autonomy of Cabinet Ministers in the French Fifth Republic." In *Cabinet Ministers and Parliamentary Government,* ed. Michael Laver and Kenneth A. Shepsle. New York: Cambridge University Press.

Thompson, Elaine. 1980. "The 'Washminster' Mutation." In *Responsible Government in Australia,* ed. Patrick Weller and Dean Jaensch. Victoria, Australia: Drummond.

Uhr, John. 1982. "Parliament and Public Administration." In *Parliament and Bureaucracy,* ed. J. R. Nethercote. Sydney: Hale and Iremonger.

———. 1992. "Public Accountabilities and Private Responsibilities: The Westminster World at the Crossroads." Paper prepared for the annual meeting of the American Political Science Association, Chicago.

———. 1993a. "Parliamentary Measure: Evaluating Parliament's Policy Role." In *Governing in the 1990s,* ed. I. Marsh. Melbourne: Longman Cheshire.

———. 1993b. "Redesigning Accountability: From Muddles to Maps." *Australian Quarterly* 65.2 (winter): 1–16.

Volcker, Paul A. 1988. *Public Service: The Quiet Crisis.* Washington, D.C.: American Enterprise Institute.

Volcker Commission Report. 1989. *Leadership for America Rebuilding the Public Service.* Washington, D.C.: National Commission on the Public Service.

Walsh, Peter. 1995. *Confessions of a Failed Finance Minister.* Sydney: Random House Australia.

Walter, James. 1986. *The Ministers' Minders: Personal Advisers in National Government.* Melbourne: Oxford University Press.

Wamsley, Gary L., et al. 1990. "The Agency Perspective: Public Administrators as Agential Leaders." In *Refounding Public Administration,* ed. Wamsley. Newbury Park, Calif.: Sage.

Warhurst, John. 1988. "Reforming Central Government Administration in Australia." In *Organizing Governance Governing Organizations,* ed. Colin Campbell and B. Guy Peters. Pittsburgh: University of Pittsburgh Press.

Waterford, Jack. 1996. *Ministerial Responsibility for Personal Staff.* Senate Occasional Lecture Series. May.

Weber, Max. 1958a. "Politics as a Vocation." In *From Max Weber,* ed. H. H. Gerth and C. Wright Mills. New York: Oxford University Press.

———. 1958b. "Bureaucracy." In *From Max Weber,* ed. H. H. Gerth and C. Wright Mills. New York: Oxford University Press.

Weko, Thomas J. 1995. *The Politicizing Presidency: The White House Personnel Office, 1949–1994.* Lawrence: University Press of Kansas.

Weller, Patrick. 1983. "Transition: Taking over Power in 1983." *Australian Journal of Public Administration* 42.3 (September): 303–19.

————. 1989. "Politicisation and the Australian Public Service." *Australian Journal of Public Administration* 48.4 (December): 369–81.

West, William F. 1995. *Controlling the Bureaucracy: Institutional Constraints in Theory and Practice*. Armonk, N.Y.: M. E. Sharpe.

Wildavsky, Aaron. 1987. "Foreword: The Human Side of Government." In *Steering the Elephant: How Washington Works,* ed. Robert Rector and Michael Sanera. New York: Universe Books.

Wilson, James Q. 1989. *Bureaucracy: What Government Agencies Do and Why They Do It*. New York: Basic Books.

————. 1994. "Reinventing Public Administration." *PS: Political Science and Politics* 27.4 (December): 667–73.

Wilson, Woodrow. 1992. "The Study of Administration." Originally appeared in *Political Science Quarterly* 2.1 (June 1887). In *Classics of Public Administration,* ed. Jay M. Shafritz and Albert C. Hyde. 3rd ed. Pacific Grove, Calif.: Brooks/Cole.

Winter Commission Report. 1993. *Hard Truths/Tough Choices: An Agenda for State and Local Reform.* (A summary may be found in *Governing,* August 1993.) Albany, N.Y.: Nelson A. Rockefeller Institute of Government.

Wood, B. Dan, and Richard W. Waterman. 1994. *Bureaucratic Dynamics: The Role of Bureaucracy in a Democracy*. Boulder, Colo.: Westview Press.

Yeend, G. J. 1979. "The Department of the Prime Minister and Cabinet in Perspective." *Australian Journal of Public Administration* 38.2 (June): 133–50.

Young, Hugo, and Anne Sloman. 1982. *No, Minister*. London: BBC.

Index

Aberbach, Joel, 19, 27, 31; and
  Rockman study, 148
Abney and Lauth study, 168
Academics. *See* University scholars
Accountability, 11, 15, 37, 65, 166; of
  bureaucracy, 2, 66, 68; of bureaucracy to elected officials, 35–38; of
  bureaucracy to public at large, 2, 39–
  41, 66–67; definition of concept, 19,
  35, 167; of department secretary to
  minister, 65, 68, 71; mechanisms, 39,
  40–42, 167; of ministerial staff, 103–
  04, 107; model proposed in Gore
  report, 171; and need of strong
  direction, 150–51; reduced by
  political appointees, 29; and responsibility, 37–38, 70, 163–67, 170–71;
  and responsiveness, 36; in
  Westminster system, 169
*Accountability in the Commonwealth
  Public Sector* (MAB report), 11, 64
Administration and politics dichotomy.
  See Politics-administration relationship
Advisory bodies, external, 123
Advisory Council, 123
Appointment process, 10, 16, 121. *See
  also* Political appointees

Attlee, Clement, 69; and role of minister,
  61, 115
Australian Capital Territory, 4
Awards, and accountability, 36

Backbenchers, 7, 52, 169
Barzelay, Michael, 39
BBC: report on civil service, 115–16;
  Yes, Minister, 120–21
Budget: approved, 5–6; cuts, 139;
  developing, 57
Bureaucracy, 12, 19, 27, 132, 153, 167;
  and accountability, 18, 39–40, 169;
  conservatism of, 20; discretion of, 32,
  37–38, 41–42, 129, 158, 164;
  experience in, 56–58, 113; and
  government, 139, 144, 155, 169; and
  institutional memory, 76, 111, 147;
  needing clear directives, 125–28, 151;
  neutral competence of, 146, 153–59,
  164; and policy advice, 111, 113,
  116, 118; and policy development,
  145, 147, 151, 153, 156–57, 159,
  161–63, 165–66; and resistance to
  minister, 139, 142, 145; responsibility
  of, 41–42; and responsiveness to
  minister, 26, 56–58, 125, 163–64;
  how to establish role of, 1–2. *See also*

Career officials; Public service
   officials; United States bureaucracy
Bureaucrat bashing: in Great Britain,
   116; in United States, 8, 115, 155–56,
   170
Bureaucratic government. *See* Government styles
Bureau of Prisons, 33
Bush administration, 24

Cabinet, 6, 51, 94–95, 144; and
   ministerial staff, 74, 108; in parliamentary system, 5–6, 11; submissions,
   57, 142, 160
Cabinet government. *See* Government
   styles
Cabinet ministers, 98, 131, 138–40;
   interviewed, 13–14; length of service
   of, 46, 133–34, 172; and portfolio,
   134, 142. *See also* Junior ministers;
   Ministers; Prime minister; Senior
   ministers
Campbell, Colin. *See* Campbell and
   Halligan study; Campbell and Wilson
   study
Campbell and Halligan study, 8, 27, 59,
   78, 90; and bureaucratic accountability, 40, 68; and ministers in Hawke
   government, 50, 109, 124, 131, 150
Campbell and Wilson study, 120, 122
Canada, democracy studied, 12, 39
Canberra Times, 107
Career officials, 145, 165; and elected
   officials, 8, 19, 21, 30–34, 70, 147,
   149, 166; and policy process, 16, 22,
   26–28; and political appointees, 20,
   21, 173. *See also* Laver and Shepsle
Castles, Francis, 13
Caucus, 6, 94–95, 108, 144
Chief executive officer. *See* Department
   heads
Citizenship, notion of, 171
Civil service reforms. *See* United States,
   reforms
Coalition, 3–4; in government, 6, 14,
   63, 118, 120, 127, 139, 145, 149,
   164; in the House, 4; in opposition,
   6–7; in the Senate, 5
Communication: department and
   ministerial staff, 91; elected officials

and bureaucracy, 26, 70, 140, 151–
   52, 155; facilitated by ministerial
   staff, 108; long chain of, in United
   States, 22; in policy formulation,
   124–25; value of, 148, 165
Competency. *See* Neutral competence
Conflict, interdepartmental, 128
Congress: and bureaucracy, 30–31; and
   neutral competence, 154; reduced
   impact on agency action, 32–33; in
   United States, 31, 33, 167–70
Constitution, Australian, 4
Constitution, U.S., 21
Consultants, use of, 27, 74, 123, 146,
   161, 172. *See also* University scholars
Cooperation, value of, 21, 145–46

Defence Department, Australia, 127,
   136
Democratic politics, values, 19
Democratic theory, 1–2, 15, 19; and
   bureaucratic responsiveness, 34
Democrats, in Australia, 4–5, 89
Department heads, 7–8, 10, 14, 154;
   and clear communication from
   minister, 126–28, 164; effect of
   Howard government terminations on,
   62–63; length of service of, 43–36,
   134, 152; in policy process, 146, 158,
   160; and responsibilities, 11, 146,
   159–60; role of, in Westminster
   system, 168–69. *See also* Department
   secretaries
Department Liaison Officer, 74
Department of Art, Sports, and
   Environment, Australia, 94
Department of Employment, Education,
   and Training, Australia, 50
Department of Finance, Australia, 44, 95
Department of Foreign Affairs, Austra-
   lia, 136
Department of Foreign Affairs and
   Trade, Australia, 50
Department of Health, Education, and
   Welfare, United States, 33
Department of Primary Industries,
   Australia, 94
Department of Prime Minister and
   Cabinet, Australia, 10–11, 44, 66, 95,
   136, 158

Department of Social Security, Australia, 130

Department of Transport and Communications, Australia, 50, 136

Departments, 130; consolidated, 50; and ministers, 47–48, 132, 133, 138–39, 166; in parliamentary system, 5; in policy process, 111, 131, 145–46, 167

Department secretaries, 9, 13, 25, 35, 121–22, 150, 172; accountability of, 64–65, 164–66, 169; administering department, 73, 110; coordinating portfolio, 46, 73; discretion of, 70–71; and ministerial staff, 89–90, 92–93, 146; and policy process, 48–50, 59–63, 73, 111, 146, 160; relationship with ministers, 56, 68–73, 91, 119, 126–27, 131, 137–39; and multiple ministers, 51–55; on leave to department, 146

Deputy prime minister, Australia, 3

Deputy secretaries, Australia, 43, 121

DiIulio, John, study of Bureau of Prisons, 33

Discretion of bureaucracy, 37; Finer and, 37–38; Friedrich and, 38; ministers' views of, 129; Woodrow Wilson and, 110

Dorothy Dixes, 7, 99–101. *See also* Question time

Durant, Robert, 20–21, 148

Educators, 157–59

Elected officials, 20; and career officials, 8, 19, 21, 30–34, 70, 147, 149, 166; and political direction, 127, 145, 151, 163; relationship with appointed officials, 33. *See also* Laver and Shepsle; Ministers

Ethics, 66, 157

Europe, ministerial service in, 134

Executive branch, in United States, 25; defining accountability of, 167; and neutral competence, 154; and political appointees, 24–26, 28–29; and responsiveness of bureaucracy, 21–22

Executive power, in parliamentary system, 5

Expenditure Review Committee, 57, 138

Expertise. *See* Professional expertise

Federalism, 3

Federal regulatory agencies, studies of, 33–34

Fesler, James, 22

Finer, Herman: and accountability, 37–40; and external controls, 103–05, 158, 163–65, 170

First assistant secretaries, 43, 121

Fraser, Malcolm, 9, 162

Frederickson, George, 158

Freedom of information requests, 106–07

Friedrich, Carl: and bureaucratic accountability, 37–40; and internal guidance systems, 65–66, 103, 105, 163–65, 169–70

Gaebler, Ted, *Reinventing Government*, 170

Garvey, Gerald, and neutral competence, 155, 157

Gaus, John, 38

Gilmour, Robert, 31, 33

Goodnow, Charles, 159

Gore, Al, 170

Gore report. *See* National Performance Review

Gormley, William, and U.S. congressional reforms, 32

Government agencies, and reform proposals, 170–71

Government styles, 144–45

Great Britain: BBC report on civil service, 115–16; Campbell and Wilson study, 120, 122; compared with the United States, 12; Westminster system in, 2–3

Green Party, Australia, 4

Halley, Alexis, 31–33

Halligan, John. *See* Campbell and Halligan study

Hawke, Robert: administration, 57, 136; Labor government of, 9, 62, 107, 133–35; as prime minister, 3, 131. *See also* Hawke reorganization

Hawke-Keating governments: brokering, 97; ministerial staff, 90, 134–35;

programs cut, 139. *See also* Hawke reorganization; Keating, Paul

Hawke reorganization, 50–51, 56, 59, 89, 97, 139–40; effects of, 108, 118, 121, 130–31, 157–58, 160, 166

Heclo, Hugh, 23, 26, 28, 134, 147, 168, 172; *A Government of Strangers,* 24; proposal of middle-range tenure, 173; and Wildavsky study, 165

House of Representatives, Australia, 4, 6, 11; question time, 7, 99

Howard, John, 4; Coalition government of, 10, 46, 51, 62, 97, 118, 139–40; ministerial staff and, 108; and terminated department heads, 152

Hyneman, Charles, 40–41

Hyslop study, 68, 108

Independents, 4–6, 89

Information, value of, 19, 46, 56–58, 65, 160

Ingraham, Patricia, 23, 25, 34, 148; and need for training political appointees, 173

Institutional memory, value of, 76, 111, 147

Institutions, study of, 12

Interest groups, 67, 101

Interpersonal skills, value of, 148

Interstate Commerce Commission, 34

Jones, Charles, 25, 29, 167, 168

Junior ministers, 13–14, 51, 53, 131, 140–41. *See also* Cabinet ministers; Ministers; Senior ministers

Kaufman, Herbert, 25; study of bureau chiefs, 30–31, 168

Keating, Michael, 65–67; and advisers, 158–59

Keating, Paul, 149; Labor government of, 9, 50, 107, 133–34, 158, 166; as prime minister, 3. *See also* Hawke-Keating governments

Kernaghan, Kenneth, 39–40

Krislov, Samuel, 32

Labor government, 6, 8–9, 13–14, 74, 90, 97, 122; and bureaucracy, 120;

and department secretaries, 9–10; making changes, 57, 65, 145; and ministers, 48, 149, 172; mistakes of, 107

Labor Party, Australia, 3; factions in, 51, 88–89; in the House, 4–5; in opposition, 6–7, 9; and ministers, 5, 138; in the Senate, 5

Langford, John, 39–40

Larsson study of Sweden, 150

Laver and Shepsle, model of relationship between elected and career officials, 144

Legislative branch, United States: and congressional reforms, 29–30; system of responsibility and accountability in, 167, 168; neglect of, 170; and responsiveness, 21–22, 29

Legislative committees, 11

Legislative government. *See* Government styles

Legislative power, in parliamentary system, 5

Legislature, state, 168, 173

Length of time in service. *See* Tenure (length of time in service)

Liberal Party, Australian, 3, 5, 51

Liberal-National Coalition. *See* Coalition

Light, Paul, 25–26, 28, 148

Lilla, Mark, 157

Long, Norton, 162

Lowi, Theodore, 40

Lynn, Laurence, 27

MAB. *See* Management Advisory Board

Madisonian plan of checks and balances, 21

Management Advisory Board (MAB), 11, 168. *See also Accountability in the Commonwealth Public Sector* (MAB report)

Maranto, Robert, 20, 24, 26, 134

Media: leaks to, 139; and question time, 7; as source of sanctions, 36

Meetings, 19; to coordinate portfolio, 53–54, 97

Michaels, Judith, 24

Miller, James, and neutral competence, 156

Ministerial government. *See* Government styles

Ministerial staff, 54, 74–76, 131, 160, 172; and accountability, 107, 166; as advisers, 74–75, 78–83, 96; brokering positions, 94–99; and bureaucracy, 107, 113, 120; coordinating portfolio, 93–94, 97–101, 108, 142; between department and minister, 81–85, 87, 140; and department, 76–78, 87–88, 105–06, 128; discretion of, 103–05; effect of increased numbers of, 9, 11, 50, 152, 160; evaluation and facilitation role, 79–80, 84–88, 146; and information, 101–02, 106–07; and minister, 74, 101–02, 163–65; mistakes, 107; morale of, 156–57; oversight function of, 129, 146; and policy, 9, 50, 87, 92, 107, 129; and question time, 99–101

Ministers, 5–6, 12, 57, 109–11, 136–37, 159, 161, 172; as accountable to parliament, 169; and advisers, 89, 90–91, 104, 107, 121; and bureaucracy, 50, 119–22, 125–28, 132, 144, 150, 153; and bureaucratic responsiveness, 9, 118–19, 139, 142–43, 166; and bureaucratic resistance, 116–18, 119, 142, 145; and cabinet, 6, 166; Coalition, 109, 119, 141–42; and departments, 51, 113–15, 118, 122, 128–29, 130, 133; Hawke government, 109, 124, 150; multiple numbers of in a department, 52–56; and policy advice, 112–14, 116, 145, 158; in policy development, 109, 111, 124–25, 130; and policy implementation, 112, 129; and policy process, 50, 115, 136, 138, 146; and portfolios, 5–6, 51, 132–33, 136, 140, 148–49; preferences expressed, 126, 127; relationship with department secretaries, 8, 46–48, 68–73, 121, 131, 139, 160–61, 166–67; and responsibility, 11, 111, 122, 140, 143; tactical skills of, 138–39; time in service of, 130, 132–38; in Westminster system, 169. *See also* Cabinet ministers; Senior ministers;

Junior ministers

Montjoy and Watson study, 161

Mosher, Frederick, 36

National Performance Review, 170–71

National Labor Relations Board, 34

National Party, Australia, 3, 5, 51

Neustadt, Richard, 12

Neutral competence, 16, 149, 161–62, 169; Garvey and, 155, 157; Miller and, 156; political appointments and, 154; respect for, 153–59, 166–67; Rourke and, 21, 27, 154

New Institutionalism, 12

New Zealand, democracy studied, 12

Nixon administration, 33

Non-elected officials. *See* Bureaucracy; Career officials; Department heads; Department secretaries; Ministerial staff

Northern Territory, Australia, 4

Objectives: need to define, 167; value of, 150, 165

Occupational Safety and Health Administration, 34

Office of Surface Mining, 34

Opinion polls, 3

Opposition, in Australia, 6–7, 95, 106, 118, 169; coming to power of, 132, 155

Orientation, training needed for political appointees, 173

Osborne, David: *Reinventing Government,* 170; and Gaebler, 171

Paperwork: for portfolio, 97; staff prioritization of, 101–02

Parliament, in Westminster system, 169

Parliamentary committees, 11, 39

Parliamentary democracy, 3, 5, 15

Parliamentary secretaries, 6, 51, 75, 98, 131; in portfolio, 53, 97. *See also* Cabinet ministers; Ministers

Parliamentary systems, 2–3, 5, 68–69; and public servant, 39; accountability and responsibility of, 167

Party caucus. *See* Caucus

Party government. *See* Government styles

Permanent Heads. *See* Department secretaries
Peters, Guy, 12
Pfiffner, James, 23, 153
Policy: in cabinet, 6; implementation of, 33, 112, 129; ministers advancing changes in, 116–17; objectives, 124–27
Policy advice: bureaucracy and, 111–13, 116, 118; from careerists, 26–27; and department secretaries, 46; from external sources, 27, 122–24, 161; ministerial staff and, 9, 50, 78–83, 87, 92, 107; ministers and, 112–14, 116, 145, 158
Policy advisers: Attlee and, 115; ministers and, 89–91, 104, 107, 121; ministerial staff and, 74–75, 78–83, 96
Policy development, 8; bureaucracy and, 145, 147, 151, 153, 155–57, 159, 161–63, 165–66; ministers and, 109, 111, 124–25, 130; political appointees and, 25
Policy making, 19, 27; collaborative, 114–15, 169; and political appointments, 26, 153
Policy process: career officials and, 16, 22, 26–28; department heads and, 146, 158, 160; departments' role in, 111, 131, 145–46, 167; department secretaries and, 48–50, 59–63, 73, 111, 146, 160; dependent on cooperation, 148; ministers and, 50, 115, 136, 138, 146; politicians and, 2; president and, 33
Political appointees, 22–24, 28, 134, 152, 153; and bureaucracy, 20–21, 25–26, 151–53, 157, 167; and neutral competence, 154; proliferation of, 170; tenure of, 172; turnover of, 133
Political direction, 111, 128, 149
Politicians: to develop initiatives, 153; in the policy process, 2. *See also* Elected officials
Politics-administration relationship, 2, 8, 11, 15, 142, 147, 172–73; dichotomy of, 16, 19, 29–30, 93, 106, 150, 159–63; and role of legislature, 168; studies of, 13; symbiotic, 142; in

United States, 2, 12, 26, 169
Portfolio, 118–19; department secretaries and, 46; ministers moving between, 133, 134–38, 148–49, 172; in parliamentary system, 5; at question time, 99; shadowed, 7; shared between ministers, 52–56, 140–42, 149
President: and bureaucratic responsiveness, 22, 29; and Congress, 33, 39; and political appointees, 25; as power center, 169; role of, 29
Prime Minister, Australia, 3–4, 57; and cabinet, 10–11, 13; and staff, 10, 74, 78. *See also* Cabinet ministers; Department of Prime Minister and Cabinet; Junior ministers; Ministers; Senior ministers
Prime-ministerial government. *See* Government styles
Professional expertise, 66, 73, 122–23; and bureaucracy, 19, 27, 146–47, 155. *See also* Neutral competence
Progressive tradition, 168; and reforms, 21, 154
Proportional representation, 4
Public administration theory, 15
Public bureaucracy, comparative studies of, 12
Public policy, comparative studies of, 13
Public servants, 16, 41, 63, 88; and discretion, 37–38
Public service, 8, 13, 122; and party platforms, 110, 123; responsible for policy advice, 111–12
Public Service Board, 10

Question time, 7, 57–58, 99–101

Randall, Ronald, 33
Reagan, Ronald: administration, 20, 24, 27, 34, 134; political appointees, 20, 24–26
Reform: agenda from outside sources, 124, 172; in Australia, 8–9, 140; congressionally imposed, 29; and department heads, 10, 122; in United States, 8, 12, 170–73
Responsibility, 15, 70, 167; and accountability, 37–38; of bureaucracy

2, 150–51; of cabinet minister and parliamentary secretary, 98; concept of, discussed, 35–38, 163–67; discrete areas of, 140, 160; external and internal controls blurred, 105; of minister and bureaucracy, 159; ministerial staff and, 107; Woodrow Wilson and, 110
Responsiveness, 89; of administration to elected officials, 103–04; in Australia and United States, 11–12; of bureaucracy, 2, 11, 21–22, 29–30; of bureaucracy to elected officials, 33–34; of bureaucracy to ministers, 8–9; of bureaucracy to president and Congress, 33–34; as democratic value, 19; of departments, 9; of department secretaries, 73; not resulting from political appointments, 25–26
Richardson, Graham, 138
Rockman, Bert, 19, 27, 31
Rose, Richard, 27–28, 40, 151
Rosenbloom, David, 32
Rourke, Francis E., 21, 25, 32; and neutral competence, 27, 154
Rubin, Irene, 27

Sanctions, 36
Sanders, Ronald, 162
Securities and Exchange Commission, 34
Senate, Australia, 4, 6, 11, 89, 169; estimates committees, 64; question time, 7, 99; proportional representation, 4–5
Senior advisers, interviewed, 13
Senior ministers, 53, 140–41; interviewed, 13–14. See also Cabinet ministers; Junior ministers; Ministers
Separation of powers, United States, 8, 15, 31, 39, 150, 162–63, 167, 171–72
Shadow ministers, 7, 107
Staff members, 7; interviewed, 13–14; resources increased, 9
Stein, Lana, 34
Submissions to cabinet. See Cabinet, submissions
Sundquist, James, 23
Sweden, Larsson study of, 150

Tange, Arthur, 41, 149
Task forces, in policy advice, 123
Tenure (length of time in service), 122; in cabinet, 43–46, 133–34; of department secretaries, 9, 43–46, 65, 121, 166–67; Heclo and, 172–73; ministers and, 130, 166–67, 172; for political appointees, 24–25, 172
Think tanks, as source of policy advice, 27
Training programs, needed for appointees, 170, 173
Treasurer, Australia, 57
Treasury, Australia, 44, 95, 136

Uhr, John, 37
United States, 3, 6, 15, 20, 21–22, 74, 167, 171; Congress, 30, 33, 167–70; democracy studied, 12; executive branch, 21–22, 25, 167; legislative branch, 21–22, 29–30, 167, 168, 170; neutral competence, 154, 162; policy process in, 27, 169; political appointees in, 22–26, 134, 151–52, 153, 157; reforms in, 8, 29–30, 32, 154, 170–73. See also Separation of powers, United States
United States bureaucracy, 22, 142; elected officials' dissatisfaction with, 166; and politicians, 152; and Congress in, 169; postwar, 18; discretion limited in, 32, 41–42. See also Bureaucrat bashing
University scholars, for policy advice, 27, 123, 161

Volcker, Paul, 28
Volcker Commission, 170

Walter study, 78, 96–97
Wamsley, Gary, 40
Washminster system, 3
Waterford, Jack, 107, 165
Waterman, Richard, 34
Weber, Max, 18
Weko, Thomas, and political appointees, 25
Western Europe, and ministers' tenure, 134
Westminster-based systems, 4, 47

Westminster model, accountability in,
   11, 168–69
Westminster system, 2–3, 5, 63;
   accountability in, 168–69; professional competence in, 7–8; responsibility in, 122
White House, 22, 26, 31, 33; and
   political appointees, 25, 154; staff,
   23, 170
Whitlam, Gough, Labor government, 9

Wildavsky, Aaron, 25–26
Wilson, Graham. *See* Campbell and
   Wilson study
Wilson, James Q., 29–31, 171
Wilson, Woodrow, 48, 110–11, 159–60
Winter, William, 170
Winter Commission, 171
Wood, Dan, 34

Yes, Minister, 120–21